MEDIA AND PUBLIC SHAMING

'In the post-Leveson world of on- and offline media, where rumour and disinformation as much as news create headlines in seconds, the relationship between individual privacy, public interest and press freedom has never been so ethically complex or more radically contested. Julian Petley has brought together a distinguished group of journalists and journalism scholars to analyse, debate and disentangle these complexities and identify possible ways forward in a shifting world of press regulation. *Media and Public Shaming* is a significant and timely book. It should be read by everyone interested in the future of journalism and news media; we all have interests in democracy.'

Bob Franklin, Professor of Journalism Studies, Cardiff University

MEDIA AND PUBLIC SHAMING

DRAWING THE BOUNDARIES OF DISCLOSURE

Edited by JULIAN PETLEY

REUTERS
INSTITUTE for the
STUDY of
JOURNALISM

Published by I.B.Tauris & Co. Ltd in association with
the Reuters Institute for the Study of Journalism, University of Oxford

The Reuters Institute would like to acknowledge the assistance of Robert G. Picard and John Lloyd as readers on behalf of the Institute.

Published in 2013 by I.B.Tauris & Co. Ltd
6 Salem Road, London W2 4BU
175 Fifth Avenue, New York NY 10010
www.ibtauris.com

Distributed in the United States and Canada Exclusively by Palgrave Macmillan
175 Fifth Avenue, New York NY 10010

ISBN: 978 1 78076 586 0 (HB); 978 1 78076 587 7 (PB)

A full CIP record for this book is available from the British Library
A full CIP record is available from the Library of Congress

Library of Congress Catalog Card Number: available

Typeset by 4word Ltd, Bristol

Printed and bound in Great Britain by T.J. International, Padstow, Cornwall

MIX
Paper from
responsible sources
FSC
www.fsc.org
FSC® C013056

Contents

List of Contributors

Simon Dawes works as an editorial assistant for the journals *Theory, Culture and Society* and *Body and Society*, and has taught at Derby University, the University of Leicester, and Nottingham Trent University in the UK. He is currently researching theories of privacy and the public sphere in broadcasting and press regulation.

Hanne Detel is a research associate at the Department of Media Studies, Tübingen University, Germany. Her research examines mediatisation processes and the social web, visibility in the digital age, internet shaming, and cyber bullying. Together with Bernhard Pörksen, she recently wrote the book *Der entfesselte Skandal: Vom Ende der Kontrolle im digitalen Zeitalter* (*The Unleashed Scandal: The End of Control in the Digital Age*).

Tim Dwyer is a senior lecturer in the Department of Media and Communications, University of Sydney. His recent books are *Media Convergence* (Open University, 2010) and *Legal and Ethical Issues in the Media* (Palgrave, 2012).

Romayne Smith Fullerton, PhD, is an associate professor of Journalism and Media Studies at Western University, London, Ontario. She is an interdisciplinary scholar whose research interests encompass gender, minority issues, and journalism ethics. Most recently, she edited a book titled *Covering Canadian Crime: What Journalists Know and the Public Should Question*.

Julia Lefkowitz is completing her Master's degree in the Department of Global Communications at the American University of Paris. Her research focuses on contemporary media discourse and material culture in the context of globalisation and postmodern consumer culture.

John Lloyd is a contributing editor for the *Financial Times*, co-founder and Director of Journalism at the Reuters Institute for the Study of Journalism at the University of Oxford, Chairman of the advisory board of the Moscow School of Political Studies, and an associate fellow of Nuffield College, Oxford. He is also a columnist for *La Repubblica* of Rome and a columnist for Reuters.com. His books include *Loss without Limit: The British Miners' Strike* (1986), *Rebirth of a Nation: An Anatomy of Russia* (1997), and *What the Media are Doing to Our Politics* (2004).

Heng Lu is a PhD candidate in the Department of Media and Communication, City University of Hong Kong. His research interest covers online public opinion, online user behaviour, and online sampling techniques.

Maggie Jones Patterson, Professor of Journalism at Duquesne University, was a reporter for the *Pittsburgh Press*. She writes about media ethics and gender issues. She co-authored *Art Rooney: A Sporting Life*; *Behind the Lines: Case Studies in Investigative Reporting* and *Birth or Abortion? Private Struggles in a Political World*.

Julian Petley is Professor of Screen Media in the School of Arts, Brunel University. A former journalist, he is a member of the editorial board of the *British Journalism Review*, co-chair of the Campaign for Press and Broadcasting Freedom, and a member of the advisory board of Index on Censorship. His most recent publication is *Film and Video Censorship in Contemporary Britain* (2011). He gave written and oral evidence to the Leveson Inquiry and is a contributor to the edited collection *After Leveson* (2012).

Adrian Quinn is a member of the Institute for Communications Studies at the University of Leeds. A reporter by training, he is a graduate of the Centre for Journalism Studies in Cardiff, Wales, and he recently completed his PhD with the Glasgow University Media Group.

Kevin Rafter is the author of eight books and is the editor of *Irish Journalism before Independence: More a Disease than a Profession* (Manchester University Press, 2011) and co-editor of *Independent Newspapers: A History* (Four Courts, 2012). He previously worked as a political journalist including with the *Irish Times* and RTÉ. He joined Dublin City University in 2010 as a senior lecturer in political communication and journalism.

Jacob Rowbottom is a tutorial fellow in Law at University College, Oxford. He is the author of *Democracy Distorted* (2010) and writes on areas of constitutional law, media law, and freedom of expression.

Jingwei Wu is a PhD candidate in the Institute for Media and Communication Studies, Free University Berlin. Her research interests include social interaction and online public opinion, media effects, and intercultural communication.

Foreword

Hugh Tomlinson QC

In the first decade of this century the appetite of the British tabloid press for private information appeared to be insatiable. Large sums of money were expended on private detectives or 'kiss and tell' informants. Information was often gathered by illegal means. The public interest in individual privacy was consistently ignored and the voices of the victims of press intrusion were largely unheard. The close relationship between the press and politicians meant that there was no political will to take remedial action. When criminal misuse of data and interception of voicemail messages were exposed, compliant or intimidated prosecuting authorities confined themselves to minimalist responses.

The Human Rights Act provided the means for the victims to fight back. In a number of landmark cases – particularly those brought by Naomi Campbell and Max Mosley – the tabloid press suffered reverses. A body of privacy law began to develop. One important consequence – which continues to be of political significance – was the resulting sustained press attack on human rights. The judiciary were not spared. The conflict between the tabloid press and the law was at its most intense during the so-called 'Super-Injunction Spring' of 2011. Over a period of a few months the granting of a small number of anonymised privacy injunctions led to a press campaign of civil disobedience, supported by Twitter leaks and compliant Parliamentarians. Although the rhetoric was of press freedom, the press rarely sought to argue that the information was not private or that there was a public interest in disclosure. Rather, the argument was 'might is right': this information has been forced into the public domain so it ought to be there.

Everything changed during a ten-day period in July 2011. This began with the *Guardian*'s disclosure that the *News of the World* had hacked

Milly Dowler's mobile phone and ended with the setting up of the Leveson Inquiry into the culture, practices, and ethics of the press. Since then privacy intrusion – and privacy injunctions – has become increasingly rare. At the time of writing, politicians are still considering how to deal with the recommendations of the Leveson report. A new phase may be about to begin in which, for the first time, the press is subject to a proper and effective regulatory regime, a development which, predictably, most newspapers are resisting with all their might.

This valuable and important book comes, therefore, at a pivotal moment. The essays which it collects were prepared during the 'Leveson truce'. The book's editor, Julian Petley, has gathered an impressive array of scholars who reflect on the privacy intrusion issues which were thrown into sharp focus by the events of 2011. The book was prompted by the 'Media and the Boundaries of Disclosure: Media, Morals, Public Shaming and Privacy' conference organised by the Reuters Institute for the Study of Journalism, University of Oxford, in February 2012.

The practicalities of privacy injunction procedures have meant that English lawyers and judges have often had to deal with complex issues of policy and balance at short notice, and with very limited time for reflection. The press megaphone has meant that the terms of the debate have often been skewed and distorted – with privacy interests often being downgraded when measured against unexamined assumptions about public attitudes to morality and the value of 'entertainment journalism'.

Any new press regulator must grapple with the important issues which are analysed in these essays. It will have to recast the balance between the general, democratic, interest in a vibrant and challenging press on the one hand and the public interest in individual privacy on the other. These issues have, over many years, been distorted by a self-interested tabloid press. They are thoughtfully and insightfully considered in this book, one which needs to be placed on the regulator's reading list.

Careful academic reflection has a crucial role to play in the privacy debate. If these issues are to be properly analysed, then discussion of the kind found in this book is crucial. I commend it to lawyers, judges, and all students of the law of privacy.

Matrix Chambers
January 2013

Introduction

Julian Petley

The genesis of the idea for this book lay in what has come to be known as 'Super-Injunction Spring', a period in the first half of 2011 when most of the UK press (and vast swathes of the blogosphere) claimed that an increasing number of celebrities were successfully applying for super-injunctions in order to prevent the press from exposing details of their private lives. As it turned out, the stories (of which there were 200 in the national press in one week alone in April) were wildly inaccurate. Either through ignorance or, more likely, wilfully – in order to exaggerate the alleged threat to press freedom and to agitate yet again against any form of privacy law being introduced – the papers had confused super-injunctions (an injunction which prevents the reporting of its own existence, as in the Trafigura case) with anonymised privacy injunctions, in which the media are prevented, either temporarily or permanently, from naming the person who has applied for the injunction. In point of fact, as was stated in the *Report of the Committee on Super-injunctions,*[1] which was published on 25 May 2011 largely as a result of the press hullabaloo: 'The recent case law shows that far from becoming common place super-injunctions are rarely applied for and rarely granted.' Indeed, the Committee discovered that only two super-injunctions had been granted since January 2010, one of which was set aside on appeal, and the other was in force for a mere seven days.

It therefore seemed timely to try to cut through the fog of disinformation and self-interest which characterised most press reporting of 'Super-Injunction Spring' and to attempt to tease out the many issues around privacy which this affair raised. For example, are these merely parochial concerns, or do they find resonance elsewhere in the world? In a European context, how can the individual's right to privacy, enshrined in Article 8 of the European Convention on Human Rights, be reconciled with the media's right to freedom of expression under Article 10? Do new forms of media, and especially social media such as Twitter and Facebook, make it impossible to protect privacy online, and, furthermore, do they constitute 'unfair' competition to older forms of media, and especially the popular press, when it comes to reporting matters pertaining to people's private lives? Can invading somebody's privacy ever be justified in terms of serving the public interest, and, if so, what is generally meant by the public interest? If the media publicly shame individuals who, they claim, have behaved immorally, are they acting in the public interest? And, finally, what can the analysis of individual cases of public exposure of private lives contribute to attempting to answer the broad questions raised above?

Shaming is the subject of Jacob Rowbottom's chapter, which usefully unpacks the various meanings which attach to the notion of 'naming and shaming' so beloved by newspapers of a certain kind. As he explains, this activity can have three different functions: to punish informally a named individual; to inform the public about their actions or conduct; and to criticise and express disapproval of them. In practice, Rowbottom argues, the three are difficult to separate and all may arguably be served by the same media campaign. However, each can be separated analytically and each poses its own difficulties, which Rowbottom explores with the aid of various recent examples taken mainly from the British press.

Newspapers frequently argue that each of these 'naming and shaming' functions is in the public interest, whilst their critics claim that such stories merely appeal to what interests sufficient numbers of people to make it profitable to publish them. Meanwhile, newspapers themselves (along with the odd judge) are apt to claim either that the public interest is impossible to define, or that that the distinction between the public interest and what interests the public is a spurious one, not least because if papers did not publish stories which are 'merely interesting', they would be out of business and therefore unable to publish stories which are genuinely in the public interest. A discussion of what actually constitutes the public interest is thus clearly called for, and this is provided by my first chapter, which argues that there already exist various workable definitions of the public interest which could be drawn upon in order to introduce a public-interest defence for serious journalism in all laws which pertain to media content of one kind or another. I also draw attention to a number of empirical studies (almost wholly ignored by the press) which suggest that when newspapers claim that they are merely 'giving the public what it wants', they are actually on very shaky ground.

As both Rowbottom and myself point out, newspapers are keen to claim their right to freedom of expression under Article 10 of the European Convention of Human Rights. But the Convention also protects, under Article 8, the individual's right to privacy – and this includes privacy from media intrusion. The scene is thus set for a clash of conflicting rights in which, increasingly, the courts are the final arbiter. Stories which involve 'naming and shaming' are particularly prone to becoming embroiled in such a legal conflict, although stories which are 'merely' intrusive frequently do so too. However, Simon Dawes suggests that reducing the privacy issue to a legal question of balancing the right to a free press and the right to privacy fails to address a more fundamental issue. Liberal theory concerning both the freedom of the press and the freedom of the individual to lead a private life conceives of freedom as primarily freedom from the state; a freedom that is guaranteed and protected by and within a free market. But, according to Dawes, what the phone hacking scandal demonstrates has less to do with insufficient freedom from the state than with insufficient freedom from the market, since it was the demands of market-driven journalism which led journalists to behave unethically and, indeed, illegally. He thus suggests replacing a liberal approach to balancing the rights to privacy and freedom of expression with a civic republican approach that takes both the market and the state into its account of freedom. In particular, this approach recognises that there are occasions when the state needs to regulate the press in the interests of press freedom – when, for example, that freedom is threatened by oligopoly or overweening proprietor power. Dawes argues that press freedom is best defended by recourse to Jürgen Habermas's concept of the public sphere, a realm free from both state and market influence, in which the democratic role of the media is privileged over its commercial function, and the public is seen as being composed of people who are first and foremost citizens. Crucially, this emphasis on citizenship also has the effect of drawing attention to the private realm's importance for the public realm, avoiding the tendency to reduce privacy to simply an individualistic and depoliticised value.

Both Rowbottom and Dawes mention the importance of John Stuart Mill to debates about privacy and press freedom, and Mill looms large in my second chapter, which explores the contribution which philosophy can make to these debates. It does so in two ways. First, it examines Samuel D.

Warren and Louis D. Brandeis's 1890 essay 'The Right to Privacy', which is as much a philosophical as a legal text, in that it explores the fundamental issues underlying such a right and is thus as relevant today as when it was first written. Since this article actually gave birth to the legal recognition of privacy in the US, it also usefully gives the lie to British journalists' frequent claims that there is no privacy legislation in that country. Second, it examines Max Mosley's case against the *News of the World* in the light of Mill's *On Liberty*, asking in particular whether the newspaper's actions could be considered as so harmful in Mill's terms as to warrant legal sanction. It also asks to what extent Mill's ideas on freedom of expression are still valid in the modern media age.

The new media are the subject of both Hanne Detel's chapter and that by Jingwei Wu and Heng Lu. The former is concerned with how the internet and other digital technologies have helped to bring about a condition known as the 'new visibility', something which affects not only prominent people such as politicians but ordinary citizens as well. Under the conditions of this new form of mediated visibility, the features of shaming processes and scandals have been significantly transformed. First, a much wider range of people than journalists, the former gatekeepers in this area, are able to disclose transgressions, as well as to determine who and what kinds of behaviour are susceptible to shaming. Second, the diffusion of scandal-inducing content evolves as an interplay between the traditional and the new media. Although the former have lost their monopoly on invoking and perpetuating scandals they still play a major role by intensifying the impact of the transgressions first disclosed on the internet. Third, the audience is no longer passive, but can intervene by expressing moral outrage directly via the new media. Finally, compared to scandals in the traditional media, the scope of shaming processes has become less predictable and the potential damage to reputation more extensive. This is because shaming content can be accessed from anywhere in the world, and can be spread and shared extremely rapidly. Moreover, because this kind of material can remain indefinitely on the internet, transgressions revealed there can ruin reputations for years.

Discussions of privacy and the new media frequently revolve around the issue of whether certain users effectively 'invade' their own privacy by making so much material about themselves publicly available. In their chapter, Jingwei Wu and Heng Lu are concerned with self-disclosure on social networking sites, and reveal the results of research which they undertook to try to discover whether there are gender differences in self-disclosure on such sites and, if so, whether these vary across cultures. They found that the users from cultures which they term 'individualistic' are more willing to disclose themselves online than are users from cultures which they describe as 'collectivist'. They also found that, unlike in offline situations, men are more willing to disclose themselves online than are women. They conclude that gender differences in online self-disclosure do indeed vary across different cultural contexts, in that within individualistic cultures, men are more willing to disclose themselves, whilst within collectivist cultures, women are more willing to do so.

The above two chapters also introduce a useful international element to the debate about privacy which, in the UK, can sometimes seem distinctly parochial. This element continues in two cross-cultural studies of press journalism. The first, by Romayne Smith Fullerton and Maggie Jones Patterson, compares the attitudes to personal privacy displayed by crime reporting in Sweden, the Netherlands, and the UK. The research on which this is based involved four strands: a close reading of the reporting of certain high-profile crimes by news organisations in the three countries concerned; in-depth interviews with journalists and scholars about press practices and cultural values in their particular countries; analysis of prevailing ethics codes and accountability practices of national professional organisations, press councils, and journalists' unions; and an exploration via the interviews and already-existing literature of the pressures that threaten to iron out national story-telling differences and to lead to a default tell-all style. At the same time, however, the authors make clear that there still exist significant differences in crime reporting in papers that adhere to the North Atlantic liberal model (in this case, those of the UK) and those that adhere to the North/Central European corporatist model (here, those of Sweden and the Netherlands).

The second cross-cultural chapter is Julia Lefkowitz's study of coverage of the Dominique Strauss-Kahn scandal in *Le Monde* and the *New York Times* (*NYT*), a study which, utilising the concept of authenticity, reveals significant differences in journalistic norms between the two papers, as well as wider cultural and ideological differences between France and the US. Lefkowitz argues that the *NYT*'s claims to authenticity are based on the appearance of accurate and neutral reporting, but that the authenticity which the *NYT* purports to offer is one which is in fact very much in line with the dominant cultural values of its US audience. Accordingly, it repeatedly depicts Strauss-Kahn as inauthentic, drawing attention to mismatches between surface and reality, or words and actions, so that he comes across as not only a hypocritical socialist who is linked with acts of sexual misconduct, but a French 'other'. By contrast, *Le Monde*'s coverage is more overtly polemical and, in this sense, subjective; however, because of the transparency of the ways in which these qualities are conveyed, they are apparent to the reader. So whereas the *NYT* uses language in such a way as to disguise its various subjectivities and viewpoints, *Le Monde* encourages audience engagement through openly presenting opinions which can serve as a stepping stone for wider public debate. *Le Monde* thus puts authenticity to an end that is more democratic, encouraging readers to come up with their own and, in this sense, authentic, viewpoints.

The next three chapters are studies of specific cases of privacy intrusion. Kevin Rafter provides a cross-cultural overview of media attitudes towards reporting politicians' states of health before focusing on the revelation in December 2009 by Ireland's TV3 channel that Irish Finance Minister Brian Lenihan had been diagnosed with pancreatic cancer. The broadcaster was the subject of considerable criticism and censure, although there were a number of supportive voices too, and complaints to the Compliance Committee of the Broadcasting Authority of Ireland were not upheld. Rafter himself concludes that politicians have a right to be sick in private but, because of their role and their responsibilities to citizens, lose the right to withhold disclosure of their medical condition.

Following this, Tim Dwyer turns his attention to a specific case of media 'outing', in this instance that of David Campbell, the transport minister in the former New South Wales Labour government led by Kristina Keneally, who was outed as a gay man by Channel Seven, a commercial, free-to-air television station. The incident quickly became a *cause célèbre* for privacy and gay rights advocates, and also served to highlight the fact that Australia has no general tort for breach of privacy either at common law or in statute. Dwyer himself argues that the journalist concerned (and Seven Network in broadcasting the item) had acted unethically in assembling a patchwork of assertions and smear in order to carry out a media scalping. However, he also notes that the Australian Communications and Media Authority, which supervises the *Commercial Television Industry Code of Practice*, refused to uphold the complaints which it received about the broadcast; although it agreed that Campbell's privacy had indeed been breached, it found this to be justified on the grounds that there was 'an identifiable public interest' for doing so. This again raises the whole question of the public interest which is the subject of my first chapter, but does so in an Australian context and with regard to a specific case, which is extremely useful. Dwyer concludes that the whole affair exposed a convenient alliance of commercially competitive media interests, regulatory supervision, and moral judgement that shelters behind the rhetoric of acting in the public's interest.

The final case study is Adrian Quinn's detailed analysis of the 'naming and shaming' of the former television presenter John Leslie in the closing months of 2002 for being the perpetrator of a 'date rape' which Ulrika Jonson describes (but without naming the rapist) in her autobiography *Honest*. Once Leslie had been inadvertently fingered as the culprit by Matthew Wright on his Channel 5 show *The Wright Stuff*, 30 other women came forward with similar claims, and what the *Observer* journalist Mary Riddell called 'the alternative tribunal' and *Independent* editor Simon Kelner 'the most powerful court in the land' swung into action. The *Sun* even published an appeal headlined in capital letters: 'HAVE YOU BEEN A VICTIM OF JOHN LESLIE? CALL THE SUN NEWS DESK.' What emerges from this chapter is a frightening picture of Leslie being tried by the media, effectively for failing to defend himself against an allegation of sexual assault for which he never faced charge or trial. Few, including Leslie himself, emerge with much credit for this story, but it also demonstrates that the laws on both libel and contempt are of little practical help to victims of this kind of 'naming and shaming'.

Finally, John Lloyd returns us to some of the more general themes explored in the opening chapters of this book. But if the focus there was on issues raised by 'Super-Injunction Spring', Lloyd's concern is with those emanating from the phone-hacking scandal and the consequent Leveson Inquiry into the culture, practices, and ethics of the press. Borrowing from C. P. Snow, Lloyd argues that there are essentially two quite different cultures at work in the British press, and indeed in the wider society. One sees personal privacy as something needing to be preserved, by regulation and by law, from intrusion by the press. The other sees such intrusion as desirable, since its object is to expose moral turpitude. The first view is held, broadly speaking, by the 'establishment' – politicians, the judiciary, the upmarket press; the second by the tabloids. But as Lloyd makes clear, the division between the two cultures of journalism lies deeper than in simply their different attitudes to privacy – what we have here, in many people's eyes, are two quite different, indeed conflicting, kinds of journalism: the one responsible, truthful, reliable, evidence-based, and concerned with the serious issues facing society; the other irresponsible, untruthful, unreliable, gossip-based, and concerned only with the trivia of celebrity culture.

At this point, and by way of a conclusion, I would suggest that those seriously concerned with the future of journalism really do need to grasp the normative nettle and to argue that there is a clear distinction between good and bad journalism. Or rather, between journalism and non-journalism. As Brian Cathcart has put it, there is actually a vast gulf between journalism, which is demonstrably valuable to society in that 'it tells us what is new, important and interesting in public life, it holds authority to account, it promotes informed debate, it entertains and enlightens' (2011: 35), and simply intruding into people's personal lives for the purpose of profit. In the latter case:

> The subject matter is almost never important – except to the victims, whose lives may be permanently blighted – and while a story may entertain, it does so only in a way that bear-baiting or public executions used to entertain. The whole activity exists on the border of legality, skipping from one side of the line to the other at its own convenience and without sincere regard for the public interest. (Ibid. 36)

As the government ponders its response to Lord Justice Leveson's Report, making this distinction and acting on its consequences are of fundamental importance. Even before Leveson had reported, the entirety of the newspaper press had drawn its wagons tightly in a defensive circle, national press lined up firmly with local, tabloid with broadsheet, journalist with privacy invader. In the early days of Leveson the old Fleet Street bruisers Paul Dacre and Kelvin McKenzie were loudly in evidence, but, as publication of the report neared, the megaphone was increasingly handed to journalists perceived to have more gravitas, such as Peter Preston, Nick Cohen, Simon Jenkins and Raymond Snoddy, all now getting hot under the collar in a Melanie Phillips vein. The bitter enmity between the liberal and illiberal press seemed to have been conveniently forgotten in the greater battle against what was grossly misreported by the papers as 'state regulation'. However, once the report was published, and the government came up with the idea of a royal charter to underpin a new self-regulatory system, dissent broke out in the ranks, with the *Guardian, Independent* and *Financial Times* showing themselves willing at least to consider the idea, whilst the rest of the press stamped its feet and threw its toys out of the pram. At the time of writing, what is going to happen next is unclear.

However, the end of the unholy alliance between the liberal and the illiberal press is wholly to be welcomed, since this was a tactic fraught with danger for journalism. As Cathcart argues: 'If journalists, for reasons of nostalgia, inertia, confusion, or misplaced loyalty, choose to keep swimming with the privacy invaders, they may well drown with them' (2011: 45). The press may well succeed in bullying the government into kicking Leveson's recommendations into the long grass, but it cannot escape the following facts: the British public has an extremely low opinion of journalists and journalism *as a whole*, its members are buying ever fewer papers, and a significant proportion of it would support forms of privacy legislation which, even if inadvertently, would almost certainly hamper serious investigative journalism along with the prying and snooping of the privacy invaders. Another press scandal of phone-hacking proportions, or perhaps further shocking revelations from the numerous phone-hacking trials, could make it impossible for the government to resist demands for such regulation – and one very much doubts that it would be unduly concerned about the dangers to investigative journalism, which it all too obviously regards as a thorn in its side.

There is a pressing need, then, to be clear about what journalism actually is, and how best to go about defending it. In this, as in so much else, we are most emphatically not 'all in this together'. Lines have to be drawn, and judgements and choices made. Non-journalism threatens the existence of proper journalism, and for the latter to throw in its lot with the former in the face of an alleged 'threat' to press freedom, which is actually no such thing, is little short of suicidal. These tasks are particularly urgent in the UK in the wake of Leveson, but, as various contributions to this book make clear, the problems facing journalism in Britain are hardly unique, even if they exist in a particularly exacerbated form there. If the chapters in this book help readers, wherever in the world they may be, to think about what should be the functions of journalism, and about how journalism which serves the public interest can best be protected and promoted, then they will have served their purpose.

Note

1   http://www.judiciary.gov.uk/Resources/JCO/Documents/Reports/super-injunction-report-20052011.pdf.

Reference

Cathcart, Brian (2011) 'Code breakers', *Index on Censorship*, 40(2): 35–45.

1

To Punish, Inform, and Criticise: The Goals of Naming and Shaming

Jacob Rowbottom

Freeloading MPs, businesses with poor customer service, sex offenders, under-performing schools, and wayward footballers may appear to have little in common, but all can find themselves subject to a media 'name and shame' campaign. The term 'name and shame' is often used loosely by the media, and can arise in a wide range of contexts and serve a number of different goals. In this chapter, three goals for naming and shaming will be explored: (1) to punish informally a named individual; (2) to inform the public about their actions or conduct; and (3) to criticise and express disapproval of them. In practice, the three are difficult to separate and all may arguably be served by the same media campaign. However, each can be separated analytically and each poses its own difficulties.

To 'name and shame' is to disclose information about an identified person or body, which either seeks to induce shame in that person, or at least express a judgement that the person ought to feel ashamed of themselves (on the differences between shame, shameful, and shaming, see Massaro, 1997: 672). If the practice succeeds in inducing a sense of shame, it can lead to feelings of exclusion and isolation for the named person. Even if a naming and shaming practice does not succeed in inducing shame, it can lead to a loss of status or reputation in the eyes of others. A person may feel no shame about their sexual behaviour, but may still want to avoid public disapproval among those who believe that behaviour to be immoral.

Naming and shaming by the media is distinct from publishing a story that invades a person's privacy (Massaro, 1997: 665–6). When a newspaper reveals that a celebrity is in the early stages of pregnancy, that story will invade the celebrity's privacy but may not seek to induce shame. Conversely, a newspaper might name and shame a person convicted of a criminal offence, but normally that would not be private information. While the two are distinct, they can overlap. When such overlaps occur, legal conflicts can follow in which the courts have to consider the strength of the privacy right over the possible justification for the naming and shaming practice. This chapter does not seek to resolve such questions of balance, but instead seeks to identify and explore three types of goal that may underlie naming and shaming. There are other reasons why the media might wish to name and shame a person, such as to boost profits or to entertain, but the focus here is on the goals that may justify the practice in certain circumstances (over and above general arguments for free speech and the right to convey accurate information).

To punish

Naming and shaming can be seen as a form of punishment for those who deviate from certain standards. In some cases, public authorities use publicity as a formal sanction. For example, section 66 of the Financial Services and Markets Act 2000 provides that the Financial Services Authority can, as one of its disciplinary powers, publish a statement that a person is guilty of misconduct (Cartwright, 2012). Section 10 of the Corporate Manslaughter and Homicide Act 2007 allows courts to impose publicity orders for corporate manslaughter and homicide convictions. Under such orders, the company can be required to publicise the fact of its own conviction (possibly through newspaper advertisements), giving details of the offence and the fine imposed. The official use of naming and shaming penalties may be potent in the context of corporate activity, given the importance of reputation and the limited effectiveness of fines (Macrory, 2006). However, arguments have been made for shaming penalties to be used more widely in criminal law, in relation to the activities of individuals (Braithwaite, 1989; Kahan, 2005). For example, in the US, one court has required convicted sex offenders to purchase advertisements in newspapers to highlight their crime and to encourage others to seek treatment (McAlinden, 2005: 378). In the UK, former minister Ann Widdecombe was quoted by the *Telegraph*, 24 April 2012, as arguing that people found very drunk in public should, following a court hearing, be named and shamed in the press.

Advocates of shaming penalties argue that publicity can serve various justifications for punishment. Most obviously, it can provide a deterrent. The loss of reputation, status, and social opportunities that can follow negative publicity may deter individuals from engaging in a criminal act. Aside from the potential for social disapproval, the practice of shaming (and also repentance) can 'build consciences which internally deter criminal behaviour even with the absence of external shaming' (Braithwaite, 1989: 75). The consequences that flow from being named and shamed may also constitute a form of retribution for the wrongdoing. Furthermore, a formal publicity sanction can serve the expressive function of punishment that publicly condemns certain conduct and signals that disapproval to the offender (Feinberg, 1965). Publicity can also communicate the censure of the criminal to third parties, which 'conveys the message that the conduct is reprehensible, and should be eschewed' (Von Hirsch, 1993: 11).

While the legal authority can provide publicity through its own press releases and websites, it can be more effective if the publicity is carried in the media. By reaching a wide audience through the media, the impact of the publicity sanction on the company or individual's reputation may be greater. In this way, the media can assist where a legal authority has decided to 'name and shame' as a formal penalty. However, in the UK, publicity sanctions are not the norm. Instead, the role of the media in publicising legal wrongs is more informal.

The most obvious example of informal publicity arises when the media report the fact of a person's criminal conviction and the surrounding details. The publicity is not part of the formal punishment, but can still serve the deterrent, retributive, and expressive goals of punishments, in the same way as a formal publicity sanction. While publicity from crime reporting can serve certain punitive goals, it is important to note that publicity is not necessary for an effective punishment. Publicity is not the norm for minors convicted of criminal offences, whose identities are not normally disclosed in the absence of strong countervailing reasons. Lord Bingham stated that for convicted minors publicity should not be used 'as an additional punishment' and that it is 'very difficult to see any place for "naming and shaming"' (*McKerry v Teesdale & Wear Valley Justices*, 2000). Furthermore, in certain European countries, such as Sweden, the media do not normally publicise the names of adults convicted of criminal offences, reflecting an effort to reduce the level of stigmatisation.

When reporting trials and convictions, the primary function of the media is to inform people about the criminal justice system, a function that will be considered in the next section. However, it often seems that the media intend their reports to have a punitive effect. The goal can be inferred from the condemnatory tone used by the media, and especially the press, when reporting certain criminal convictions. Serious criminals are sometimes described as 'fiends' or 'monsters', which promotes their exclusion from society. The media themselves refer to naming and shaming. For example, on the *Manchester Evening News* website, under the heading 'Locked Up', the paper states that it is 'naming and shaming criminals convicted of serious offences' in the previous month.[1] It displays a photograph of the convicted individual and a summary of the crime committed. The use of the term 'shaming' itself suggests that the media are doing more than merely reporting, and are seeking to impose a social penalty.

Media publicity surrounding a conviction does not constitute punishment in the usual sense of the word, which refers to sanctions 'imposed and administered by an authority constituted by a legal system' (Hart, 2008: 5). The courts have stressed that only they have the power to punish people for a crime (*R. (on the Application of Ellis) v Chief Constable of Essex* [2003] EWHC 1321 (Admin) at [30]). In this view, it is for the courts to decide what sanction is appropriate and proportionate. Despite this, informal publicity has some connection with punishment. John Spencer (2000: 466) has written that, for adults, '[t]he unspoken premise seems to be that being named in the newspaper is a part of the sanction, and the risk of public shame is part of the law's system of deterrents'. If this were to be more openly recognised, then the courts could consider the harsh effects of publicity when deciding the formal sanction. The court has on occasion mentioned the high levels of shame caused by publicity as a mitigating factor in sentencing (*R v Oliver* [2011] EWCA Crim 3114), although it is not clear when the courts will rely on such a factor. The US scholar Douglas Husak (2010) has argued that a more explicit connection between publicity and punishment should be made, calling for the level of stigma generated by the media to be taken into account when deciding the severity of the sentence. However, if such an approach were to be taken, it would raise concerns about equity of treatment if those criminals suffering the greatest reputational losses, such as businessmen or celebrities, were to receive shorter jail terms.

While distinct from the formal penalty, media publicity can provide a supplementary informal sanction for a violation of the law. By acting in this way, the media engage in a voluntary collaboration with the state.

The media may be reluctant to emphasise such a function, as it points in the opposite direction to the classic view of the media as an independent watchdog over the state. By naming and shaming the convicted criminal, the media advance rather than check the interests of the state, and seek to encourage compliance with the laws. That may be no bad thing, and on many occasions cooperation between the media and the state will be expected. For example, the media may publicise statements from the police about a spate of crimes in a particular area. Crime reporting can be supportive of the state in more general ways, given the tendency of the media to 'exaggerate the threat of crime and in the main promote policing and punishment as the antidote' (Greer and Reiner, 2012: 269). Of course, not all crime reporting is supportive of existing policies. Certain parts of the media advance a 'tough on crime' agenda and criticise judges for imposing 'soft' sentences. While taking a critical stance, such reports still seek to further the interests underlying the legal rule by asking how it can be better enforced. The relationship between the media and crime raises many complex issues, but the central point made here is that the reporting of convictions is one way that the media can informally collaborate with the state to further certain punitive goals.

There are a number of criticisms that can be advanced against publicity as a formal or informal sanction (Kahan, 2005). It is not clear whether naming and shaming will be effective and the publicity may be counterproductive. Being named as guilty of particular conduct may fail to trigger the desired social response and be regarded as a badge of honour among some people. Naming and shaming may also highlight the frequency with which the norm is broken, and thereby normalise and make more acceptable the very behaviour regarded by the authorities as shameful. A contrasting line of criticism is that naming and shaming practices may be too effective and undermine the goal of rehabilitation. The social stigma generated by naming and shaming an individual may be so great that the person has difficulty putting past mistakes behind them and being accepted by the wider community. Where the public has a strong reaction to a particular crime, the effects of publicity may be disproportionate to the wrong in question (Cartwright, 2012). Given the unpredictability of the public response to a person being named and shamed, it is likely that publicity can both under- and over-punish in different circumstances. So far the discussion has focused on a simple example of naming and shaming by communicating details of a criminal conviction. This should arguably be the least controversial example of punitive naming and shaming, as the legal authorities have made a public finding of a legal wrong that deserves punishment. However, as the discussion above shows, it raises a number of difficulties. Deeper problems arise when the media act more independently of the state and take a proactive role in deciding when people should be subject to censure and stigmatised as criminals. The famous *News of the World* campaign to name and shame convicted child sex offenders went beyond the reporting of convictions, and included details of the crimes, and photographs and addresses of the offenders, labelled all the people into one category and had a strong emotive tone. Far from aiding law enforcers, it was condemned by the police and was criticised by many as leading to vigilantism. Other examples include the media naming someone they believe to have committed a crime, even though that person has not been convicted in a court. In these examples, the media target what they take to be a breach of a criminal standard, but do so independently of the legal authorities.

While the independent actions of the media raise all the problems of shaming penalties discussed earlier, there are further criticisms of such methods. The individual named by the media prior to prosecution or conviction may not be guilty and may be subject to unfair criticism (Braithwaite, 1989: 158). The media are not subject to strict evidential requirements before condemning an individual. Where the media publish information beyond the details of a conviction, there are dangers that the publication will interfere with other legal rights, such as the right to privacy (Corbett, 2011). Finally, there is the questionable legitimacy of the media's authority to invoke informal punishments. As stated earlier, the courts have stressed that only they have the power to punish people for a crime. While publishing allegations of criminal activity independently of legal proceedings may be justified, shaming as a form of punishment does not offer such a justification.

In other examples, the media may seek to shame as a way of punishing violations of non-legal standards. For example, a newspaper might decide to name companies that have used overseas contractors with a poor record on labour standards. While that publication serves an informational role in advising on consumer choices, there is also an element of censure, in which the actions of the company are condemned. Where the conduct violates widely accepted standards, there may be little objection to such social censure. However, in a speech to the Society of Editors in 2008,[2]

Daily Mail editor Paul Dacre made a broader argument defending the media's role in enforcing social standards:

> *Since time immemorial public shaming has been a vital element in defending the parameters of what are considered acceptable standards of social behaviour, helping ensure that citizens – rich and poor – adhere to them for the good of the greater community. For hundreds of years, the press has played a role in that process. It has the freedom to identify those who have offended public standards of decency – the very standards its readers believe in – and hold the transgressors up to public condemnation.*

One difficulty with this approach lies in determining what social standards should be upheld in this way. In some cases, it is debatable whether a wrong has arisen, such as where a newspaper 'shames' a celebrity for having an affair. There are further reasons for caution about such informal publicity sanctions, given that Mill warned of 'the moral coercion of public opinion' which could lead to a 'social tyranny more formidable than many kinds of political oppression' (1991: 8, 14). However, if there is to be a sanction of public opinion in certain cases, it should not be unilaterally imposed by media that decide what the standards are, whether they have been breached, and what penalty should be imposed. The media still have a role in expressing and persuading others of their view about such conduct, which in turn can create a social pressure to conform, but that will be considered below as part of the freedom to criticise, rather than to punish.

Several punitive functions of the media have been outlined. To critics of the media, these functions may be unattractive in so far as they assign to the media a power that is open to abuse. If there is a punitive aspect to the media naming and shaming, there are dangers if this power is left to the discretion of editors. The punitive functions of the media are also unattractive for the media industry because they stand in tension with the classic liberal account of the press as a check on the state. However, discussion of a punitive function at least recognises the power of the media to have a negative impact on a person's life and the informal role they play in social control. It is arguable that the media have some value in this role when they act in collaboration with the state. However, a punitive role for naming and shaming in the media can be justified, if at all, only in limited circumstances. Greater exploration of this function in future might identify possible safeguards and conditions that can be attached to this power of the media.

To inform

A second goal of naming and shaming is to provide information. A simple example is where a local paper names and shames restaurants with the worst results recorded by food hygiene inspectors, as in the case of the *South Wales Echo*, 15 August 2011. The purpose of the publicity is not to punish or embarrass the restaurant, but to allow people to make an informed choice when deciding which restaurant to visit. This goal arises in circumstances where the audience members might face a choice or decision for which that information may be relevant. The justification can arise in a wide range of circumstances. When the *Daily Telegraph* named and shamed those MPs who had abused the expenses system, it was justified not as a punitive measure (although it had a punitive effect on certain MPs), but as providing information so that people could decide for themselves whether a penalty should be imposed via the ballot box. When the government introduced a programme for publishing details of criminal convictions, the primary aim was to secure public confidence in the criminal justice system by providing information about its workings (Home Office, 2009).

In practice, naming and shaming can be both punitive and informational. Reporting criminal convictions can provide an informal punishment, while at the same time informing the public about the workings of the justice system. A distinction can, however, be drawn between the two in the abstract. When naming and shaming seeks to punish, the information is expected and hoped to trigger a social sanction. The naming and shaming fails in its punitive goal if it produces no such reaction. By contrast, with an informational goal, it is for the recipients of the information to decide for themselves how to react. If someone decides to continue going to a restaurant that has been shamed for poor hygiene, or if a person still votes for a politician who has been shamed for making extravagant expenses claims, the media will not have failed in their informational goal.

If the goal is merely to facilitate people's decisions or choices, it begs the question of what role shaming has to play. Instead, the neutral provision of information without any condemnatory tone would be sufficient to inform people. If the goal of the *News of the World*'s campaign on child sex offenders was solely to inform and warn parents about people living in their neighbourhood, then there would be no need to describe the individuals as 'fiends' or 'monsters' (Thomas, 2004: 349). There are two responses as to why shaming may play a role in the informational goal.

The first is that the condemnation may be necessary to add colour to the story (*R (on the application of Stanley, Marshall and Kelly) v Metropolitan Police Commissioner* [2004] EWHC 2229 (Admin) at [40]). If a story has a sensationalist tone, it is more likely to attract attention and engage readers. It may also give greater context to the story, enabling people to understand its importance (*Jameel v Wall Street Journal* [2006] UKHL 44 at [51–2]). On this view, the element of shaming is ancillary to the core informational goal. Second, when providing information, the media are not neutral regarding how that information should be used, and seek to advise their audiences to respond in a particular way. The idea that a person has been shamed is itself a steer to the audience to react negatively. Such advice, however, remains something that the audience can take or leave.

Both of these responses are premised on an assumption that the condemnation entailed by naming and shaming does not distort the information being conveyed. For example, a sensational story about a sex offender living in a certain locality may lead readers to over-estimate the risk posed. In such circumstances, the shaming may hinder rational decision-making. Even where there is no sensationalism in the reporting, naming and shaming stories tend to be selective in advancing a negative angle and can give a skewed picture to the audience. For example, where the media name and shame a failing school, the story may lack context or an explanation of why a school is failing. While naming and shaming may provide a way of communicating information that is more likely to seize the audience's attention, it is less likely to provide a contextualised and rounded understanding of more complex issues.

The goal of providing information is connected to the classic justification of media freedom. The Strasbourg Court has repeatedly stated that freedom of expression is of particular importance for the media, as 'it is incumbent on them to impart information and ideas' on matters in the public interest, and to perform the role of a public watchdog (*The Observer and the Guardian v United Kingdom* (1992) 14 EHRR 153 at [59]). In the domestic courts, Lord Bingham has emphasised the need to allow the press to alert and inform citizens of 'matters which call or may call for consideration and action' (*McCartan Turkington Breen (A Firm) v Times Newspapers Ltd* [2001] 2 AC 277 at [290]), and of the 'role of the press in exposing abuses and miscarriages of justice' (*R v Shayler* [2002] UKHL 11 at [21]). The informational role can sometimes be performed in cooperation with the state; for example, where the media publish information released by a regulator, which will be useful to consumers in that it names and shames companies in breach of certain standards. However, naming and shaming practices can in certain contexts fulfil the watchdog function of the media. The publication of MPs' expenses claims ensured that elected officials were held to account. Justifying the disclosure of information in this way has a strong appeal for those working in the media, in so far as it portrays them as serving the needs of the public and helping the audience to make their own minds up. These arguments acknowledge the power of the media, but claim that it is used to empower the audience.

While the media are normally free to provide information, difficult questions arise when naming and shaming discloses information that is normally private or confidential in law. To address such a conflict, the court will normally ask whether disclosure is in the public interest. When applying this standard, there are a number of factors that the court takes into account, including: the subject matter of the disclosure (giving strongest protection to information on political issues (*R (ProLife Alliance) v BBC* [2003] UKHL 23 at [6]) and matters of public importance, but also extending to commercial information); whether the disclosure relates to a public figure; or whether it exposes some form of wrongdoing or hypocrisy. If these factors are present, then the court will place greater emphasis on the right to publish. Most obviously, where the information relates to a politician, it may have some value in helping people make their choice at the ballot box, or holding the politician to account (*Von Hannover v Germany* at [64], citing *Plon (Société) v France* [2004] ECHR 58148/00). By contrast, gossip is frequently given little weight when balancing rights to privacy and reputation with freedom of expression. Baroness Hale has spoken dismissively of 'vapid tittle-tattle' about the activities of footballers' wives and girlfriends (*Jameel v Wall Street Journal* [2006] UKHL 44 at [147]), and noted that:

> *The political and social life of the community, and the intellectual, artistic or personal development of individuals, are not obviously assisted by pouring [sic] over the intimate details of a fashion model's private life.*
> (*Campbell v MGN* [2004] UKHL 22 at [149])

This approach attempts to identify those areas on which the public has a need or right to be informed, which should be given priority over other competing rights. But there are a number of difficult boundary issues that arise with this approach. First of all, it is not clear what types of expression are deemed to be political or a matter of public importance. At its narrowest it could mean those issues on which a political decision is to be taken, or at its broadest any issue that can impact on the formation of political opinions. Second, it is not clear who is a public figure. In some cases, the courts have taken a sceptical view of arguments that a person's private life is relevant simply because he or she is a talented footballer or singer (*McKennitt v Ash* [2006] EWCA 1714). However, more recent decisions have held that, in some cases at least, there will be expectations of behaviour attached to certain roles, such as captain of the England football team (*Ferdinand v MGN* [2011] EWHC 2454 (QB) at [90]). Third, even if we can identify a public figure, it is not clear how much information can be disclosed about such a person. Revealing that a politician has a drink problem which is hampering the performance of their work might be justified, but the interest of the public would not go as far as knowing their full medical history. The European Court of Human Rights has accepted that there are limits to what information can be revealed about a politician. Under the Court's current approach, it is not simply a matter of letting the public decide for themselves what information is relevant for political decisions (Fenwick and Phillipson, 2007: 791). Finally, there is debate about the types of wrongdoing about which the public should be informed.

Debates about privacy laws tend to revolve around the informational value (or the lack of such a value) of the disclosure. Framing the debate in this way is popular with the media as it portrays them as serving the audience, whether as voters or consumers. Emphasising the provision of information thus helps to legitimise the power of the media. Informational value also provides a focus for privacy campaigners, who question the necessity for audiences to be informed of trivia and gossip. Both sides agree on the importance of the informational function, but disagree over what disclosures it justifies. Questions about whether information is of sufficient value to justify publication as being in the public interest is a matter of judgment on which there is considerable disagreement. Given the difference of views, the courts accept that a degree of leeway should be given to journalists to decide what is a matter of public importance (*Ferdinand v MGN* [2011] EWHC 2454 (QB) at [64]). This area of dispute gives the media scope to argue that practices of naming and shaming are justified as a means of communicating information, even when the element of shaming is largely ancillary to the primary goal of informing people.

To criticise

The third goal of the media in naming and shaming is to criticise a person's conduct. This goal often goes hand-in-hand with the informational goal. For example, when a newspaper names and shames a bank for a breach of professional ethics, it will both convey details that inform the public of the wrongdoing, and also convey the newspaper's views on the bank's conduct and any lessons to be learned. Offering an opinion and its own interpretation of events is a core part of the media's role in disseminating diverse views and ideas. It is also part of the classic watchdog function of the media to be free to criticise government and other powerful institutions. This is, of course, subject to the condition that multiple voices are being communicated in the media system as a whole. If there is a sufficient range of voices, then conduct criticised in one media entity can be defended in another. It also needs to be borne in mind that the broadcast media are bound by law to remain impartial on matters of political controversy, whereas the press is free to be as partial as it chooses.

In certain cases it will be debatable whether the person being criticised has done anything of which to be ashamed. Examples include media stories naming and shaming doctors who have performed a large number of abortions, lab workers who have conducted tests on animals, businessmen who pay low wages to staff, and celebrities who have affairs. In each of these cases, the morality and ethics of such activities are the subject of disagreement. Where there are high levels of disagreement, exposure in the media is not expected to induce feelings of shame in the individual. Instead, by indicating that they believe a person ought to feel shame, the media express their disapproval and seek to convince others that this view is correct. Here the media act not as authority figures censuring an individual, nor as public servants telling people what they need to know, but as speakers in their own right expressing a point of view. The argument is not that the public *needs* to know a particular piece of information, but that the media would like to disclose the information in order to convey a viewpoint.

Difficulties arise when the media seek to criticise a person by publishing information that would normally be protected by legal rights of confidentiality or privacy. In such cases, the courts have to decide whether the rights of the media or of the person being criticised should prevail. In resolving such questions, the courts will normally look at whether the disclosure is in the public interest, relying on the criteria discussed in the previous section. Two contrasting approaches to the public interest can be found in the cases concerning the public exposure of sexual behaviour. In *Mosley v News Group Newspapers* [2008] EWHC 1777 (QB), Eady J. stated that it is now recognised that 'sexual conduct is a significant aspect of human life in respect of which people should be free to choose' and that 'it is not for the state or for the media to expose sexual conduct which does not involve any significant breach of the criminal law' (at [125] and [127]). This view suggests that lawful sexual activity should be engaged in without the risk of being named and shamed, save in exceptional circumstances. In this case, Eady J. found that there was no public interest in publishing details of Max Mosley's sexual activities.

The approach of Eady J. has come under attack from those who believe the media should be free to express their disapproval of certain conduct, an attack that has been led by Paul Dacre, whose views were cited earlier. Dacre may take some comfort from the position of Tugendhat J. in *Terry (formerly LNS) v Persons Unknown* [2010] EWHC 119 (QB) at [104]:

> *There is much public debate as to what conduct is or is not socially harmful. Not all conduct that is socially harmful is unlawful, and there is often said to be much inconsistency in the law. For example, some commentators contrast the law on consumption of alcohol with that on other intoxicating substances. The fact that conduct is private and lawful is not, of itself, conclusive of the question whether or not it is in the public interest that it be discouraged. There is no suggestion that the conduct in question in the present case ought to be unlawful, or that any editor would ever suggest that it should be. But in a plural society there will be some who would suggest that it ought to be discouraged. That is why sponsors may be sensitive to the public image of those sportspersons whom they pay to promote their products. Freedom to live as one chooses is one of the most valuable freedoms. But so is the freedom to criticise (within the limits of the law) the conduct of other members of society as being socially harmful, or wrong. Both the law, and what are, and are not, acceptable standards of lawful behaviour have changed very considerably over the*

years, particularly in the last half century or so. During that time these
changes (or, as many people would say, this progress) have been achieved
as a result of public discussion and criticism of those engaged in what
were, at the time, lawful activities.

Tugendhat J.'s comments have been approved in later cases (e.g. *Hutcheson v News Group Newspapers* [2011] EWCA Civ 808), but have also been subject to academic criticism (Wragg, 2010). The above passage can be interpreted in two ways. The first is that the courts should grant leeway to the media to decide what information will be valuable to the public. Under this view, the media should be given discretion to decide what actions amount to a wrongdoing of which the public has a right to be informed. That interpretation is supported by Nicol J. in *Ferdinand* (at [64]), who stated that the public interest should be treated broadly to allow room for competing views on the breadth of that standard. A second interpretation is that criticism from the media is a contribution to a prior debate about what constitutes the public interest. That a person has an affair may not be seen as self-evidently harmful, but the press may seek to persuade others that it should be viewed in that way. Similarly, we might accept that there is normally a public interest in knowing that a person has committed a crime. However, criticising people's lawful actions can contribute to a discussion of what actions should be criminalised.

In *Goodwin v NGN* [2011] EWHC 1437, Tugendhat J. stated that the newspapers should be able to report that Sir [at that time] Fred Goodwin had an affair with a colleague because it 'is in the public interest that newspapers should be able to report upon cases which raise a question as to what should or should not be a standard in public life' (at [133]). In other words, even if an affair with a colleague is not in breach of professional ethics, by publicising such facts the media express an opinion about what the professional standards in this instance should be. When he talks of the subject being in the public interest, Tugendhat can be understood as referring to a contribution to a prior debate about what constitutes a wrongdoing and what types of behaviour it is in the public interest to discourage. The public interest is not static and the media can shape its boundaries. So even when arguments for naming and shaming based on the informational role fail, on this view the right to criticise provides a broader justification.

There are, however, difficulties in asserting the right to criticise in this way. First, it is unclear whether criticism of an individual is necessary for a contribution to a debate about moral or ethical standards. A point about the morality or ethics of a particular activity can be expressed without naming and shaming a person. However, the argument will be less vivid or memorable without specific details. Furthermore, providing a concrete example through naming and shaming helps to show that the activity is actually taking place, rather than merely hypothetical. Second, a right to criticise is expansive (Wragg, 2010). Most instances of naming and shaming will do something to shape our views about what rules ought (or ought not) to regulate behaviour, or what types of activity are 'socially harmful, or wrong'. Naming and shaming a tobacco smoker who is receiving treatment for lung cancer at the state's expense will highlight the potential harms and costs to society of smoking. That, however, would take the right to criticise too far and mark a serious inroad into the confidentiality of medical information, which has been viewed as being at the core of privacy interests. To give priority to a very expansive right to criticise would stop other rights and interests getting a look in.

Maybe we should accept these drawbacks and tolerate a certain amount of naming and shaming, accepting that the criticism of lawful activities of others is valuable as a contribution to a debate about standards in society. Such criticism can also play a role in maintaining certain social standards. These points are arguably stronger when considering criticisms made in the course of conversations among individuals. Individuals will often exchange information and gossip with one another as a way of forming views about social standards, as well as developing social bonds. Criticising others and being subject to criticism is part of the cut and thrust of day-to-day life.

Different considerations, however, apply to the media, as they are not like any other participant in a conversation. While the media can stimulate debate among the public by expressing an opinion, they wield far greater power than an individual speaker when they do so. When the media name and shame they do more than add their voices to a debate on public standards: they effectively enforce their view through the power of publicity. For example, when naming and shaming an individual, a national newspaper is not just contributing to a debate about what is in the public interest, it is deciding that disclosure of the information is in the public interest and acting upon that conclusion. By publicising details about a person's sex life in order to name and shame them, the newspaper does not merely indicate what types of behaviour the editor thinks should be discouraged, but it actually discourages that behaviour through adverse publicity to a wide audience. Naming and shaming people such as Max Mosley in a newspaper does not simply express a view about his sexual behaviour, but creates a strong pressure that might deter him (and others) from engaging in such activities.

However, the right to criticise should not be lightly dismissed. The power to name and shame should not be limited to conduct that is in breach of the law or of some clearly accepted ethical standards. The media have a role in expressing different viewpoints and illustrating their arguments. However, the view of the media acting as mere participants adding their voice to a debate about ethics is difficult to square with their communicative power. The discussion here does not seek to resolve this tension between criticism and other legal rights, but rather seeks to identify the powerful arguments on either side. Nonetheless, if the media assert their right to criticise, there are arguments that this right should be subject to responsibilities and restraints in order to redress the imbalance of power.

Conclusion

Naming and shaming practices of the media have been examined from three perspectives. The punitive function casts the media as authority figures engaging in a type of public censure. Although that role may be justified in a limited set of circumstances, there are serious questions about the legitimacy of the media assuming that position of authority. By contrast, naming and shaming as a form of criticism avoids that question, as it gives the media no special authority and views the media like any other speaker who wishes to express an opinion about behaviour. The difficulty faced by this argument is that it is unrealistic to ignore the reach and impact of disclosures in the media. Both the punitive and critical goals face problems of media power, which the former fails to legitimise and the latter tries to ignore. The informational function seeks to legitimise the power of the media by portraying them as a servant of the people. In this view, naming and shaming can provide an audience with what they need to know, or at least provide advice that will assist their decisions in their capacity as citizens or consumers. It is not clear, however, what range of information people need to know in order to assist their decisions and choices. All of these goals come with their own problems, but each assigns a separate function for the media, which the term 'naming and shaming' tends to obscure.

Notes

1 http://menmedia.co.uk/manchestereveningnews/news/crime/s/1503205_locked-up-in-may-12 (accessed July 2012).
2 http://www.pressgazette.co.uk/story.asp?storycode=42394 (accessed July 2012).

References

Braithwaite, John (1989) *Crime, Shame and Reintegration* (Cambridge: Cambridge University Press).

Cartwright, Peter (2012) 'Publicity, Punishment and Protection: The Role(s) of Adverse Publicity in Consumer Policy', *Legal Studies*, 32(2): 179–201.

Corbett, Val (2011) 'The Illusion of Safety: The Right to Privacy of Sex Offenders', *Journal of Media Law*, 3: 89–115.

Feinberg, Joel (1965) 'The Expressive Function of Punishment', *The Monist*, 49: 397–423.

Fenwick, Helen, and Phillipson, Gavin (2007) *Media Freedom under the Human Rights Act* (Oxford: Oxford University Press).

Greer, Chris, and Reiner, Robert (2012) 'Mediated Mayhem: Media, Crime, Criminal Justice', in Mike Maguire, Rod Morgan, and Robert Reiner (eds), *The Oxford Handbook of Criminology* (Oxford: Oxford University Press).

Hart, Herbert L. A. (2008) *Punishment and Responsibility* (Oxford: Oxford University Press).

Home Office, Ministry of Justice and Attorney General's Office (2009) *Publicising Criminal Convictions* (London: Home Office).

Husak, Douglas (2010) *Philosophy of Criminal Law: Selected Essays* (Oxford: Oxford University Press).

Kahan, Dan (2005) 'What's Really Wrong with Shaming Sanctions', *Texas Law Review*, 84: 2075–95.

McAlinden, Anne-Marie (2005) 'The Use of "Shame" with Sex Offenders', *British Journal of Criminology*, 45(3): 373–94.

Macrory, Richard (2006) *Regulatory Justice: Making Sanctions Effective, Final Report* (London: Cabinet Office).

Massaro, Toni (1997) 'The Meanings of Shame', *Psychology, Public Policy, and Law*, 3: 645–704.

Mill, John Stuart (1991) *On Liberty and Other Essays* (Oxford: Oxford University Press).

Spencer, John (2000) 'Naming and Shaming Young Offenders', *Cambridge Law Journal*, 59(3): 466–8.

Thomas, Terry (2004) 'When Public Protection Becomes Punishment? The UK Use of Civil Measures to Contain the Sex Offender', *European Journal on Criminal Policy and Research*, 10(4): 337–51.

Von Hirsch, Andrew (1993) *Censure and Sanctions* (Oxford: Oxford University Press).

Wragg, Paul (2010) 'A Freedom to Criticise? Evaluating the Public Interest in Celebrity Gossip After Mosley and Terry', *Journal of Media Law*, 2(2): 295–320.

2

Public Interest or Public Shaming?

Julian Petley

On 4 July 2011 the *Guardian* revealed that journalists at the *News of the World* had hacked into the mobile phone of the schoolgirl Milly Dowler, who had gone missing in March 2002, and whose murdered body was discovered in November that year. The hacking had taken place in the immediate aftermath of her disappearance, and it was at first believed (wrongly, in fact) that the hacking had caused some of her voicemails to be deleted, thus giving her parents the false hope that she might still be alive. Public revulsion at the newspaper's behaviour in this case led directly on 13 July to the government setting up the Leveson Inquiry into the culture, practices, and ethics of the press.

Up until this point, most of the national press had spent much of the year noisily obsessing about injunctions taken out mainly by celebrities in order to stop various stories about their private lives appearing in print. Indeed, in one week alone in April there were over 200 stories about injunctions in the national press. Typically, the majority of these stories generated a great deal more heat than light. Most British newspapers are not exactly renowned for their accuracy, and stories which concern their own interests are particularly prone to distortion, if not outright fantasy. In this instance, certain newspapers repeatedly conflated super-injunctions (whose terms mean that their very existence cannot be reported, and which are granted extremely rarely) and anonymised injunctions (whose existence can be reported as long as the person granted the injunction is not identified), often wildly exaggerating the numbers of both in existence and even drawing on anonymous and entirely unreliable Twitter sources to back up their inflated and spurious claims.

The reasons for such a campaign of misinformation are not particularly difficult to pinpoint. First, newspapers whose commercial lifeblood consists of kiss 'n' tell stories are going to be extremely hostile to any measure which interferes with their ability to run such stories. Second, although the Milly Dowler story had not yet broken, the phone-hacking saga was gradually clawing its way out of the pages of the *Guardian* and breaking the *omertà* which the rest of the national press had appeared to impose on it over the previous two years, bringing with it calls for select committee hearings, public inquiries, and statutory regulation. (For a detailed discussion of the way in which the subject was ignored, see Bennett and Townend, 2012.) What better than a carefully orchestrated furore against the development of privacy law to deflate these calls? This was given added urgency by the fact that judgment was looming at the European Court of Human Rights in a privacy case brought by Max Mosley, the former president of the governing body for Formula One racing and the youngest son of the fascist leader Sir Oswald Mosley, arising out of an article in the *News of the World* in March 2008 which had alleged that he had taken part in a 'sick Nazi orgy with five hookers'. And, finally, the fact that the privacy injunctions in question were made possible only by the existence of Article 8 of the European Convention on Human Rights, which states that 'everyone has the right to respect for his private and family life, his home and his correspondence', enabled Europhobic newspapers to hitch their anti-privacy crusade to their raucous and long-running campaigns against both the Human Rights Act 1998 and the hated 'Europe' in general. (For an account of the former, see Petley, 2006.)

As self-interested, inaccurate, and ideologically driven as much of the coverage was in what came to be known as Super-Injunction Spring, it did nonetheless raise several important issues. One of these concerned the dearth of any hard and fast evidence about the number of injunctions, of any kind, actually in existence. So, for example, *The Times* could claim on 2 April 2011 that 'celebrities, sportsmen and financiers have succeeded in winning at least 30 orders to stop press publicity about their private lives in the past two years', the *Star* could state on 25 April that 'a staggering 240 injunctions have been granted to the rich and famous to hide behind in the last three years', and the *Telegraph* could confidently tell its readers on 13 May that 'the rich and the famous have obtained almost 80 gagging orders in British courts in six years, blocking the publication of intimate details about their private lives'. Now admittedly the *Star*, like other British tabloids, is not necessarily a trustworthy source of news, but the fact is that there are no official figures against which to measure these claims. As it happens, this very point was addressed by the Committee on Super-Injunctions, which was set up in April 2010 and whose report was published in May 2011 at the height of the hullaballoo. This noted that it had been able to discover only two super-injunctions granted since January 2010, but also added:

> *The current absence of any data renders it impossible to verify whether and to what extent super-injunctions and anonymised injunctions are being granted by the courts. Equally, it renders it impossible to verify whether claims of the existence of as many as 200–300 such orders refer to super-injunctions, anonymised injunctions, a combination of the two, is based on double counting orders made first at a without-notice hearing and then continued at a with-notice notice hearing, or is simply an exaggeration. Given the lack of a uniform definition of the term super-injunction, this is a particularly acute concern, not least because recent reports assert that 30 super-injunctions are thought to have been issued in the last three years, when it is clear that many of those orders referred to are in fact anonymised injunctions and not super-injunctions. (Master of the Rolls, 2011: 54)*

The Report thus usefully recommended 'the introduction of a data recording system to enable public, Parliamentary, and judicial scrutiny of the frequency with which super-injunctions, and injunctions containing publicity restrictions, are applied for and granted' (ibid.).

The public interest

Another positive consequence of what was otherwise largely an exercise in barely disguised self-interest and self-regard was a debate about the nature of the public interest. This was largely because certain newspapers tried to defend their thwarted attempts to intrude into people's privacy on the grounds that these were in the public interest, although it has to be admitted that the defence was generally mounted in an *ex post facto* manner so half-hearted that even those advancing it appeared not to believe in it. Furthermore, the debate took place largely outside the pages of the national press (with the exception of the *Guardian/Observer* and the *Independent*) and in places such as the special issue of *Index on Censorship*, devoted to privacy (2011), and blogs such as Inforrm.

This chapter is intended as a contribution to that still ongoing debate and, as a first step, it will lay out a number of already-existing definitions of the public interest. Since we are concerned here mainly with the press, let us start with the Press Complaints Commission, even though at the time of writing its future is uncertain. Distinctly unhelpful, *The Editors' Codebook* states:

> *The public interest is impossible to define. So the Code does not attempt to do so. Instead it provides a flavour of what it regards as the public interest – a non-exhaustive list that attempts to reflect the values of the society the British press serves:*
>
> • *Detection or exposure of crime or serious impropriety;*
> • *Protection of public health and safety;*
> • *Prevention of the public from being misled;*
> • *Upholding freedom of expression. (Beales, 2009: 74)*

The public interest defence is available in the case of all or part of nine of the 16 clauses of the Editors' Code. A similarly unhelpful line was taken by the then Chairman of the PCC, Sir Christopher Meyer, when he appeared before the Department of Culture, Media and Sport Select Committee in March 2007:

> *One person's public interest is not necessarily in another person's public interest. The animated debates we have every month when the board of commissioners meets at the PCC to adjudicate on cases very often rotate around an issue of where is the line between what is properly private and what is genuinely in the public interest, and this can be very contentious and very difficult … What I am really saying is that we, any of us, will never come to an absolutely objective standard for the public interest. (Department of Culture, Media and Sport Select Committee, 2007: Ev 67)*

Moving on to broadcasting, the Ofcom Broadcasting Code is even briefer, noting in its section on privacy that 'examples of public interest would include revealing or detecting crime, protecting public health or safety, exposing misleading claims made by individuals or organisations or disclosing incompetence that affects the public' (2009: 38). With regard to privacy itself, it states:

> *Legitimate expectations of privacy will vary according to the place and nature of the information, activity or condition in question, the extent to*

which it is in the public domain (if at all) and whether the individual concerned is already in the public eye. There may be circumstances where people can reasonably expect privacy even in a public place. Some activities and conditions may be of such a private nature that filming or recording, even in a public place, could involve an infringement of privacy. People under investigation or in the public eye, and their immediate family and friends, retain the right to a private life, although private behaviour can raise issues of legitimate public interest. (Ibid.)

When it comes to defining the public interest, the *BBC Editorial Guidelines* are considerably fuller than either of the above. These state that there is no single definition, but that it includes but is not confined to:

- Exposing or detecting crime.
- Exposing significantly anti-social behaviour.
- Exposing corruption or injustice.
- Disclosing significant incompetence or negligence.
- Protecting people's health and safety.
- Preventing people from being misled by some statement or action of an individual or organisation.
- Disclosing information that assists people to better comprehend or make decisions on matters of public importance.

In terms of privacy, the *Guidelines* explain:

When using the public interest to justify an intrusion, consideration should be given to proportionality; the greater the intrusion, the greater the public interest required to justify it.

The BBC must balance the public interest in freedom of expression with the legitimate expectation of privacy by individuals. Any infringement of a legitimate expectation of privacy in the gathering of material, including secret recording and doorstepping, must be justifiable as proportionate in the particular circumstances of the case.

We must balance the public interest in the full and accurate reporting of stories involving human suffering and distress with an individual's privacy and respect for their human dignity.

We must justify intrusions into an individual's private life without consent by demonstrating that the intrusion is outweighed by the public interest.

> *We normally only report the private legal behaviour of public figures*
> *where broader public issues are raised either by the behaviour itself or by*
> *the consequences of its becoming widely known. The fact of publication by*
> *other media may not justify the BBC reporting it. (BBC, n.d.)*

Finally, in our consideration of how media organisations define the public interest, it is worth turning to the *Guardian's* editorial guidelines, whose sections on protecting privacy were strengthened in September 2011. These acknowledge that much journalism *may be intrinsically intrusive*, but they also state that a person's privacy must not be invaded unless there is a clear public interest in doing so. To help journalists decide whether or not material is intrusive, the *Guardian* developed five core principles, which are based on the work of Sir David Omand, a former intelligence officer. Since these clearly have a bearing on the definition of the public interest, they are worth noting here:

1. There must be sufficient cause – the intrusion needs to be justified by the scale of potential harm that might result from it.
2. There must be integrity of motive – the intrusion must be justified in terms of the public good that would follow from publication.
3. The methods used must be in proportion to the seriousness of the story and its public interest, using the minimum possible intrusion.
4. There must be proper authority – any intrusion must be authorised at a sufficiently senior level and with appropriate oversight.
5. There must be a reasonable prospect of success; fishing expeditions are not justified. (Inforrm, 2011)

Moving away now from the sphere of media organisations, let us turn to the guidelines issued to prosecutors in September 2012 by the Director of Public Prosecutions. These are intended to help them assess the public interest in cases affecting the media. The guidelines acknowledge that 'the public interest served by freedom of expression and the right to receive and impart information has never been defined in law', but they also provide examples of conduct which is capable of serving the public interest, namely:

(a) Conduct which is capable of disclosing that a criminal offence has been committed, is being committed, or is likely to be committed.

(b) Conduct which is capable of disclosing that a person has failed, is failing, or is likely to fail to comply with any legal obligation to which s/he is subject.

(c) Conduct which is capable of disclosing that a miscarriage of justice has occurred, is occurring, or is likely to occur.

(d) Conduct which is capable of raising or contributing to an important matter of public debate. There is no exhaustive definition of an important matter of public debate, but examples include public debate about serious impropriety, significant unethical conduct, and significant incompetence which affects the public.

(e) Conduct which is capable of disclosing that anything falling within any one of the above is being, or is likely to be, concealed. (Director of Public Prosecutions, 2012)

The Information Commissioner's Office also concerns itself with the public interest, since this is a matter which it must take into account when trying to decide whether a public authority should or should not accede to a request for information under the Freedom of Information Act 2000. In his Introduction to that Act the Commissioner lists the following public interest factors that would encourage the disclosure of information:

• Furthering the understanding of and participation in the public debate of issues of the day.

• Promoting accountability and transparency by public authorities for decisions taken by them.

• Promoting accountability and transparency in the spending of public money.

• Allowing individuals and companies to understand decisions made by public authorities affecting their lives and, in some cases, assisting individuals in challenging those decisions.

• Bringing to light information affecting public health and public safety. (Information Commissioner, n.d.)

As is made clear above, these considerations apply under the Act only to public authorities, but with the remorseless privatisation of so many formerly public services there is clearly a strong argument that they should apply too to private organisations performing a public function.

The Freedom of Information Act does not itself contain a definition of the public interest, nor do those few laws which actually allow those alleged to have broken them to mount a public interest defence. However, it is worth examining the Public Interest Disclosure Act 1998, which protects whistle-blowing by employees if they have a 'reasonable belief' that one or more of the following conditions is engaged, conditions which clearly relate to the public interest in the whistle being blown:

(a) that a criminal offence has been committed, is being committed, or is likely to be committed;
(b) that a person has failed, is failing, or is likely to fail to comply with any legal obligation to which he is subject;
(c) that a miscarriage of justice has occurred, is occurring, or is likely to occur;
(d) that the health or safety of any individual has been, is being, or is likely to be endangered;
(e) that the environment has been, is being, or is likely to be damaged; or
(f) that information tending to show any matter falling within any one of the preceding paragraphs has been, is being, or is likely to be deliberately concealed. (HM Government, 1998)

From the above, we can see that, *pace* the Press Complaints Commission, it is actually perfectly possible to define the public interest. This is also a matter on which judges have had a great deal to say in recent times, especially in matters regarding privacy, even though there is no privacy law as such in the UK.

For example, in the 2004 case between Naomi Campbell and Mirror Group Newspapers, which arose from the super-model suing the paper after it published photographs of her leaving a Narcotics Anonymous meeting, Baroness Hale argued:

> *There are undoubtedly different types of speech, just as there are different types of private information, some of which are more deserving of protection in a democratic society than others. Top of the list is political speech. The free exchange of information and ideas on matters relevant to the organisation of the economic, social and political life of the country is crucial to any democracy. Without this, it can scarcely be called a democracy at all. This includes revealing information about public figures, especially those in elective office, which would otherwise be private but is relevant to their participation in public life. Intellectual and educational speech and expression are also important in a democracy, not least*

because they enable the development of individuals' potential to play a full part in society and in our democratic life. Artistic speech and expression is important for similar reasons, in fostering both individual originality and creativity and the free-thinking and dynamic society we so much value. No doubt there are other kinds of speech and expression for which similar claims can be made. But it is difficult to make such claims on behalf of the publication with which we are concerned here. The political and social life of the community, and the intellectual, artistic or personal development of individuals, are not obviously assisted by pouring [sic] over the intimate details of a fashion model's private life. (Hale, 2004)

A similar approach was taken by the European Court of Human Rights in the case of *Von Hannover v Germany* (2005). This concerned pictures of Princess Caroline of Hannover and her family which had been published in the magazines *Bunte, Freizeit Revue,* and *Neue Post,* and which the German courts had refused to block. She thus appealed to Strasbourg, which upheld her case. The court argued:

A fundamental distinction needs to be made between reporting facts – even controversial ones – capable of contributing to a debate in a democratic society relating to politicians in the exercise of their functions, for example, and reporting details of the private life of an individual who, moreover, as in this case, does not exercise official functions. While in the former case the press exercises its vital role of 'watchdog' in a democracy by contributing to imparting information and ideas on matters of public interest … it does not do so in the latter case. Similarly, although the public has a right to be informed, which is an essential right in a democratic society that, in certain special circumstances, can even extend to aspects of the private life of public figures, particularly where politicians are concerned … this is not the case here. The situation here does not come within the sphere of any political or public debate because the published photos and accompanying commentaries relate exclusively to details of the applicant's private life.

It concluded that

the decisive factor in balancing the protection of private life against freedom of expression should lie in the contribution that the published photos and articles make to a debate of general interest. It is clear in the instant case that they made no such contribution, since the applicant exercises no official function and the photos and articles related exclusively to details of her private life. (ECHR, 2005)

This notion of a 'debate of general interest' has played an extremely important role in subsequent privacy cases in the UK. Thus, for example, in the *Max Mosley v News Group Newspapers* (2008) case mentioned above, Mr Justice Eady (later to be labelled 'Britain's Muzzler-in-Chief' by a *Times* editorial on 21 April 2011) pointed out that, in cases involving a person's right to privacy versus the media's right to freedom of expression:

One of the more striking developments over the last few years of judicial analysis, both here and in Strasbourg, is the acknowledgement that the balancing process which has to be carried out by individual judges on the facts before them necessarily involves an evaluation of the use to which the relevant defendant has put, or intends to put, his or her right to freedom of expression. This is inevitable when one is weighing up the <u>relative</u> worth of one person's right against those of another.

He also explained that 'it is not simply a matter of personal privacy versus the public interest. The modern perception is that there is a public interest in respecting personal privacy. It is thus a question of taking account of conflicting public interest considerations and evaluating them according to increasingly well recognised criteria.' Noting that the only circumstances under which it may be legally permissible to infringe a person's Article 8 rights are where 'there is a countervailing public interest which in the particular circumstances is strong enough to outweigh it; that is to say, because one at least of the established "limiting principles" comes into play', he went on to list the questions which a judge would ask in order to determine whether a public interest defence could be successfully run:

Was it necessary and proportionate for the intrusion to take place, for example, in order to expose illegal activity or to prevent the public from being significantly misled by public claims hitherto made by the individual concerned (as with Naomi Campbell's public denials of drug-taking)? Or was it necessary because the information, in the words of the Strasbourg court in Von Hannover ... would make a contribution to 'a debate of general interest'? That is, of course, a very high test. It is yet to be determined how far that doctrine will be taken in the courts of this jurisdiction in relation to photography in public places. If taken literally, it would mean a very significant change in what is permitted. It would have a profound effect on the tabloid and celebrity culture to which we have become accustomed in recent years.

This, as noted earlier, is the kind of thinking which drives sections of the British press into a rage against the ECHR in general and Article 8 in particular. Indeed, when Mr Justice Eady cited the European Court's judgment in the subsequent case of *Leempoel v Belgium* (2006), it can have served only to rub further salt into the wounds which newspapers believe 'Europe' has inflicted upon them:

In matters relating to striking a balance between protecting private life and the freedom of expression that the Court had had to rule upon, it has always emphasised ... the requirement that the publication of information, documents or photographs in the press should serve the public interest and make a contribution to the debate of general interest ... Whilst the right for the public to be informed, a fundamental right in a democratic society that under particular circumstances may even relate to aspects of the private life of public persons, particularly where political personalities are involved ... publications whose sole aim is to satisfy the curiosity of a certain public as to the details of the private life of a person, whatever their fame, should not be regarded as contributing to any debate of general interest to society.

Unsurprisingly, Mr Justice Eady concluded that, 'in the light of the strict criteria I am required to apply, in the modern climate, I could not hold that any of the visual images ... can be justified in the public interest', and found in favour of Max Mosley (Eady, 2008).

'What interests the public'

Debate about the public interest has frequently been marked by attempts to distinguish it from 'what interests the public' or the 'merely interesting'. Thus, for example, in *Jameel v Wall Street Journal Europe SPRL* (2006), which arose from an article alleging that the Saudi authorities were monitoring the bank accounts of prominent Saudis for evidence that they were supporting terrorism, Baroness Hale argued that the public have a right to know only if there is

> a real public interest in communicating and receiving the information. This is, as we all know, very different from saying that it is information which interests the public – the most vapid tittle-tattle about the activities of footballers' wives and girlfriends interests large sections of the public but no-one could claim any real public interest in our being told all about it.

And in the same case, Lord Bingham noted that 'it has been repeatedly and rightly said that what engages the interest of the public may not be material which engages the public interest' (*Jameel*, 2006). Similarly, in the Max Mosley case, Mr Justice Eady pointedly quoted Sir John Donaldson in *Francome v Mirror Group Newspapers* (1984) to the effect that 'the media … are peculiarly vulnerable to the error of confusing the public interest with their own interest'.

However, there have also been attempts to argue that the public interest and what interests the public may be linked. One of the best known examples of this was advanced by Lord Woolf in *A v B and C* (2002), a case involving the footballer Gary Flitcroft's attempts to keep two extra-marital affairs out of the papers, in which he argued that 'any interference with the press has to be justified because it inevitably has some effect on the ability of the press to perform its role in society. This is the position irrespective of whether a particular publication is in the public interest.' And whilst he admitted that in the case of many stories about celebrities' private lives, 'it would be overstating the position to say that there is a public interest in the information being published', he also argued:

> The public have an understandable and so a legitimate interest in being told the information. If this is the situation then it can be appropriately taken into account by a court when deciding on which side of the line a case falls. The courts must not ignore the fact that if newspapers do not publish information which the public are interested in, there will be fewer newspapers published, which will not be in the public interest. The same is true in relation to other parts of the media. (Woolf, 2002)

This was meat and drink to much of the popular press and was much quoted at the time. But although, as we have seen, this kind of approach did not survive *Von Hannover* in the courts, it is still one which is favoured, entirely unsurprisingly, by certain newspaper editors, in particular Paul Dacre, who argued in his Hugh Cudlipp Memorial Lecture in 2007 that popular papers

> *need to be sensational, irreverent, gossipy, interested in celebrities and human relationships and, above all, brilliantly entertaining sugar coated pills if they are to attract huge circulations and devote considerable space to intelligent, thought-provoking journalism, analysis and comment on important issues ... We live in a world where, frankly, many electors are more interested in Celebrity Big Brother than in affairs of state. And any paper that manages both to entertain and engage millions of readers with brilliantly written serious journalism on the great issues of the day is playing an important role in democracy. (Dacre, 2007)*

He also pursued the same line in his speech to the Society of Editors the following year, arguing:

> *If mass circulation newspapers, which, of course, also devote considerable space to reporting and analysis of public affairs, don't have the freedom to write about scandal, I doubt whether they will retain their mass circulations with the obvious worrying implications for the democratic process ... If the News of the World can't carry such stories as the Mosley orgy, then it, and its political reportage and analysis, will eventually probably die. (Dacre, 2008)*

There are, however, several substantial objections to such an approach. First, and most obviously, the *News of the World* died entirely *because of* its addiction to scandal and the illegal methods employed to research its privacy-busting stories. Second, those papers which carry the most soft news also carry the least hard news, thus badly denting the 'subsidy' argument (although, to be fair, it should be admitted that the *Sun* helps to subsidise *The Times*). Third, what hard news there is in popular papers is frequently so polluted by bias, partisanship, and editorialising as not to count as news at all. And finally, Dacre's whole approach to the issue of what is in the public interest and what interests the public is based on a very particular conception of journalism, one with which many might disagree profoundly.

The Enlightenment model

Broadly speaking, most journalism with any pretensions to seriousness adheres to the Enlightenment model. As John Lloyd argued in his Alistair Hetherington Memorial Lecture in 2007, serious journalism is itself

> *a product of the Enlightenment. It assumes a secular world, in which there is such a thing as objective truth, which can be searched for and should be searched for without hindrance from authorities who claim their higher knowledge from divinities or ideologies or even the people. Journalism as presently conceived cannot do other than that, for otherwise it has no basis for its stories – that is, they become a different kind of story, the stories that writers of fiction write … To make a stab at the truth is to enter into complexity. No account of an event, or an accident, or a war, or an individual which attempts to both tell a narrative and provide context is other than complex. (Lloyd, 2007)*

The values of such journalism are those which have come to be associated with the idea of journalism as the Fourth Estate. Nowhere have these values been more effectively summarised than in David Randall's book *The Universal Journalist*, in which he argues that the role of journalism is to:

- Discover and publish information that replaces rumour and speculation.
- Resist or evade government controls.
- Inform, and so empower, voters.
- Subvert those whose authority relies on a lack of public information.
- Scrutinise the action and inaction of governments, elected representatives, and public services.
- Scrutinise businesses, their treatment of workers and customer, and the quality of their products.
- Comfort the afflicted and afflict the comfortable, providing a voice for those who normally cannot be heard in public.
- Hold a mirror up to society, reflecting its virtues and vices, and also debunking its cherished myths.
- Ensure that justice is done, is seen to be done, and investigations carried out where this is not so.
- Promote the free exchange of ideas, especially by providing a platform for those with philosophies to the prevailing ones. (2007: 3)

One strongly suspects that most people who become journalists do so precisely because they want to fulfil this kind of role in society.

'Public ridicule and contempt'

However, in the English press at least, there is also a different, and indeed competing, conception of journalism, although it is one which tends to remain implicit and which rarely sets out its stall in the public arena. It is one particularly associated with the *Daily Mail*, but it actually underlies a great deal of what appears in the *Sun*, the *Express*, the *Star*, and the *Telegraph*, which together constitute what I would call the illiberal press. Unsurprisingly, it finds its most vocal champion in Paul Dacre, who explained this particular conception of journalism in his Society of Editors speech quoted above:

> *Since time immemorial public shaming has been a vital element in defending the parameters of what are considered acceptable standards of social behaviour, helping ensure that citizens – rich and poor – adhere to them for the good of the greater community. For hundreds of years, the press has played a role in that process. It has the freedom to identify those who have offended public standards of decency – the very standards its readers believe in – and hold the transgressors up to public condemnation.*

Equally unsurprisingly, it also features in Melanie Phillips's endless jeremiads against human rights, for example:

> *Scorn or shaming are important in reaffirming the boundaries of what is considered acceptable behaviour and helping ensure that people adhere to them. Centuries ago, this function was performed very effectively by the stocks. Today's Press fulfils much the same function. It allows individuals to identify those who they feel have wronged them and hold them up to public ridicule and contempt. (Phillips, 2006)*

But perhaps rather more surprisingly, this conception of journalism has also found an academic proponent in the shape of Tim Luckhurst, Professor of Journalism at the University of Kent. Thus, in the *Guardian*, 25 May 2011, he claimed:

In the 115 years since the birth of professional, popular journalism ordinary readers have chosen to use their favourite titles to censure and regulate the conduct of people who have grown rich on their wages. Hostility to privacy injunctions is not, as Lord Prescott fondly imagines, a conspiracy by newspapers to preserve profits. The sanction of public opinion is being applied to hypocrisy of which millions disapprove. Many Britons resent celebrities who treat publicity as a tap they can turn on and off. They accept these people as role models and brand ambassadors. They demand in return the right to scrutinise their lives.

He expanded on this theme a few days later, in the *Mail*, in a piece which was quoted at length by Paul Dacre when he appeared before the Leveson Inquiry on 6 February 2012. Here he argued:

The notion that moral failures such as adultery are entirely private and do not matter to the wider world is an affront to the very idea of community. A taste for titillation must explain some people's interest in Ryan Giggs's alleged extramarital activities. But for many others, cheap thrills were the last thing on their mind when they rebelled against privacy injunctions and remote, arrogant judges. This admirable majority resent public figures who think they can turn publicity on and off like a tap. We reserve the right to scrutinise and censure the conduct of people who have grown rich on our wages or claim authority over our lives. (Luckhurst, 2011b)

Furthermore, in Luckhurst's view, 'the community's interest in private wrongdoing delivers an emphatic public good' by exposing it to the sanction of public opinion and thus creating an incentive to behave responsibly. It is only the 'elite liberal dimwits' and 'foolish elitists' who 'fail to grasp the value of morality', and to understand that 'respect for fidelity and integrity … is the cement that keeps Britain decent and tolerant'. He concludes:

An artificial distinction between the public interest and what the public is interested in makes sense only to isolated occupants of ivory towers and wealthy enclaves. To most Britons, public virtue demands knowledge of significant private vice because the consequences of the latter can damage lives and set atrocious examples. (2011b)

Clearly, then, what for convenience I'll call the *Mail* conception of the public interest is very different from those considered (and indeed endorsed) at the start of this chapter, and it raises a number of important issues. By way of an extended conclusion, let me try to deal with these.

'An intense focus'

First, the underlying idea that the courts habitually engage in helping to cover up the private wrongdoings of public figures is simply not borne out by the facts. As Lord Steyn put it in 2004 in the case of *Re S (FC) (a child) (Appellant)*, when it comes to balancing Articles 8 and 10 of the ECHR, 'an intense focus on the comparative importance of the specific rights being claimed in the individual case is necessary', and this is exactly the procedure followed by the courts in all privacy cases. In the above-mentioned Mosley case Mr Justice Eady described this 'intense focus' on the individual facts of the specific case as a 'new methodology' which is

> *obviously incompatible with making broad generalisations of the kind which the media often resorted to in the past, such as, for example, 'Public figures must expect to have less privacy' or 'People in positions of responsibility must be seen as "role models" and set us all an example of how to live upstanding lives'. Sometimes factors of this kind may have a legitimate role to play when the 'ultimate balancing exercise' comes to be carried out, but generalisations can never be determinative. In every case 'it all depends' (i.e. upon what is revealed by the intense focus on the individual circumstances). (Eady, 2008)*

Proof that this is indeed the case was provided in July 2011 when the footballer Rio Ferdinand lost his case for misuse of private information against the *Sunday Mirror*, which had carried a kiss 'n' tell story about him. According to Judge Andrew Nicol, Ferdinand had generated a false image by embarking on a campaign since 2006 to 'project a more responsible and positive image than the reputation which he had had in the past' [2011] EHWC 2454 (QB). This campaign included a confessional interview in the *News of the World* in which he had publicly committed himself to the role of faithful family man. This was followed up by an autobiography and numerous further newspaper interviews in which the same theme was echoed. The judge also argued, rather more controversially, that, by accepting the England football captaincy when the manager, the FA chief executive, the sports minister, and numerous commentators had insisted that the incumbent must maintain high standards both on and off the field, Ferdinand was making a strong, albeit implicit, assertion that his private conduct was by that time appropriate to the role. In other words, judged solely on the *specific* facts of this *particular* case, Ferdinand's right to privacy was outweighed by the paper's right freely to express itself. The judge was not (as much of the press claimed) resurrecting the argument rejected by Mr Justice Eady, namely that 'People in positions of responsibility must be seen as "role models" and set us all an example of how to live upstanding lives', and in this respect it is highly significant that the judgment was not followed by a renewed spate of 'kiss and tell' stories in the popular press.

The public

In the *Mail* view of the public interest, generally accepted moral standards should determine the extent to which private information can be published. But this raises the question of whether such standards actually exist. Luckhurst invokes 'ordinary readers', 'most Britons', and even 'we', but all the reliable evidence (e.g. that collected annually by the British Social Attitudes Survey) suggests that views about sexual morality vary greatly across the population. Indeed, as the then Sir David Eady put it in a speech given at Gray's Inn on 12 December 2002:

> *There is no longer, if there ever was, a generally agreed code of sexual morality. Marriage no longer appears to have the particular status it used to be accorded. We are not courts of morals. Nowadays many people, particularly young people, lead lives which in the old days what would have been called 'promiscuous'. Now it is simply known as a 'sexually active' or 'fun loving' lifestyle. If a sportsman or model does not presume to preach to the general public, why should he or she have imposed upon them by anyone, let alone judges or tabloid journalists, the standards which used to be applied from behind the twitching curtains of suburbia half a century ago – on pain of prurient exposure? (Eady, 2002)*

No wonder, then, that he is such a hate figure for the *Mail*!

But if public attitudes to sexuality vary, many people do not appear to take the view of privacy which the *Mail* claims that they do. For example, in the survey which David Morrison and his colleagues carried out for their report *The Public Interest, Media and Privacy*, although 61% of respondents agreed that celebrities 'have to accept some degree of intrusion into their personal lives', and 63% felt the same about people in important positions, 27% agreed strongly and 39% agreed that 'the media should always respect people's privacy, even if this means not being able to cover an issue fully' (Morrison et al., 2007: 348). Furthermore, when asked about how much coverage the media should give to certain issues, the respondents clearly placed public interest issues over what we might call private-interest ones. Thus 42% said that details of serious crimes should receive maximum coverage, and 43% opted for quite a lot of coverage, with exposure of incompetence by officials scoring 42% and 48%, exposure of corruption and hypocrisy 40% and 38%, and exposure of fraud and cheating 37% and 42%. But, turning to the topic of the lives of ordinary people, Morrison et al. found that 49% of respondents felt that these merited a little coverage, and 15% no coverage at all. In the case of the lives of sporting personalities the figures were 54% and 26%, politicians' private lives 31% and 58%, the lives of pop stars 47% and 40%, and the lives of TV and film stars 56% and 30% (ibid. 357).

According to an Ipsos-MORI poll commissioned by the Media Standards Trust in 2009, conducted before the phone-hacking revelations came fully to light, 70% of the public believe that there are 'far too many instances of people's privacy being invaded by newspaper journalists' (Media Standards Trust, 2009: 11). Much more specific, though, were responses to a poll conducted by the *British Journalism Review* and YouGov in 2012 (Barnett, 2012). This tended to echo the findings of Morrison et al. in that there was strong support for public interest stories to be published – for example, stories about contaminated food being sold by a major supermarket (92% in favour), a High Court judge's investment in companies linked to the illegal drugs trade (82%), a schoolteacher helping her pupils to cheat in exams (70%), and a company testing drugs on animals in a cruel fashion (70%) – but very low levels of support for publishing private-interest stories. Thus 58% of respondents felt that a story about a well-known English footballer, who is married with young children, was a private matter and should not be published, 69% felt the same about a story concerning a leading politician's daughter being found drunk in public, 66% about a story featuring a member of a leading pop group having cosmetic facial surgery, and 80% about a story involving a finalist on *Britain's Got Talent* who once attempted suicide. Particularly interesting is the fact that there is little significant variation in attitudes to these private interest stories between tabloid and broadsheet readers. Needless to say, this extremely interesting piece of research, which appears to drive a coach and horses through editors' habitual protestations that they are simply 'giving the public what it wants', was entirely ignored by the national press.

Similar findings emerged from a report published by Demos and the Carnegie Trust (2012). This interrogated public attitudes towards five categories of stories: kiss and tell, lying, incompetence, making money illegally, and putting others at risk. This showed that there was least support for publishing stories about people's sex lives (whether they were stars of one kind or another or MPs), and most support for publishing stories about people (no matter who they were) putting the health and safety of others at risk. Members of the public were afforded the most protection, and MPs and local councillors the least, although as the seriousness of the stories increased, the gap narrowed considerably. On the question of information gathering, the report notes:

> *There was a clear pattern of declining support for publication as the level of intrusion involved increased, with our scale moving from standard journalistic practice (interviews with friends and neighbours) to ethical and legal grey areas (going through the bins outside of someone's house) to methods that are both illegal and highly unusual (entering premises illegally).*

Furthermore, the more intrusive the form of information gathering, the less the nature of the person who was the subject of the story mattered to those questioned. The report concluded that the public were reluctant publishers, in that:

> *Only a relatively small minority of scenarios (15 out of 90) saw at least 50% of the public backing publication. The only scenarios reaching the 50% approval mark involved the least intrusive kind of information gathering, 'interviews with friends and neighbours', and the three most serious types of revelation: 'professional incompetence', 'making money illegally', or 'putting others at risk'. On the evidence of this poll at least, the public are much more guarded about publication than many of those*

in authority – whether newspaper editors, regulators or judges – who are used to making judgements about where the public interest lies. Privacy concerns weigh especially heavily, with at least two thirds opposed to the publication of the 'kiss and tell' stories in our scenarios, regardless of which figure was involved or how the information was acquired.

Skimmington rides again

But surely the most profound question raised by the *Mail*'s conception of the public interest is whether or not journalism should be a form of public shaming for private behaviour, which is one of the central topics of this collection. Across Europe, rituals used to be enacted against traditional targets of communal resentment or hostility – lechers, promiscuous women, nagging wives, adulterers, swindlers, misers, and so on. These rituals were known in different parts of England as skimmington rides, skimmity, rough music, and riding the stang, in France as *charivari*, and in Germany as *Katzenmusik*. In a skimmington ride:

> *The victim would be visited by a boisterous crowd who would sometimes have their faces 'blacked' or disguised, terrifying effigies might be paraded or burned, stink-bombs released and missiles thrown – all to the accompanying racket of 'rough music' played on crude instruments ... In full cry the 'Skimmington' would parade an effigy of the ridiculed victim seated backwards on a donkey or a wooden pole; or the victim's person would be hauled about and made to 'ride the stang', in which case he or she might be roughly treated or ducked into a convenient pond or dung-heap. (Pearson, 1983: 197)*

In modern times, some of these functions have undoubtedly been taken over by forms of journalism, not least crime reporting in the popular press. As Steve Chibnall has pointed out, crime news 'illustrates most effectively the system of beliefs, values and understandings which underlies newspaper representations of reality ... Nowhere else is it made quite so clear what it is that newspapers value as healthy and praiseworthy or deplore as evil and degenerate in society' (1977: p. x). He continues:

> *Crime news may serve as the focus for the articulation of shared morality and communal sentiments. A chance not simply to speak to the*

community but for the community, against all that the criminal outsider represents, to delineate the shape of the threat, to advocate a response, to eulogise on conformity to established norms and values, and to warn of the consequences of deviance. In short, crime news provides a chance for a newspaper to appropriate the moral conscience of its readership ... The existence of crime news disseminated by the mass media means that people no longer need to gather together to witness punishments. They can remain at home for moral instruction. (Ibid., pp. x–xi)

These passages are surely implicitly critical of the populist and authoritarian thrust underlying much crime reporting, indeed much reporting *per se*, but clearly this is a conception of journalism with which Melanie Phillips would feel perfectly happy, given her drawing of a parallel between the stocks and the modern press. But it really does have to be asked whether such a conception of journalism is desirable in a modern democratic society, particularly one which is so heterogeneous (not to say deeply divided), tangibly uneasy, and all too readily prone to demonising those perceived as Other by the likes of the *Mail*. Many would argue that it is not, and their number would certainly include many journalists. Take, for example, two judgements which were made on 24 May 2011 at the height of the press-stoked furore of Super-Injunction Spring. Thus Terence Blacker complained in the *Independent* that 'the debate is now a perfect combination of all that is least attractive in contemporary Britain: a furtive interest in sex, a bogus and self-important moral argument, and mass bullying of individuals through the press and the internet'. Whilst Polly Toynbee in the *Guardian* 24 May 2011, in an article headed 'Superinjunctions: How the Rightwing Media Makes the Political Personal', argued:

The phoney moralising and loathing of rich stars comes from newsrooms where editors like Paul Dacre are paid millions, and whose politics decry high taxes or curbs on top earnings. Spreading jealousy taps into the social dysfunction of extreme pay inequality. Pressing everyone's nose up against impossible lifestyles, editors like to stir envy, while diverting political impulse to personal revenge.

Doubtless Tim Luckhurst would condemn all this as 'liberal elitism', but, even if he were correct, is this not preferable to populist demagoguery and putting people in the stocks – albeit metaphorical ones?

References

Barnett, Steve (2012) 'Public Interest: The Public Decides', *British Journalism Review*, 23(2): 15–23.

BBC (n.d.) *BBC Editorial Guidelines*: http://www.bbc.co.uk/guidelines/editorialguidelines/page/guidelines-privacy-introduction#the-public-interest (accessed July 2012).

Bennett, Daniel, and Townend, Judith (2012) 'Press "Omerta": How Newspapers' Failure to Report the Phone Hacking Scandal Exposed the Limitations of Media Accountability', in Richard Lance Keeble and John Mair (eds), *The Phone Hacking Scandal: Journalism on Trial* (Bury St Edmunds: Abramis).

Beales, Ian (2009) *The Editors' Codebook* (London: The Press Standards Board of Finance).

Chibnall, Steve (1977) *Law and Order News: An Analysis of Crime Reporting in the British Press* (London: Tavistock Publications).

Dacre, Paul (2007) Hugh Cudlipp Memorial Lecture: http://ukcommentators.blogspot.com/2007/01/read-whole-thing.html (accessed July 2012).

Dacre, Paul (2008) Speech to the Society of Editors: http://www.pressgazette.co.uk/story.asp?storycode=42394 (accessed July 2012).

Demos and the Carnegie Trust (2012) *Voicing the Public Interest*: http://carnegieuktrust.org.uk/publications/2012/voicing-the-public-interest (accessed July 2012).

Department of Culture, Media and Sport Committee (2007) *Self-Regulation of the Press* (London: TSO).

Director of Public Prosecutions (2012) *Guidance for Prosecutors on Assessing the Public Interest*: http://www.cps.gov.uk/legal/d_to_g/guidance_for_prosecutors_on_assessing_the_public_interest_in_cases_affecting_the_media_/#a03 (accessed July 2012).

Eady, David (2002) Speech given at Gray's Inn, 12 Dec. Quoted at http://www.carter-ruck.com/Media%20Law/publicationDetails.asp?ID=15 (accessed July 2012).

Eady, David (2008) *Max Mosley v News Group Newspapers* (2008): http://www.bailii.org/ew/cases/EWHC/QB/2008/1777.html (accessed July 2012).

European Court of Human Rights (2005) *Von Hannover v Germany*: http://www.bailii.org/eu/cases/ECHR/2004/294.html (accessed July 2012).

Hale, Baroness B. M. (2004) http://www.bailii.org/uk/cases/UKHL/2004/22.html (accessed July 2012).

HM Government (1998) Public Interest Disclosure Act: http://www.legislation.gov.uk/ukpga/1998/23/section/1 (accessed July 2012).

Index on Censorship (2011) Special issue on privacy, 40(2).

Information Commissioner (n.d.) 'Public Interest Test': http://www.ico.gov.uk/upload/documents/library/freedom_of_information/detailed_specialist_guides/awareness_guidance_3_public_interest_test.pdf (accessed July 2012).

Inforrm (2011) https://inforrm.wordpress.com/2011/09/07/news-guardian-beefs-up-its-privacy-code-jaron-lewis/#more-11259 (accessed July 2012).

Jameel (2006) *Jameel v Wall Street Journal Europe SPRL* (2006): http://www.publications.parliament.uk/pa/ld200506/ldjudgmt/jd061011/jamee.pdf (accessed July 2012).

Lloyd, John (2007) Alistair Hetherington Memorial Lecture: http://www.fmj.stir.ac.uk/hetherington/john-lloyd.php (accessed July 2012).

Luckhurst, Tim (2011a) 'Read All about it: Britons have Always Loved Scandal', *Guardian*, 25 May.

Luckhurst, Tim (2011b) 'Why Twitter Knows More About Morality than High Court Judges', *Daily Mail*, 31 May.

Master of the Rolls (2011) *Report of the Committee on Super-Injunctions: Super-Injunctions, Anonymised Injunctions and Open Justice*: http://www.judiciary.gov.uk/Resources/TCO/Documents/Reports/super-injunction-report-20052011.pdf (accessed July 2012).

Media Standards Trust (2009) *A More Accountable Press* (London: Media Standards Trust).

Morrison, David E., Kieran, Matthew, Svennevig, Michael, and Ventress, Sarah (2007) *Media and Values: Intimate Transgressions in a Changing Moral and Cultural Landscape* (Bristol: Intellect).

Ofcom (2009) *The Ofcom Broadcasting Code* (London: Ofcom).

Pearson, Geoffrey (1983) *Hooligan: A History of Respectable Fears* (London: Macmillan).

Petley, Julian (2006) 'Podsnappery: Or Why British Newspapers Support Fagging', *Ethical Space*, 3(2): 42–50.

Phillips, Melanie (2006) 'The Law of Human Wrongs', *Daily Mail*, 6 Dec.

Randall, David (2007) *The Universal Journalist*, 3rd edn (London: Pluto).

Woolf, Lord (2002) *A v B and C*: http://www.bailii.org/ew/cases/EWCA/Civ/2002/337.html (accessed July 2012).

3

Privacy and the Freedom of the Press: A False Dichotomy

Simon Dawes

More than just the actions of a single rogue reporter, the behaviour of journalists and editors of the *News of the World* (*NOTW*) has raised questions about the ethical standards of the rest of the British press, and about News International's multimedia and international interests. Alongside police investigations into phone hacking (Operation Weeting), computer hacking (Operation Tuleta), and payments to police (Operation Elveden), as well as two House of Commons Select Committees into press standards (Culture, Media and Sport, 2012) and police behaviour (Home Office, 2011), there is the Leveson Inquiry, investigating both the conduct of News International, other media organisations, police and politicians, and wider issues of the culture, practices, and ethics of the British press. Its ultimate task is to consider the implications for relationships between the media, their regulatory bodies, politicians and the police, and to propose more effective policy and regulation 'that supports the integrity and freedom of the press while encouraging the highest ethical standards'.[1]

The illegal procurement (through technological surveillance, bribery, or 'blagging') of personal information for the purpose of publishing stories that cannot convincingly be justified by recourse to a public interest defence has turned attention to the codes of conduct and the regulatory framework that are meant to guide journalists' behaviour. More particularly, it has focused interest on the balancing of the right to freedom of expression and the right to respect for private life, and on the definitions of privacy and of the public interest enshrined therein. As such, the News International phone-hacking scandal shares characteristics with the earlier MPs' expenses scandal in the UK and the Dominique Strauss-

Kahn affair in France and the US, in that all of these raise the question of where we draw the line between public and private life, and of how where that line is drawn can be to the benefit of private interests as well as of the public interest.

I argue, however, that the distinction between public and private is important in another sense, and that reducing this issue to a question of balancing the right to a free press and the right to privacy fails to address the underlying issue – the distinction between public and private in terms of the relation between the market and the state in liberal democracy. Liberal rhetoric concerning both the freedom of the press and the freedom of the individual to lead a private life sees freedom as freedom from the state, a freedom that is guaranteed and protected by and within a free market. But what the phone-hacking scandal demonstrates has less to do with insufficient freedom from the state than with exposing the need for more freedom from the market. As such, rather than attempting ineffectually to find the right balance between what are effectively two non-conflicting rights, both of which fail to account for the insidious threat from market forces, the task is to address and recast the issue in terms of both the market and the state, as well as the concepts of privacy and press freedom. With this in mind, I will suggest replacing a liberal approach to balancing these rights with a civic republican approach that takes both the market and the state into its account of freedom, and that values both privacy and the role of the press in terms of their importance for the public sphere (see also Dawes, 2013).

What this chapter offers, therefore, is a theoretical perspective on the key terms of debate, and a critique of the way in which that debate is most commonly presented. To understand why this dichotomy has become so ubiquitous, and limiting my comments to a consideration of the press at the expense of an overview of the media more generally, I will begin by reviewing the relation between privacy and the press within the legal framework of the UK. I will then look more closely at these liberal rights in turn.

The legal approach to privacy and the freedom of the press

Article 12 of the Universal Declaration of Human Rights 1948 was the first formal declaration of fundamental rights to include a right to privacy. Until 2000, however, UK citizens who felt that their right to privacy had been breached had to take their case to the European Court of Human Rights in Strasbourg, as there was no common law right to privacy in English law. This absence was highlighted by the notable case of actor Gorden Kaye, who, in 1990, was 'interviewed' and photographed by a journalist from the *Sunday Sport* while recovering in hospital from brain surgery. Because the press intrusion into Kaye's hospital room wasn't covered by the law of trespass or harassment, and because the publication of the information was not covered by the law of confidentiality and was only partially remedied by the tort of malicious falsehood, the only remedy available to Kaye was to insist that the newspaper be prohibited from suggesting that he had consented to the 'interview', as this could lower the monetary value of his story should he decide to sell it. Kaye's right to *publicity* was therefore protected by law, whereas his right to *privacy* enjoyed no such protection.

Throughout the 1990s, frustration at declining press standards and press intrusion into the private lives of public figures led to debate over ways in which specific privacy offences, or even a general privacy tort, could be introduced into law without negatively affecting press freedom. The Calcutt *Report on Privacy and Related Matters* (Home Office, 1990) criticised the decline in tabloid standards over the previous 20 years, and proposed a new privacy offence covering certain acts performed on private property, such as the placing of surveillance devices and taking photographs or recording voices without consent (Warby et al., 2002: 26–7). Despite dismissing claims that the introduction of a privacy tort would be irreconcilable with the freedom of the press, Calcutt nevertheless agreed with the then Conservative government that self-regulation would be more acceptable to the public, and so recommended the establishment of the Press Complaints Commission, a non-statutory body which would adjudicate complaints; this would replace the Press Council, which had come to be considered compromised by its dual responsibility both to adjudicate complaints and to protect press freedom (ibid. 25). The PCC was subsequently established as the press's last chance at self-regulation.

At the end of the PCC's 18-month probationary period, however, the Calcutt *Review of Press Self-Regulation* (Dept of National Heritage, 1993) noted that the regulatory body was substantially weaker than the entity which Calcutt had proposed, and that although it stressed that it was 'independent', it was neither independent of the press nor had it been proactive at initiating its own investigations. Furthermore, press intrusion had continued to occur (Sherborne and Jethani, 2002: 530–1). As he had threatened in the earlier *Report*, Calcutt thus recommended the creation of a statutory body with powers to order the press to pay fines and to apologise to its victims, as well as a general privacy tort, further specific privacy offences – namely, laws on intrusion to deal specifically with invasions of private property, surveillance devices, and taking of photographs on private property without consent and with a view to publication – and a review into other aspects related to press intrusion, such as, highly pertinently, the interception of telecommunications (Warby et al., 2002: 28).

However, the PCC responded by strengthening its code of practice (to prohibit harassment and to make invasions of privacy 'not generally acceptable'), and as the government was clearly unwilling to countenance the degree of statutory intervention proposed by Calcutt II (Bingham, 2007: 88), the proposals were rejected and the decision on whether or not to put an end to the days of self-regulation was postponed. (However, at the time of writing the PCC's future is uncertain, in the wake of its record in the phone-hacking scandal.)

The likelihood, and potentially the necessity, of further statutory regulation directed specifically at the press vanished, however, when the New Labour government implemented the European Convention on Human Rights (ECHR) into domestic law in 1998 through the Human Rights Act (HRA). This shifted the terms of the debate away from a simple choice between privacy and the freedom of the press (i.e. between, on the one hand, self-regulation of the press and no right to privacy, and, on the other, a privacy tort and a legal curb on press freedom) towards balancing twin but often conflicting freedoms (Rozenberg, 2004: 252), alongside a consideration of the 'public interest' (Warby et al., 2002: 29–30).

Since 2000, both the PCC and the domestic courts have been left to balance the freedom of the press with the right to privacy via reference to Article 8 (the right to respect for private and family life) and Article 10 (freedom of expression) of the ECHR. When deciding on cases, and particularly when balancing these two freedoms, judges are required to refer to case law pertaining to Articles 8 and 10, and also to section 12(4) (a)(ii) of the HRA 1998, which requires them (due to a passage added to the Act at the last minute following pressure from newspaper owners and editors) to also have 'particular regard to the Convention right to freedom of expression' when dealing with material which it is, or would be, in the public interest to publish (Tugendhat et al., 2002: 184). Similarly, section 55(2)(d) of the Data Protection Act 1998 (DPA) allows for the obtaining or disclosure of private data by a third party if the 'obtaining, disclosing or procuring was justified as being in the public interest. These laws do allow the media to breach personal privacy under certain circumstances, but by the same token media organisations now have to operate on the assumption that they may be called upon to demonstrate convincingly before a court of law that a particular breach of privacy serves the public interest.

The Department of Culture, Media and Sport's (DCMS) response to its own Select Committee's *Report on Privacy and Media Intrusion* (House of Commons, 2003), however, continued to emphasise the importance of a free press for democracy, and insisted that no further laws should be passed that restrict that freedom. The response also emphasised the New Labour government's preference for self-regulation, following the same line as its predecessors. But this focuses on the independence of the press only from government, ignoring other influences on the media, such as corporate power and economic forces. It also reduces the idea of the freedom of the press to a question of content and the related issue of behaviour, rather than including issues such as ownership and economic freedom, or employee rights and the freedom of journalists from their own employers. As Alan Rusbridger, the editor-in-chief of the *Guardian*, has suggested, it is thus perhaps time to look at market dominance as well as issues of content and behaviour when debating the regulation of the press (Rusbridger, 2011).

Limits to the legal approach

But over and above the legal effectiveness of balancing people's rights to privacy and the freedom of the press, there are normative implications in constructing an antagonistic dichotomy between competing public interests. Both rights are significant for free speech and are in the public interest, and it should not be assumed that they are immutable or always in conflict. As Michael Tugendhat told the DCMS Select Committee in 2003, there are many circumstances in which it is impossible to have freedom of expression without privacy; 'the most obvious examples of that', he explained, 'are when people give information to newspapers and need to protect their identities' (quoted in Rozenberg, 2004: 4). People may also feel that they require privacy if they wish to express controversial or unpopular beliefs. Again, if an individual believes that his correspondence is likely to be opened, that person cannot be free to express themselves and there can be no free exchange of ideas (Tugendhat and Coppola, 2002: 66). And sometimes the right to privacy advances the rights of others to freedom of expression, as when the whereabouts of an individual are kept secret to prevent them from harm so that they can express themselves freely and the public can receive their information (ibid. 44). Furthermore, neither article is absolute, and in cases involving one or both of these rights, the courts have to take into account the requirements of democracy. As Article 10 itself puts it: 'freedom of expression constitutes one of the essential foundations of a democratic society and one of the basic conditions for its progress'. It is on these grounds that the courts have, albeit belatedly, come to accept that journalistic sources are confidential. As the European Court put it in the case of *Goodwin v United Kingdom* in 1996: 'Without such protection, sources may be deterred from assisting the press in informing the public on matters of public interest. As a result, the vital public watchdog role of the press may be undermined' (quoted in Robertson and Nicol, 2008: 73).

That being said, it is a common mistake to conflate freedom of expression with the freedom of the press (Lever, 2012). The latter should be regarded as an instrumental good rather than as an intrinsic good (although the extent to which privacy and freedom of expression have intrinsic value is also a source of debate), where it is 'good insofar as it causes the press to act in the public interest and reinforces democratic ideals, but not good insofar as it ... impoverishes public debate' (Petley, 2011: 19). Nor is it an unconditional good. There is a difference in scope and scale between an individual's relatively unrestricted freedom of expression (which ends only where another's begins) and the freedom of an institution to disseminate commercial speech to a large audience via mediated communication (Petley, 2011: 72–3). As Onora O'Neill has argued, if newspapers act as if they have 'unrestricted rights to freedom of expression, and therefore a licence to subject positions for which they don't care to caricature and derision, misrepresentation or silence', then they would also have rights to 'undermine individuals' abilities to judge for themselves and to place their trust well, indeed rights to undermine democracy' (2002: 94). Placing more obligations and limits on the freedom of expression of the press than on that of individuals could actually help to make the press accountable, without conflicting either with freedom of expression or freedom of the press, because 'the classic arguments for press freedom do not endorse, let alone require, a press with unaccountable power' (ibid. 93).

What is more, when we expose how the two rights are reductively read from the perspective of liberal theory, both the pre-2000 approach that saw them as antagonists, 'locked in a zero-sum game, in which gains to the one can only come at the expense of costs to the other' (Lever, 2012: 41), and the post-2000 approach that has sought to find an appropriate balance between them, seem equally ineffectual. This is because within liberalism and behind the debate over market self-regulation and government intervention (Weintraub, 1997: 8) there is an implicit assumption of the 'naturally' self-interested character of individuals. Both privacy and the freedom of the press foster the same kind of individual; an individual that too often resembles a consumer more than a citizen. In contrast to the liberal conflation of citizenship with passive community membership and the freedom to make individual choices, citizenship from a civic republican perspective entails the active participation and collective decision-making of equal members of a 'willed community' (ibid. 13). Approaching both privacy and the freedom of the press from this perspective, and evaluating them in terms of their importance for the political sphere of social life – whether understood as Tocqueville's 'political society', Arendt's 'public realm', or Habermas's 'public sphere' – would avoid the trap inherent in the liberal approach of conflating them with what are in fact the private interests of the powerful.

The freedom of the press

Histories of the press vary from country to country and depending on whether a newspaper is defined in terms of its 'appearance, periodicity, content or format' (Barker and Burrows, 2002: 4), but generally they are stories of the winning of gradual independence from state power and public authority, with the market in the role of guarantor of its democratic 'fourth estate' potential. In 1855, the last of the state-imposed taxes on newspapers was abolished in England. The liberal theory of press freedom derives from this mid-Victorian era of newspapers making politics a public affair and the promise of a free market in ideas, and, as James Curran puts it, 'assumes tacitly that press freedom is a property right exercised by publishers on behalf of society' (Curran and Seaton, 2003: 346). Their actions are consistent with public opinion and the public interest, because the workings of the free market ensure that papers for which there is sufficient demand will survive. Press freedom thus becomes synonymous with the free market and self-regulation.

But although in the nineteenth century the press won its freedom from the state and political authority, and although its making politics a public affair was a significant achievement, by the end of that century the rise of the press barons and the not-unrelated decline in press standards had already weakened the freedom of the press and cast doubt upon its democratic potential. Although institutions such as the press had been originally 'protected from interference by public authority by virtue of being in the hands of private people', their critical functions have since been threatened by 'precisely their remaining in private hands' (Habermas, 1992: 188), so that, because of commercialisation and concentration, they have become 'the gate through which privileged private interests [invade] the public sphere' (ibid. 185).

As James Curran has pointed out (1979, 1991; Curran and Seaton, 2003), the liberal theory of press freedom makes a series of unconvincing assumptions. The idea of the press as a form of public opinion assumes that a market democracy is representative of the will of the people. But as well as privileging the press over other institutions of civil society that may be more or equally representative, this ignores the distorting effects of capital on the market place, and the politically charged publishing environment in the UK that, despite the rhetorical independence from politics, has tended to produce newspapers that are biased, partisan, and more susceptible to influence from both politicians and political pressure groups than they are objective or neutral. The idea of the press as an agency of information highlights its numerous successes in holding political authority to account, but ignores the reality of the full range of newspaper content and the role of the press as an entertainment industry, not to mention the increasing blurring of the boundaries between information, entertainment, and advertising. Furthermore, the view of the press as an independent watchdog assumes that it is independent of economic interests, ignoring the fact that newspapers are often a subsidiary of vast multimedia and other industries, so can rarely be said to be free of vested interests. It also assumes their political independence, ignoring the mutual advantage and lack of transparency in the relation between the press and political parties, the role of lobbying and spin, and the influence of the media on government policy and electoral results, which threatens not only the media's independence from government, but government's independence from the media.

Because liberal theory conflates the freedom of the press with that of media owners, it overlooks the employee rights of journalists and disregards their freedom from the restraints and whims of their employers; it also fails to recognise the reality of the incentives and constraints inherent in an environment of market competition that shapes journalist behaviour. Consequently, the freedom of the press from state regulation fails to protect it from the negative effects of competition and the need to cut costs and boost profits. It also allows media owners to pursue their own private interests, using their power to influence policies which further deregulate the media or other sectors in which they have vested interests, thus granting them even greater power in the name of press freedom. Such manifestations of market censorship (Jansen, 1991; Keane, 1991) undermine the liberal theory of the freedom of the press, and suggest that certain kinds of state intervention could, in ensuring that the press meet the obligations that attend its right to freedom of expression (Petley, 2011: 19), actually empower the press to free itself from the constraints imposed by market forces.

As a self-regulatory body which is far from independent of the press and such vested interests, the PCC serves to privilege a privatised and limited conception of the public interest, and potentially to further the private interests of media owners at the expense of the freedom of their journalists and newspapers. The legitimacy of a self-regulated and market-based press freedom has been weakened, not only by the rise of corporations and the dependence of newspapers upon advertising, but because the press is no longer disinterested nor accountable. Debate on the future of the role of the press and proposals for its regulation that limit themselves merely to efforts to correct instances of 'market failure', criticise occasional inaccuracies and abuses of power, and set out professional standards of journalism, though important, merely 'relegitimate' the market system. At stake is the market foundation of the theory of press freedom, a freedom which is actually undermined by economic power in the form of rampant commercial interests in an era of economic convergence (and an economically unstable climate of technological convergence), and the breakdown of channels of accountability between the press, political parties, and (in the phone-hacking scandal) the police.

In short, because the rhetoric of press freedom is blind to the effect of market censorship, press freedom often becomes little more than a mask for private interests that have little to do with either the public sphere or democracy.

Privacy

Privacy is also a concept that can serve self-interest, keeping secret what it could be inconvenient to make public, and effectively excluding certain areas of life and types of information from the public realm.

In the UK, the Freedom of Information Act 2000 has redrawn the boundaries of public and private information. But while the public interest in the use of taxpayers' money, for example, is relatively uncontroversial, the extent to which it is in the public interest to know about the private sex life of a public figure is less straightforward. The Dominique Strauss-Kahn affair, for instance, highlights the differences between French and Anglo-Saxon approaches to this issue. In France, the individual's right to a private life tends to outweigh the rights of the press to expose that life, so that rumours and allegations about Strauss-Kahn's private life remained off-limits to the French public until criminal proceedings in the US made the self-censorship of the French press untenable. It is hard to imagine the equivalent behaviour of a figure in British public life escaping the scrutiny of the tabloid press and celebrity magazines of this country. That being said, although clearly of interest to a large proportion of the tabloid-reading public, the consensus of their broadsheet-reading contemporaries would probably be that exposure of such matters is not generally in the public interest, even when they concern politicians. The contrasting ways in which different parts of the UK press reported the fall from grace of Conservative MP Liam Fox in October 2011, for example, illustrate the different approaches to the public interest of tabloids and broadsheets. When commenting on the impropriety of a Secretary of State being accompanied so often on ministerial trips by a personal friend and business associate, broadsheets like the *Guardian* focused on the distinction between Fox's government and business interests, while tabloids such as the *Sun* were more interested in investigating the personal relationship between the two men. The two newspapers were investigating the same story, but from different perspectives and with different objectives in mind, and if there is a public interest in the broadsheet's investigations, the tabloid could make the same argument. Similarly, although it might be unconvincing to claim that exposure of a footballer's extra-marital affair is in the public interest, there are times when the sex lives of individuals in positions of power can take on public significance. The Profumo Affair of 1963, for instance, where Christine Keeler's simultaneous relationships with a British government Secretary of State and a Russian spy posed a national security threat at the height of the Cold War, or the relationships in the late 1980s between Pamela Bordes and several British MPs and newspaper editors, as well as a Saudi Arabian arms dealer and a Libyan security official, are both examples of why proscribing a certain type of newspaper content could in certain circumstances potentially harm the public interest.

Although the line has to be drawn somewhere between public and private, where that line is actually drawn is a matter for permanent contestation. Some have argued against any restrictions on the type of content that can be considered to be in the public interest (Benhabib, 1992), stressing the exclusionary potential of such restrictions and the capacity of any matter to become of public concern. Women's, workers', and minorities' rights have all in the past been excluded from the public sphere because of rigid distinctions between public and private. Other material has been excluded because it has been thought to be offensive. But as John Stuart Mill (1995) argued, any criticism of the status quo or of those in power (in his example, the Church) would no doubt be considered offensive by some, especially by those subject to such criticism, but there is absolutely no reason to censor it. There should therefore be a degree of openness and flexibility regarding both the content and form of media content when it comes to considering what may or may not be in the public interest.

However, while obviously of interest to the public, the sort of information that the *NOTW* allegedly broke the law to obtain and publish, and the type of content that makes up much of the tabloid press, could barely be defended as being in the public interest. Although citizens must be free publicly to describe their lives and affairs, as well as, by extension, the lives of those with whom they've had affairs, kiss 'n' tell stories, in particular, provide 'an excellent vehicle for personal grudges' (Lever, 2012: 42). It is often in the self-interest (and frequently in the financial interest) of the source of information for such stories to be published, as well as in the commercial interests of the newspaper and its publisher to chase and solicit such material, treating the private lives of individuals as nothing more than material for the entertainment of others. Rather than prohibiting such content, it has been suggested that the frequency and intensity of the pursuit of personal information should be limited, and that the details of the fees paid for the story and whether or not it was solicited should be disclosed in the published story itself (Lever, 2012: 42–3). This would highlight the commercial motives of the industry in invading privacy in the name of the freedom of the press, and help the public to determine the difference between one newspaper's investigations into a matter merely of interest to the public and another's investigations into a matter of genuine public interest. It would also emphasise that the threat posed to privacy can be by a commercial entity as well as by the state.

The liberal theory of privacy, however, tends to limit itself to an elaboration of the right to conduct one's personal life as one chooses, free from interference or regulation by the state (Rössler, 2005: 10). In contrast to a totalitarian view, for instance, which would see the public or political realm as all-inclusive, the liberal view designates an area of life as private and not responsible to the state (Benn, 1984: 239–40). In legal discourse, particularly in the US, where recognition of the right to privacy has a longer history than in the UK, even though it has frequently been overridden by the First Amendment (Tugendhat and Coppola, 2002: 62), particularly in cases concerning the freedom of the press, this equates government and the state with 'public', and individuals and corporations with 'private'. Consequently, many protections of privacy in the US, coming indirectly from amendments to the Constitution and the Bill of Rights, have tended to protect citizens from government but not from corporations (Nissenbaum, 2010; Solove, 2008). The importance given in liberalism to freedom of expression over the right to a private life is therefore difficult to separate from that given to the rights of a corporation over those of an individual. When that corporation owns a newspaper and is further shielded from 'the Government' by the rhetoric of the freedom of the press, it is also difficult to see, from such a blinkered perspective, how privacy can be protected.

While the liberal value of privacy lies in respect for the individual and their autonomy, a civic republican approach would argue against an individualist conception of privacy, stressing the harm which it can do to the public good; instead, it would emphasise the political importance of privacy for the public good and as a shelter from the individualism of the market (Dawes, 2011). For Hannah Arendt (2003), for instance, although the personal could never be political, there was a need to stress the profound connection between public and private areas of life. Although the private realm can function very well without the public realm, the latter is founded and dependent upon the former; without a foundation in privacy, there can be no public realm of politics, no public interest, and therefore no freedom (Kumar, 1997: 212–13). Such an approach would distinguish between public (state) and private (market) influence on society, and explore the ways in which privacy should be protected from the market as well as from the state. And in emphasising the public interest in privacy and its importance for democracy, it would also avoid the other tendency in liberalism for privacy to be used individualistically as a shield for keeping from the public what it is in the private interests of a few to keep secret.

Conclusion

The dichotomy between the freedom of the press and the individual's right to privacy therefore does not stand up to scrutiny, and is particularly inappropriate as a framework within which to understand the issues raised by the News International phone-hacking scandal. The behaviour of journalists, the content of tabloid newspapers, and the routine invasions of privacy are the result of commercial forces; the consequences of a 'free press' as envisioned by liberal fourth estate theory. In the name of this theory, the power of the unions has been weakened, the training of journalists has been watered down, and the converged media sector has been progressively deregulated to create levels of market concentration unimaginable 150 years ago. While concepts such as press freedom and privacy (and indeed the public interest) have been used to maintain or further press proprietors' self-interest, their redundancy is more fundamental than their misuse. The very theories behind the concepts are under the spotlight. Theories of both press freedom and privacy see freedom in terms of freedom from the state, with freedom from the state being guaranteed by the operations of a free market. What the phone-hacking scandal demonstrates, however, is the lack of freedom of both the press and of individuals from a deregulated market, and that what is required is a little *less* freedom from the state – that is, from a certain level of state intervention – in order to curb the threat to press freedom posed by the market. Unlike liberal theory, which seeks to limit and check state power only, the civic republican perspective that sees freedom in terms of both the state and the market appears to be more appropriate to understanding and remedying the current crisis in press regulation. Rather than having recourse to empty fourth-estate rhetoric, the freedom of the press can better be defended by reference to the concept of Habermas's public sphere, a realm free from both state and market influence, in which the democratic role of the media is privileged over its commercial function, and the public is seen as being composed of people who are first and foremost citizens. Crucially, this emphasis on citizenship and the deposition of market logic and private interests would also have the effect of casting privacy in light of the private realm's importance for the public realm, avoiding the tendency to reduce privacy to an individualistic and depoliticised value. Instead of seeking to strike a balance between two liberal rights that are both equally blind to the inadequacy of the market as a guarantor of freedom, approaching the scandal in terms of its effect on the public sphere would recognise that the market is the cause of the crisis, and would enable remediation by casting in a different light many of the arguments made in the name of the freedom of the press, turning attention to the lines of accountability between media, state, society, and market.

The reluctance of politicians to regulate the press industry does little to benefit a truly free press. Allowing commercial pressures and the private interests of media owners to have such an unfettered influence over journalism, politics, and the private lives of public figures is detrimental not only to privacy, but also to the freedom of the press and, ultimately, to democracy itself.

Note

1   http://www.levesoninquiry.org.uk (accessed Jan. 2012).

References

Arendt, Hannah (2003) 'The Public and the Private Realm', in Peter Baehr (ed.), *The Portable Hannah Arendt* (London: Penguin Books), 182–230.

Barker, Hannah, and Burrows, Simon (2002) *Press, Politics and the Public Sphere in Europe and North America, 1760–1820* (Cambridge: Cambridge University Press).

Benhabib, Seyla (1992) 'Models of Public Space: Hannah Arendt, the Liberal Tradition, and Jürgen Habermas', in Craig Calhoun (ed.), *Habermas and the Public Sphere* (Cambridge, MA: MIT Press), 73–98.

Benn, Stanley (1984) 'Privacy, Freedom and Respect for Persons', in Ferdinand D. Schoeman (ed.), *Philosophical Dimensions of Privacy: An Anthology* (Cambridge: Cambridge University Press), 223–44.

Bingham, Adrian (2007) '"Drinking in the Last Chance Saloon": The British Press and the Crisis of Self-Regulation, 1989–95', *Media History*, 13(1): 79–82.

Culture, Media and Sport Select Committee (2012) *News International and Phone-Hacking* (London: TSO).

Curran, James (1979) 'Press Freedom as a Property Right: The Crisis of Press Legitimacy', *Media Culture and Society*, 1: 59–82.

Curran, James (1991) 'Rethinking the Media as a Public Sphere', in Peter Dahlgren and Colin Sparks (eds), *Communication and Citizenship: Journalism and the Public Sphere* (London: Routledge), 27–57.

Curran, James, and Seaton, Jean (2003) *Power without Responsibility*, 6th edn (London: Routledge).

Dawes, Simon (2011) 'Privacy and the Public/Private Dichotomy', *Thesis Eleven*, 107(1): 115–24.

Dawes, Simon (2013) 'Press Freedom, Privacy and the Public Sphere', *Journalism Studies*: http://dx.doi.org/10.1080/1461670X.2013.765637 (accessed Feb. 2013).

Department of National Heritage (1993) *Review of Press Self-Regulation* (London: HMSO).

Habermas, Jurgen (1992) *The Structural Transformation of the Public Sphere* (Cambridge: Polity Press).

Home Affairs Select Committee (2011) *Unauthorised Tapping into or Hacking of Mobile Communications* (HC; London: TSO).

Home Office (1990) *Report on Privacy and Related Matters* (Calcutt Report; London: HMSO).

House of Commons Culture, Media and Sport Committee (2003) *Privacy and Media Intrusion* (London: TSO).

Jansen, Sue Curry (1991) *Censorship: The Knot that Ties Power and Knowledge* (Oxford: Oxford University Press).

Keane, John (1991) *The Media and Democracy* (Cambridge: Polity Press).

Kumar, Krishan (1997) 'Home: The Promise and Predicament of Private Life at the End of the Twentieth Century', in Jeff Weintraub and Krishan Kumar (eds), *Public and Private in Thought and Practice: Perspectives on a Grand Dichotomy* (Chicago: University of Chicago Press), 204–36.

Lever, Annabelle (2012) *On Privacy* (Abingdon: Routledge).

Mill, John Stuart (1995) *On Liberty* (London: Penguin).

Nissenbaum, Helen (2010) *Privacy in Context: Technology, Policy, and the Integrity of Social Life* (Stanford, CA: Stanford University Press).

O'Neill, Onora (2002) *A Question of Trust: the BBC Reith Lectures 2002* (Cambridge: Cambridge University Press).

Petley, Julian (2011) 'Press Freedom: A Democratic Rubric', Leveson Inquiry, 8 Dec: http://www.levesoninquiry.org.uk/evidence/?witness=professor-julian-petley (accessed Jan. 2012).

Robertson, Geoffrey, and Nicol, Andrew (2008) *Media Law*, 5th edn (London: Penguin).

Rössler, Beate (2005) *The Value of Privacy* (Cambridge: Polity Press).

Rozenberg, Joshua (2004) *Privacy and the Press* (Oxford: Oxford University Press).

Rusbridger, Alan (2011) 'Hacking Away at the Truth: Alan Rusbridger's Orwell lecture': http://www.guardian.co.uk/media/2011/nov/10/phone-hacking-truth-alan-rusbridger-orwell (accessed Nov. 2011).

Sherborne, David, and Jethani, Sapna (2002) 'The Privacy Codes', in Michael Tugendhat and Iain Christie (eds), *The Law of Privacy and the Media* (Oxford: Oxford University Press), 519–64.

Solove, Daniel (2008) *Understanding Privacy* (Cambridge, MA: Harvard University Press).

Tugendhat, Michael, and Coppola, Anna (2002) 'Principles and Sources', in Michael Tugendhat and Iain Christie (eds), *The Law of Privacy and the Media* (Oxford: Oxford University Press), 43–72.

Tugendhat, Michael, Sherborne, David, and Barnes, Jonathan (2002) 'Data Protection and the Media', in Michael Tugendhat and Iain Christie (eds), *The Law of Privacy and the Media* (Oxford: Oxford University Press), 153–94.

Warby, Mark, Christie, Iain, and Wolanski, Adam (2002) 'Context and Background', in Michael Tugendhat and Iain Christie (eds), *The Law of Privacy and the Media* (Oxford: Oxford University Press), 3–42.

Weintraub, Jeff (1997) 'The Theory and Politics of the Public/Private Distinction', in Jeff Weintraub and Krishan Kumar (eds), *Public and Private in Thought and Practice: Perspectives on a Grand Dichotomy* (Chicago: University of Chicago Press), 1–42.

4

On Privacy: From Mill to Mosley

Julian Petley

Ever since the death of Princess Diana in 1997 there has been considerable public debate in the UK about the extent to which the media are, or should be, entitled to encroach on people's privacy, and in particular that of celebrities of one kind or another. Recently that debate has been ratcheted up a notch by the *News of the World* phone-hacking scandal, by the *Sun* publishing pictures of Prince Harry frolicking naked in Las Vegas in August 2012, and, one might add, by the refusal of British papers to print the photos of a topless Duchess of Cambridge which appeared in France in *Closer* magazine and in Italy in *Chi* the following October.

Shortly after Diana's death, the terms of the privacy debate in Britain were somewhat changed by the incorporation of the European Convention on Human Rights into UK law via the passing of the Human Rights Act 1998. This brought with it a right to privacy, albeit a qualified one. This lays down that:

> *Everyone has the right to respect his privacy and family life, home and his correspondence ... there shall be no interference by a public authority with the exercise of this right except such as is in accordance with the law and is necessary in a democratic society in the interests of national security, public safety or the economic well-being of the country, for the prevention of disorder or crime, for the protection of health or morals, or for the protection of the rights and freedom of others.*

However, Article 10 of the ECHR acknowledges that 'everyone has the right to freedom of expression', which immediately raises the question of how these two rights can be reconciled. How far should the press go in publishing private information about individuals, and how far can the individual go in claiming the right to privacy?

As Eric Barendt notes:

> There is an enormous philosophical and legal literature that explains why privacy is a fundamental human right. It provides a space for individuals to think for themselves and to engage in creative activity, free from observation and supervision. Further, personal relationships could not develop if the participants felt that every move was watched and reported. This applies most obviously, but not exclusively, to intimate, sexual relationships. Like the right to reputation protected by defamation laws, privacy is an aspect of human dignity and autonomy. It enables individuals to exercise a degree of independence or control over their lives. Privacy, therefore, entails rights to be alone and to keep confidential personal correspondence and other documents, and to ensure that intimate activity is not filmed or reported. (2002: 14–15)

However, it should also be noted that concern with privacy and its protection is a relatively recent notion, and emerged only with the modern separation of life into public and private zones. As Raymond Wacks explains:

> The emergence of the nation-state and theories of sovereignty in the 16th and 17th centuries generated the concept of a distinctly public realm. On the other hand, the identification of a private domain free from the encroachment of the state emerged as a response to the claims of monarchs, and, in due course, parliaments, to an untrammelled power to make law. In other words, the appearance of the modern state, the regulation of social and economic activities, and the recognition of a private realm are natural prerequisites to this separation. (2010: 33)

This separation of the public and the private, and in particular where the line between the two should be drawn, is also central to liberalism. Indeed, as Steven Lukes argues: 'Liberalism may be said largely to have been an argument about where the boundaries of [the] private sphere lie, according to what principles they are to be drawn, whence interference derives and how it is to be checked' (1973: 62). It is thus no accident that the last part of this chapter is devoted to a discussion of how the ideas of one of the greatest liberal thinkers, John Stuart Mill, might best be applied to the privacy issue today.

Philosophical-legal perspectives

Mill wrote *On Liberty* at the end of the 1850s, shortly before the birth of the modern press in the UK. And it was the birth of the modern press, with its emphasis on delving into the private sphere and its obsession with 'personalities' of one kind or another, which led to growing concern about its intrusiveness. Given that the modern press developed rather earlier in the US than in the UK, it is perhaps unsurprising that it was in the former that the first article was published which examined, from a legal-philosophical perspective, the whole issue of privacy and the press; indeed, it gave birth to the legal recognition of privacy in the US. This was 'The Right to Privacy' by Samuel D. Warren and Louis D. Brandeis,[1] which was published in 1890 in the *Harvard Law Review*, and is still cited in legal judgments today. The UK and other European countries may have adopted different legal means in order to protect privacy, but what I want to consider here are Warren and Brandeis's underlying arguments for the protection of privacy, which are broadly philosophical in nature and thus by no means confined to the specific conditions of the press in late nineteenth-century America.

Warren and Brandeis argue that privacy is vital to human existence, and never more so than in modern times when 'the intensity and complexity of life, attendant upon advancing civilisation, have rendered necessary some retreat from the world, and man, under the refining influence of culture, has become more sensitive to publicity, so that solitude and privacy have become more essential to the individual'. However, it is at precisely this moment that individual privacy has come under increased threat, thanks mainly to the modern media: Instantaneous photographs and newspaper enterprise have invaded the sacred precincts of private and domestic life; and numerous mechanical devices threaten to make good the prediction that 'what is whispered in the closet shall be proclaimed from the house-tops'. In their view:

> *The press is overstepping in every direction the obvious bounds of propriety and of decency. Gossip is no longer the resource of the idle and of the vicious, but has become a trade, which is pursued with industry as*

> well as effrontery. To satisfy a prurient taste the details of sexual relations are spread broadcast in the columns of the daily papers. To occupy the indolent, column upon column is filled with idle gossip, which can only be procured by intrusion upon the domestic circle.

As in any other business, demand creates supply, in that

> each crop of unseemly gossip, thus harvested, becomes the seed of more, and, in direct proportion to its circulation, results in a lowering of social standards and of morality. Even gossip apparently harmless, when widely and persistently circulated, is potent for evil. It both belittles and perverts. It belittles by inverting the relative importance of things, thus dwarfing the thoughts and aspirations of a people. When personal gossip attains the dignity of print, and crowds the space available for matters of real interest to the community, what wonder that the ignorant and thoughtless mistake its relative importance. Easy of comprehension, appealing to that weak side of human nature which is never wholly cast down by the misfortunes and frailties of our neighbors, no one can be surprised that it usurps the place of interest in brains capable of other things. Triviality destroys at once robustness of thought and delicacy of feeling. No enthusiasm can flourish, no generous impulse can survive under its blighting influence.

In Warren and Brandeis's view, 'the legal doctrines relating to infractions of what is ordinarily termed the common-law right to intellectual and artistic property are ... but instances and applications of a general right to privacy, which properly understood afford a remedy' for invasions of privacy. As they point out, 'the common law secures to each individual the right of determining, ordinarily, to what extent his thoughts, sentiments, and emotions shall be communicated to others', and this right is forfeited only when the individual themselves communicates their thoughts to the public by publishing them in some form or other. And 'publication' is to be understood here in a very broad sense, in that

> the same protection is accorded to a casual letter or an entry in a diary and to the most valuable poem or essay, to a botch or daub and to a masterpiece. In every such case the individual is entitled to decide whether that which is his shall be given to the public. No other has the right to publish his productions in any form, without his consent. This right is wholly independent of the material on which, the thought, sentiment, or emotions is expressed.

The right which is being protected here is not a property right (although it may additionally be so in certain instances). Rather, as Warren and Brandeis explain:

The protection afforded to thoughts, sentiments, and emotions, expressed through the medium of writing or of the arts, so far as it consists in preventing publication, is merely an instance of the enforcement of the more general right of the individual to be let alone. It is like the right not be assaulted or beaten, the right not be imprisoned, the right not to be maliciously prosecuted, the right not to be defamed. In each of these rights, as indeed in all other rights recognized by the law, there inheres the quality of being owned or possessed – and (as that is the distinguishing attribute of property) there may some propriety in speaking of those rights as property. But, obviously, they bear little resemblance to what is ordinarily comprehended under that term. The principle which protects personal writings and all other personal productions, not against theft and physical appropriation, but against publication in any form, is in reality not the principle of private property, but that of an inviolate personality.

They are at pains to point out, however, that 'the right to privacy does not prohibit any publication of matter which is of public or general interest', that there are those who, 'in varying degrees, have renounced the right to live their lives screened from public observation', and that 'peculiarities of manner and person, which in the ordinary individual should be free from comment, may acquire a public importance, if found in a candidate for public office'. But their central point is:

The design of the law must be to protect those persons with whose affairs the community has no legitimate concern, from being dragged into an undesirable and undesired publicity and to protect all persons, whatsoever; their position or station, from having matters which they may properly prefer to keep private, made public against their will. It is the unwarranted invasion of individual privacy which is reprehended, and to be, so far as possible, prevented.

In the years following the publication of Warren and Brandeis's article, the American (but not the British) courts steadily extended the protection of privacy, and in 1960 the torts scholar William Prosser argued that four torts of privacy had emerged as a result of this judicial activity:

> The law of privacy comprises four distinct kinds of invasion of four different interests of the plaintiff, which are tied together by the common name, but otherwise have almost nothing in common except that each represents an interference with the right of the plaintiff, in the phrase coined by Judge Cooley, 'to be let alone'. Without any attempt to exact definition, these four torts may be described as follows:
>
> 1. Intrusion upon the plaintiff's seclusion or solitude, or into his private affairs.
> 2. Public disclosure of embarrassing private facts about the plaintiff.
> 3. Publicity which places the plaintiff in a false light in the public eye.
> 4. Appropriation, for the defendant's advantage, of the plaintiff's name or likeness. (Prosser, 1960: 389)

More recently, in order to confront the privacy problems spawned by new information technologies, Daniel J. Solove has created a 'new taxonomy to address privacy violations for contemporary times' (2008: 101). Briefly, Solove constructs four groups of harmful activities, each of which consists of different related subgroups of harmful activities. These are:

1. Information collection. (Surveillance, interrogation.)
2. Information processing. (Aggregation, identification, insecurity, secondary use, exclusion.)
3. Information dissemination. (Breach of confidentiality, disclosure, exposure, increased accessibility, blackmail, appropriation, distortion.)
4. Invasion. (Intrusion, decisional interference.) (Ibid., 101–70)

The issues raised by Warren and Brandeis are as relevant today as when they first wrote about them – the need for personal privacy, especially in a highly mediatised world; the intrusiveness of media driven by purely commercial values; the edging aside of hard news by soft; the importance of protecting journalism which is genuinely in the public interest – and Prosser and Solove have usefully tabulated the specific issues relating to privacy concerns which have arisen since Warren and Brandeis first published their seminal article. It might also be added that they give the lie to British journalists' frequent claims that the US is free from privacy legislation. Like so much that appears in British newspapers, this is simply untrue. It may indeed be the case that the First Amendment means that certain privacy actions which succeed in the UK might fail in the US, but that's as far as it goes.

However, let us now return to the UK and try to apply a particular philosophical perspective, namely that of John Stuart Mill, to a specific case of privacy invasion, in order to see whether it clarifies the matter concerned.

Mill, Mosley, and the *News of the World*

In the UK, the philosopher who is most frequently cited in debates concerning freedom of expression is John Stuart Mill, and the work which is most often quoted is *On Liberty*, first published in 1859. Mill announces his subject as 'the nature and limits of the power which can be legitimately exercised by society over the individual' (1985: 59), and argues that the only valid reason for restricting individual liberty is in order to prevent harm being done to others. As he puts it: 'The only purpose for which power can be rightfully exercised over any member of a civilised community, against his will, is to prevent harm to others. His own good, either physical or moral, is not a sufficient warrant' (ibid. 68). So could it be argued that the right to privacy should take priority over the right to freedom of expression if breaching someone's privacy can be shown to harm them?

At first sight, this may seem plausible enough, but an initial problem is that the harm principle as enunciated by Mill is not without its difficulties. As John Gray has pointed out:

> *There are real problems surrounding Mill's use of the term. Does he intend the reader to understand 'harm' to refer only to physical harm or must a class of moral harms to character be included in any application of the liberty principle? Must the harm that the restriction of liberty prevents be done directly to identifiable individuals, or may it also relevantly be done to institutions, social practices and forms of life? Can serious offence to feelings count as harm in so far as the restriction of liberty is concerned, or must the harm be done to interests, or to those interests the protection of which is to be accorded the status of a right? ... These difficulties express a philosophical difficulty in the analysis of the*

concept of harm – a difficulty emerging from the fact that judgements
about harm are often controversial as between exponents of different
moral outlooks. (1983: 49)

However, this should not discourage one from at least posing the
question of whether it is more harmful to expose someone's private life
in the media, thus possibly harming them, than to fail to expose it, or to
be prevented from doing so, thus possibly harming the public's right to
know about matters which are genuinely in the public interest, as well as
harming freedom of expression – something which Mill held very dear –
into the bargain.

In this last respect, it is important to note that Mill argues that
freedom of thought and freedom of expression belong to 'a sphere of
action ... comprehending all that portion of a person's life and conduct
which affects only himself', a sphere which he calls 'self-regarding' and
which we would describe as private. He continues:

This, then, is the appropriate region of human liberty. It comprises, first,
the inward domain of consciousness, demanding liberty of conscience in
the most comprehensive sense, liberty of thought and feeling, absolute
freedom of opinion and sentiment on all subjects, practical or speculative,
scientific, moral or theological. The liberty of expressing and publishing
opinions may seem to fall under a different principle, since it belongs to
that part of the conduct of an individual which concerns other people,
but, being <u>almost</u> of as much importance as the liberty of thought itself
and resting <u>in great part</u> on the same reasons, is practically inseparable
from it. (emphases added; 1985: 71)

But what needs to be noted here is that Mill does not endow expression
with the absolute liberty which he accords to thought. As he put it:

No one pretends that actions should be as free as opinions. On the
contrary, even opinions lose their immunity when the circumstances
in which they are expressed are such as to constitute their expression a
positive instigation to some mischievous act ... Acts, of whatever kind,
which without justifiable cause do harm to others may be, and in the more
important cases, absolutely require to be, controlled by the unfavourable
sentiments, and, when needful, by the active interference of mankind.
(Ibid. 119)

Interestingly, Mill argues that 'an opinion that corn dealers are starvers of the poor' should be legal if expressed in a newspaper, but should incur punishment 'when delivered orally to an excited mob assembled before the house of a corn dealer' (ibid. 119). However, it is difficult to understand why publishing an article in a newspaper (or, for that matter, anywhere in the media) should not be considered, for the purposes of this argument, as an 'action'. However, this may well be one of those instances in which Mill's arguments need to be revised in the light of the development of the modern media, and in which recourse to actual examples of possibly harmful action by the media can help both to elucidate and to test Mill's admittedly elusive ideas about harm.

Consider, for example, the campaign launched by the *News of the World* in July 2000 to 'name and shame' paedophiles, which led to vigilante violence against a convicted paedophile in the Paulsgrove area of Portsmouth, and against several victims of mistaken identity, including a paediatrician in Newport. Equally seriously, the campaign led to sex offenders breaking off contact with their probation officers, moving from addresses that were monitored by police, altering their appearance, and failing to attend treatment programmes, in an attempt to shield themselves from vigilante action. In so doing, of course, they made it far more difficult for their behaviour to be monitored. If such a campaign cannot be considered as a harmful action, it would be hard to know what can.

But let us return to the more general question of what actions, according to Mill, may be forbidden, and indeed punished, on the grounds that they are harmful to others. Mill states:

> *Everyone who receives the protection of society owes a return for the benefit, and the fact of living in society renders it indispensable that each should be bound to observe a certain line of conduct towards the rest. This consists, first, in not injuring the interests of one another, or rather certain interests which, either by express legal provision or by tacit understanding, ought to be considered as rights. (Ibid. 141)*

In his view:

> *The acts of an individual may be hurtful to others or wanting in due consideration for their welfare, without going to the length of violating any of their constituted rights. The offender may then be justly punished by opinion, though not by law. As soon as any part of a person's conduct*

affects prejudicially the interests of others, society has jurisdiction over it, and the question of whether the general welfare will or will not be promoted by interfering with it becomes open to discussion. (Ibid. 141)

This then raises the question of what actions are prejudicial to the interests of others. According to Mill, these are:

Encroachment on their rights; infliction on them of any loss or damage not justified by [the inflicter's] own rights; falsehood or duplicity in dealing with them; unfair or ungenerous use of advantages over them; even selfish abstinence from defending them against injury – these are fit objects of moral reprobation and, in grave cases, of moral retribution and punishment. (Ibid. 145)

In Mill's view, to engage in such acts is to infringe the rules necessary for the protection of one's fellow human beings, individually or collectively, and society, 'as the protector of all its members', must retaliate and inflict pain on the offender 'for the express purpose of punishment, and must take care that it be sufficiently severe' (ibid. 146).

We do, of course, need to bear in mind that, as already noted, Mill's notion of harm is not as clear as it might be, that he is concerned to keep restrictions on freedom of expression to a bare minimum, and that his philosophical position on such freedom was developed before the development of the media as we know them today. However, with these caveats in mind, we can still enquire whether Mill's ideas are helpful to current debates about competing rights to privacy and press freedom. To try to answer this question, let us turn again to a specific case, namely the treatment of Max Mosley by the *News of the World* and his subsequent legal action against the newspaper.

On 30 March 2008, the *News of the World* reported, under the headline 'F1 Boss has Sick Nazi Orgy with Five Hookers', that Max Mosley, head of Formula One and of the Fédération Internationale de l'Automobile (FIA), had been involved in what it described as a 'Nazi-themed sadomasochistic sex orgy'. On its website the paper also published a video secretly recorded by one of the women present. The following week it published a story headed 'My Nazi Orgy with F1 Boss'. The *News of the World* variously claimed that Mosley had specifically ordered a Nazi or concentration camp scenario, and that this had involved 'mocking the humiliating way Jews were treated' and 'parodying Holocaust horrors' by 'acting out his vile death-camp fantasies in a torture dungeon orgy with five hookers'. It argued that its revelations were in the public interest partly because they cast doubt on Mosley's suitability as President of the FIA and partly because he was the son of fascist leader Sir Oswald Mosley. Mosley sued the paper for gross invasion of privacy and was awarded £60,000 damages in July that year. During the course of the trial it became abundantly clear that the so-called 'orgy' had no Nazi overtones whatsoever.

The first, and most obvious, point to be made here is that Mosley's activities took place fairly and squarely in the 'self-regarding' or private realm. These may have been distasteful to many people, but the key point is that they did not take place in any way in public – they were *made* public, entirely against the wishes of all but one of the participants involved, by the actions of the *News of the World*. Thus only in a very limited sense could Mosley be said to be the architect of his own misfortunes. Nor could the paper possibly avail itself of any countervailing argument that it was, in the public interest, exposing activities which were in any way harmful, because these were neither illegal nor did they have the Nazi overtones which it claimed. Nor could the paper claim that it was revealing Mosley to be a hypocrite, since he had never publicly spoken out against engaging in sadomasochistic or extra-marital sexual activity.

Second, the judge in the case, Mr Justice Eady, made it abundantly clear that Mosley's rights, and in particular his right to privacy, had been encroached upon.[2] As he put it:

> There is now a considerable body of jurisprudence in Strasbourg and elsewhere which recognises that sexual activity engages the rights protected by Article 8 … People's sex lives are to be regarded as essentially their own business – provided at least that the participants are genuinely consenting adults and there is no question of exploiting the young or vulnerable.

Given that this is indeed the case, he went on:

> It is not for the state or for the media to expose sexual conduct which does not involve any significant breach of the criminal law. That is so whether the motive for such intrusion is merely prurience or a moral crusade. It is not for journalists to undermine human rights, or for judges to refuse to enforce them, merely on grounds of taste or moral disapproval. Everyone is naturally entitled to espouse moral or religious beliefs to the effect

> that certain types of sexual behaviour are wrong or demeaning to those participating. That does not mean that they are entitled to hound those who practise them or to detract from their right to live life as they choose … The fact that a particular relationship happens to be adulterous, or that someone's tastes are unconventional or 'perverted', does not give the media carte blanche.

Turning now to the matter of inflicting loss or damage, it is important to note that Mr Justice Eady argued that 'the scale of the distress and indignity in this case is difficult to comprehend. It is probably unprecedented', adding that Mosley was 'hardly exaggerating when he says that his life was ruined'. He continued:

> Whereas reputation can be vindicated by an award of damages, in the sense that the claimant can be restored to the esteem in which he was previously held, that is not possible where embarrassing personal information has been released for general publication. As the media are well aware, once privacy has been infringed, the damage is done and the embarrassment is only augmented by pursuing a court action.

As Mosley himself put it in his witness statement to the Leveson Inquiry, the experience was 'indescribably distressing'.[3] As he described it:

> Every time I visit a restaurant or shop anywhere in the world, I have to prepare myself that the individuals working there or other customers know. I am openly mocked by newspaper editors such as Paul Dacre. I have to steel myself to this and, in some cases respond as best I can. Whilst I have developed my ability to deal with this, the effect of the intrusion and the damage to my reputation is devastating. I have continued to campaign for privacy, because I know what it is like to be a victim and I have the resources to do this, but the Inquiry should be in no doubt that the victim of an invasion of privacy suffers a terrible penalty. It is comparable to the penalties the courts can impose on convicted criminals, if not worse.

Furthermore, Mosley's position in the FIA was put in very considerable jeopardy, and in this respect it is important to note that the *News of the World* instructed their solicitors, Farrer & Co., to send an unedited copy of the covert video, lasting several hours, to Michael Boeri, the president of the FIA senate. And finally, there was the harm done to his son, Alexander, by the newspaper's revelations. As Mosley told the Inquiry:

> *In May 2009 my eldest son Alexander, who suffered from depression, died of a drug overdose. Although it is true to say that he had struggled with drug addiction prior to publication of the Article, I strongly believe its publication and the coverage that followed played a significant part in exacerbating Alexander's depression and contributed to the circumstances which led to his death.*

It is also important to note in respect of the loss and damage inflicted on Mosley that Mr Justice Eady explicitly rejected the argument that this was in any way justified by the paper's Article 10 rights – that is, he asserted that Mosley's right to privacy was not trumped by the *News of the World*'s right to express itself freely.

The *News of the World* also dealt with Mosley in a manner that can justly be described as false and duplicitous. First of all, there is the matter of the clandestine filming. This the paper attempted to justify on the grounds that it was revealing a matter of public interest, namely a Nazi-themed orgy involving Max Mosley. But, as we have already seen, there was no Nazi theme. As noted above, one of the participants (known in court as Woman E) was paid by the *News of the World* secretly to film the proceedings, and was coached in her role by Neville Thurlbeck, the paper's chief reporter. We know from evidence given by Thurlbeck at the trial that he borrowed the jacket which she was to wear at the orgy, in order to have it fitted with a hidden camera, and that he therefore must have known that the garment had no Nazi connotations. And we also know from the unedited footage taken by Woman E that, whilst Thurlbeck was instructing her how to use the camera, he told her: 'When you want to get him doing the Sieg Heil it's [the camera] about 2.5 to 3 metres away from him and then you'll get him in – no problem.'[4] From this one could infer that Thurlbeck was trying to induce the woman to make Mosley give a Nazi salute and thus to give credence to the central claim which the paper would subsequently make, namely that the party had a Nazi theme. The fact that she failed to encourage Mosley to give any such salute may be one of the reasons why the £25,000 which she was originally offered by the paper for her services was reduced to £12,000. She also failed to turn up to give evidence in the court case, and subsequently confirmed to Sky

News that the Nazi allegation was completely untrue; she also apologised for making the video.

This brings us on to the matter of whether the paper was 'unfair or ungenerous' in its 'use of advantages' over Mosley. Of course, it has to be admitted that Mosley is extremely wealthy – otherwise he could never have afforded to sue the *News of the World* in the first place. However, his riches pale into complete insignificance when compared to those of the paper's parent company, News International, behind which stands the global might of News Corporation. Thus the paper clearly had a very considerable advantage over Mosley in terms of the financial resources at its disposal. As to whether it used its advantage unfairly or ungenerously, consider the following.

The video footage was initially removed by the *News of the World* at the request of Mosley's lawyer the day after it first appeared. The paper's representatives agreed to give his lawyers 48 hours notice if it was intended to restore the video to the website. When such notice was given later in the week, Mosley instructed his lawyers to apply for an injunction to prevent it appearing. The injunction application was made late on a Friday afternoon and judgment was reserved over the weekend. In spite of the fact that the paper was awaiting judgment, and in spite of Mosley's flat denials that the orgy had had a Nazi theme, the paper effectively ran the story again that weekend. As Mosley himself put it in his witness statement to the Leveson Inquiry:

> I took this follow up article to be intended as a threat to me. In essence the NotW was showing me that they had the power and resources to write what they wanted to an audience of millions. Having published their original article and seen that I was prepared to sue them, they were now seeking to use every means to put me under the utmost pressure. I believe they intended to crush me and make an example of me to others who might contemplate suing or criticising them.[5]

There seems no good reason to disagree with this assessment.

On 9 April, Mr Justice Eady gave judgment in respect of Mosley's application for an injunction. According to Mosley's above-mentioned witness statement, he stated that although he could see no legitimate public interest in the story, he felt that he had to refuse the application, 'with some reluctance', on the grounds that the 'damn had effectively burst' as a result of the global dissemination of the video on the internet.

Despite Mr Justice Eady stating that 'there [was] no legitimate element of public interest which would be served by the additional disclosure of the edited footage, at this stage, on the Respondent's website', the *News of the World* immediately reposted it. We have already noted that it also sent the unedited footage to the president of the FIA senate. In addition, in the week before the second story was published, Thurlbeck contacted two of the women involved in the orgy and offered them £8,000 for an interview – presumably in an attempt to stand up the 'Nazi' allegation. In return, their faces would be pixelated in the photographs accompanying the forthcoming article, and their names not mentioned. As Mr Justice Eady put it in his judgment: 'This would appear to contain a clear threat to the women involved that unless they cooperated with Mr Thurlbeck (albeit in exchange for some money) their identities would be revealed the following Sunday.' Courageously, they resisted what could be regarded as a crude attempt at blackmail. And although Mr Justice Eady politely referred to 'these blandishments', he also added that the fact that the paper's editor, Colin Myler, 'did not consider that there was anything objectionable about Mr Thurlbeck's approach ... discloses a remarkable state of affairs'.

Reading Mr Justice Eady's lengthy and highly detailed judgment it is hard not to come to the conclusion that the *News of the World* was, for whatever reason, determined to publish the Mosley story, and then landed on different so-called justifications for doing so that Mr Justice Eady said 'somewhat shifted as matters have developed', although elsewhere Myler and Thurlbeck's evidence is variously described as 'disingenuous' (twice), 'hard to swallow', 'especially unconvincing', 'erratic', and 'remarkably vague'. Mosley's QC, James Price, is quoted as accusing Thurlbeck of 'making it up as he went along'. If all this does not count as the *News of the World* being 'unfair or ungenerous' in its 'use of advantages' over Mosley, then it's hard to understand what could constitute such behaviour.

As noted elsewhere in this book, apropos the *Daily Mail* in particular, there is a certain kind of British newspaper which sees its job as attempting to enforce what it regards as conventional morality (especially in the sexual sphere), and which viciously excoriates those whom it perceives as departing from the norm. And, for all their superficial salaciousness, this is also very much the stock in trade of papers like the *Sun* and the late, unlamented *News of the World*. Mill's *On Liberty* is, as we have seen, a book not without its problems, but one of its most attractive aspects is its warnings against the tyranny of the majority, a majority on behalf of which populist papers always insist that they are speaking (albeit usually with precious little evidence), and whose raucous, bullying, censorious voice was very much in evidence during the Mosley affair – and by no means simply in the *News of the World*. It would therefore be fitting to conclude by quoting a passage from Mill which does not actually mention privacy specifically, but is remarkably germane to the matters discussed in this chapter:

> *Protection … against the tyranny of the magistrate is not enough. There needs protection also against the tyranny of the prevailing opinion and feeling, against the tendency of society to impose, by other means than civil penalties, its own ideas and practices as rules of conduct on those who dissent from them; to fetter the development and, if possible, prevent the formation of any individuality not in harmony with its ways, and compel all characters to fashion themselves upon the model of its own. There is a limit to the legitimate interference of collective opinion with individual independence; and to find that limit, and maintain against its encroachment, is as indispensable to a good condition of human affairs as protection against political despotism. (1985: 63)*

Like Warren and Brandeis, Mill brings a judicious and above all rational voice to the debate, attempting to tease out the fundamental principles underlying the issues at stake in it, thus giving the discussion a relevance that extends far beyond the shores of the UK. Many of the chapters in this book are concerned, quite correctly, with analysing the laws and other regulations which govern the extent to which the media may or may not intrude on privacy, but philosophy digs beneath specific laws and regulations to discover the ethical principles on which these rest and from which they derive. And philosophy, like all journalism worthy of the name, is concerned above all else to discover the truth, something which is all too frequently lacking in discussions about privacy and the media. As is pointed out in several chapters in this book, the media, and in particular newspapers, are all too frequently unreliable (and that's putting it politely) when it comes to discussing matters pertaining to themselves, since self-interest all too often fogs the debate – for example, in the case of the UK, there was the 'Super-Injunction Spring' which contained a dramatic dearth of super-injunctions. A philosopher would never have made quite such an elementary categorical mistake.

Notes

1   http://groups.csail.mit.edu/mac/classes/6.805/articles/privacy/Privacy_brand_
    warr2.html (accessed Aug. 2012).
2   http://image.guardian.co.uk/sys-files/Media/documents/2008/07/24/
    mosley_v_news_group.pdf?intcmp=239.
3   http://www.levesoninquiry.org.uk/wp-content/uploads/2011/11/Witness-
    Statement-of-Max-Mosley.pdf.
4   http://image.guardian.co.uk/sys-files/Media/documents/2008/07/24/
    mosley_v_news_group.pdf.
5   http://www.levesoninquiry.org.uk/wp-content/uploads/2011/11/Witness-
    Statement-of-Max-Mosley.pdf.

References

Barendt, Eric (2002) 'Media Intrusion: The Case for Legislation', in Clare Heyward and Damian Tambini (eds), *Ruled by Recluses?* (London: Institute for Public Policy Research).

Gray, John (1983) *Mill on Liberty: A Defence* (London: Routledge).

Lukes, Stephen (1973) *Individualism* (Oxford: Basil Blackwell).

Mill, John Stuart (1985) *On Liberty* (London: Penguin).

Prosser, William L. (1960) 'Privacy', *California Law Review*, 48(3): 383–423.

Solove, Daniel J. (2008) *Understanding Privacy* (Cambridge, MA: Harvard University Press).

Wacks, Raymond (2010) *Privacy: A Very Short Introduction* (Oxford: Oxford University Press).

Warren, Samuel, and Brandeis, D. Louis (1890) 'The Right to Privacy', *Harvard Law Review*, 4(5): http://www.jjllplaw.com/The-Right-to-Privacy-Warren-Brandeis-Harvard-Law-Review-1890.html (accessed Oct. 2012).

5

Disclosure and Public Shaming in the Age of New Visibility

Hanne Detel

This chapter is based on the assumption that the internet and other digital technologies can be considered as the cause of a phenomenon that John B. Thompson (1995, 2000, 2005) has called the 'new visibility'. Under these conditions the features of scandals have been transformed as well. Fates such as the one suffered by a young South Korean demonstrate this amplified significance for scandal processes of the new forms of visibility created by the internet and other digital technologies.

Seoul in 2005. A young woman refused to clean up after her dog, which had defecated in a subway. Another passenger took a photo of her and the dog and posted it on a popular Korean blog – labelling her 'Dog Poop Girl'. By displaying the photographed proof of the transgression on the internet he made it visible to a large audience. Within days the picture and the story spread all over the internet, the young woman was identified, and her personal data were circulated. Users were outraged about her behaviour and insulted her in an extreme manner. Local as well as international 'old' media took notice and reported on the case. As a result, the young South Korean dropped out of university.

The case of the Dog Poop Girl stands for a number of similar new forms of scandals: norm violations committed by hitherto unknown people are disclosed on the internet, leading to major moral outrage. However, as internet scandals such as this have barely been studied, there is thus far little understanding of this new phenomenon, and in particular of how internet scandals typically develop. This chapter therefore aims to examine how the shaming process has been transformed due to the appearance of the new media, thus contributing to a better understanding of this new phenomenon.

In the first part of this chapter, the concept of the new visibility is explained and developed further with regard to the internet and other digital technologies. Next, information concerning gatekeeper scandals is provided in order to be able to compare older forms of shaming with internet scandals. After the formulation of research questions a number of case studies are undertaken, and comparisons between these various studies will allow deductions to be made about the main differences between scandals in the new and the traditional media.

New visibility in the digital age

According to Thompson (2005: 35), 'visible' means that which can be perceived via the sense of sight. A more precise definition has been developed by Erving Goffman (1963/86: 48), who argued that, since the human senses are not limited to the sense of sight, 'the more general term, "perceptibility" would be more accurate, and "evidentness" more accurate still'.

Thompson (2000: 40) has shown that because of the mass media, visibility, and especially the visibility of political leaders, has increased radically: 'The development of new communication media thus gave rise to a new kind of despatialized publicness which allowed for an intimate form of self-presentation freed from the constraints of co-presence.' The term 'new communication media' refers here mainly to print media, radio, and television; the new media in a more contemporary sense are mentioned only in one short paragraph. But elsewhere, Thompson (2005) has expanded upon how internet and other digital technologies make it much more difficult for those in power to control one's image, because a much larger group of people can create and distribute content.

This chapter argues for a stronger focus on the internet and its impact on visibility. This is because the internet and other digital technologies have changed the scope of visibility in a fundamental way – not only for prominent people in powerful positions, but also for ordinary people.

The information technology bringing about this change is digitisation. In digital form, data can be haphazardly copied, saved, linked, shared, modified, and remixed – and the physical and material limitations of images and sounds, texts and films, disappear. Thus the original context of words and actions can easily be shifted in terms of space, time, audience, and modality. The result of what Wesch (2009: 23) calls such a 'context collapse' is that words and actions which were intended for a certain context can easily be made persistently visible to a potentially large audience. This applies to harmless texts, photos, or videos, as well as to textual, audio, or audiovisual evidence depicting transgressions and norm violations. This makes it possible for everyone easily to shame other people and thus, possibly, to bring about a scandal. Furthermore, it makes everyone – not just those in power – prone to becoming the object of scandal.

The characteristics of gatekeeper scandals

To be able to study how the features of scandals have changed under the influence of the new visibility created by the internet and other digital forms of communication, it is necessary to look at 'old' scandals first – here referred to as 'gatekeeper scandals', because journalists, the so-called gatekeepers, select which transgressions are worth making the object of scandal and which are not.

According to Thompson (2000: 13), the word 'scandal' refers to 'actions or events involving certain kinds of transgressions which become known to others and are sufficiently serious to elicit a public response'. Most of those researching scandal are of the same opinion, and argue that scandals entail typically at least three features: a norm violation (1) is disclosed by the old media (2) to a huge audience, which is morally outraged (3) at the transgression (see, for example, Burkhardt, 2006; Kepplinger, 2005).

Gatekeeper scandals target people in positions of power and never ordinary people (Gross, 1965: 400; Hondrich, 2002: 40). An empirical study of 326 scandals between 1910 and 1998 by Kurt Imhof (cited in Burkhardt, 2006: 123) supports this finding: Imhof came to the conclusion that, in 82.2% of the cases examined, politicians were the objects of the scandal, followed by prominent figures in the entertainment industry and the nobility (5.2%).

In the case of gatekeeper scandals, transgressions and norm violations are always disclosed and spread by journalists, although in many cases the scandalous content originates from whistle-blowers or campaigning organisations such as Greenpeace (Kepplinger, 2005: 27–8). According to

Steffen Burkhardt (2006: 141), the audience plays a somewhat passive role, but recipients can influence the scandal-making process through their purchasing power and reception behaviour – such as writing letters to the editor to express their point of view.

The consequences of gatekeeper scandals range from damage to the reputation of the person concerned to resignation, psychological problems, and criminal sanctions. Thompson (2000: 22–3) points out various strategies of possible scandal management: engaging a lawyer and going to court, denying the allegation (which carries with it the danger of a second-order transgression if a lie has been told or a false denial made), or admitting the transgression publicly.

Research questions

The main interest of this study is to provide a preliminary understanding of the new phenomenon of internet scandals, and thereby to identify how scandal-making processes have changed under the influence of the internet and other new digital forms of communication.

The main focus will be on how internet scandals typically develop. Who first discloses a transgression? What types of inducement to revealing scandals exist? What means are used for disclosure? How does the shaming content disseminate on the internet? How do other internet users react to the revelation? How do they express their moral outrage? What is the role of the old media? And finally, what are the consequences of an internet scandal for the person targeted?

Method

The object of this study is relatively new. Therefore, in order to gain a preliminary understanding of the phenomenon, an explorative qualitative approach was taken. According to Philipp Mayring (2002: 149–50), each research subject requires its own specific method of cognition. Thus, it is important, especially in qualitative research, not only to adopt proven research approaches on a one-to-one basis, but also to apply procedures appropriate to the specific subject.

The case-study approach was chosen in order to allow a detailed examination of the research questions. This chapter follows the definition of Yin (2009: 18) in regarding a case study as 'an empirical inquiry that investigates a contemporary phenomenon in depth and within its real-life context, especially when the boundaries between phenomenon and context are not clearly evident'. The approach is particularly suitable to questions of how and why a certain social phenomenon works. In addition, case-study research is relevant to questions requiring an in-depth description of the social phenomenon examined.

The reconstruction and analysis of a single case is not enough to draw a conclusion about the complexity of a social phenomenon, because the focus lies in the specifics of the case. Therefore, a multiple case study was conducted in order both to address the specifics of the individual cases and to include the contrasting analysis of certain cases.

In this study, internet scandals were the unit of analysis. Therefore, cases had to meet at least the basic requirements of a scandal as defined by Thompson (above). This requires that the disclosure of an alleged transgression must have taken place and caused widespread moral outrage. Furthermore, the disclosure of the norm violation and parts of the public expression of indignation must have happened on the internet or through other digital forms of communication. A list of 70 potential cases was compiled. From this list, 14 were chosen, following Glaser and Strauss's (1967/98) concept of theoretical sampling. They represent the full range of disclosure modes, scandal inducements, forms of new media, expressions of moral outrage, and consequences of public shaming which could be found in the 70 cases. The most recent case is from 2011, the oldest from 1998. Five of the 14 cases are scandals targeting prominent people, the other nine concern transgressions committed by ordinary people.

In a next step, the cases were reconstructed in detail by analysing various materials (online writings, photos, and videos, as well as relevant newspaper articles and other forms of coverage in the traditional media, along with interviews with the people involved). Finally, the comparative case method was applied. As Eisenhardt (1989: 541) explains: 'Overall, the idea behind these cross-case searching tactics is to force investigators to go beyond initial impressions, especially through the use of structured and diverse lenses on the data.' For that reason, this last step provided additional insight into the phenomenon of internet scandals, and typical patterns regarding the research questions could be identified.

Single-case reconstruction

Presenting the entire reconstruction process and the analysis of the cases would go beyond the scope of this chapter. Therefore, only a short description of each case examined is provided in Table 5.1, in order to give an idea of the findings that the case comparison yielded. The cases are in chronological order. Some of the more sensitive cases are anonymised so as to protect the people concerned.

Findings of the case comparison

Under the conditions of a new form of mediated visibility, the features of shaming processes and scandals have been transformed. The findings of the study allow for a typology of how shaming and the manufacture of scandal on the internet usually proceed. From a comparison of the case studies, five different phases can be identified, although these overlap in most of the cases: the original disclosure of the transgression; the diffusion of the shaming material; the formation of a cyber mob; the intervention of the traditional media; and the consequences of internet scandals. Set out below, these five phases are described and illustrated with examples from the case studies.

The original disclosure of the transgression

In the digital age, journalists – the former gatekeepers – are no longer alone in their ability to publish shaming and scandal-inducing material, as every internet user, alone or in groups, can do so as well. On the other hand, it is not just those in powerful positions who become the target of scandals, but rather everyone living in societies in which people use mobile phones, digital cameras, and the internet. The scope of what is seen as a transgression is also relevant, for the scope of scandal-making has widened. Nowadays, even minor norm violations can ignite scandals. Several separate factors involving disclosure could be identified: modes of disclosure, amplifying factors, the means used for revelation, and the audio, audiovisual, or written evidence for the transgression, as well as uncertainty regarding the credibility of the shame-inducing content.

Table 5.1 Overview of the Case Studies

Cases	Short descriptions of the cases
Case 1: **Clinton-Lewinsky** **(1998)**	On 17 January 1998, Matt Drudge first revealed the Monica Lewinsky scandal in his Drudge Report, which had begun as an email sent out to a couple of friends. He reported that the magazine *Newsweek* had stopped a story 'that was destined to shake official Washington to its foundation: A White House intern carried on a sexual affair with the President of the United States'. The story was based on a tip and Drudge did not waste much time in carrying out additional research except for talking to Lucianne Goldberg, a literary agent who was in contact with Linda Tripp, a friend of Monica Lewinsky. Within eight hours of the publication of Drudge's story numerous people had visited the website and read it. He received 15,000 emails commenting on the disclosure. The story circulated on the internet until it spilled over into the traditional media on 21 January.
Case 2: **Washingtonienne** **(2004)**	Jessica Cutler from Washington, DC, wrote a blog about her sexual experiences with several men including colleagues. Famous US-blog Wonkette found the blog, called Washingtonienne, and linked to it. Within minutes thousands of internet users found their way to Cutler's blog. She deleted it, but it was too late. A number of people had already copied the blog entries and spread them on the internet. As a result, she was fired and one of her former lovers sued her for circulating intimate information about him. She later wrote a book about her story.
Case 3: **Abu Ghraib** **(2003/4)**	In 2003 military police officers committed various forms of torture and prisoner abuse in Abu Ghraib prison in Iraq. Between 18 October and 30 December 2003, more than 1,000 photos and about 100 video clips were taken by the officers, documenting what they had done. Accidentally, a CD with some of the pictures fell into the hands of army reserve specialist Joseph Darby, who informed the US Army Criminal Investigation Command. Later on, articles describing the prisoner abuse, as well as some of the pictures, were published. Today, many of the pictures can be found online. In this case the transgressions were not disclosed on the internet first; however, digital technologies were used to capture photo evidence of the abuse and to shift it into new contexts.

Cases	Short descriptions of the cases
Case 4: **Broken laptop** **(2005/6)**	Thomas Sawyer, from Exeter, Devon, bought a laptop at an internet auction from Amir Tofangsazan. After transferring the necessary funds to Tofangsazan's account, it took almost two months until he received the laptop, which was broken. Sawyer tried to talk to Tofangsazan, but without success. Indignant, Sawyer set up a blog where he uploaded personal information about and pictures of Tofangsazan, recovered from the laptop's hard drive; these included a scan of his passport and his CV. He sent an email to all the contacts on Tofangsazan's Hotmail account to inform them of the existence of the blog. Within three and a half weeks, the website had had about 2.3 million page views. Although Sawyer was never refunded, he did make money by placing advertisements on his website (Allgöwer, 2006; Bigge, 2006).
Case 5: **Mis-sent email** **(2006)**	Two female staff members at an employment agency in south Germany exchanged emails about their sex lives during working hours. By accident one of the two women sent the whole email conversation to a staff mailing list. Within hours, this was forwarded to numerous colleagues, and over the next few days to thousands of people outside the company, who were both outraged about the employees writing private emails during working hours and amused by the mishap – and the bad spelling. Newspapers and TV reported the story. As a result, both women changed their jobs.
Case 6: **Bus uncle (2006)**	Roger Chan Yuet-tung, from Hong Kong, was on his way home, talking loudly on his mobile phone, when 23-year-old Elvis 'Alvin' Ho tapped him on the shoulder and asked him to lower his voice. Chan became angry and shouted at Ho for six minutes. A third bus passenger, Jon Fong, recorded the rant secretly with his mobile phone and posted it on YouTube for everyone to see. The original video alone – without counting the various copies – has had 4.1 million page views to date. Comments show that people were both outraged and amused by Chan's behaviour. Numerous mashups of the video were created, users wrote about 'bus uncle' on the web, local and international media reported the incident, and T-shirts and bags emblazoned with phrases from Chan's rant appeared on the market. Eventually, reporters from *Next* magazine found and interviewed the unemployed man.

Cases	Short descriptions of the cases
Case 7: **Rant about** **earthquake** **victims (2008)**	After the Sichuan earthquake in 2008, China began a three-day period of national mourning. Even on the internet, several entertainment websites were blocked and so 21-year-old Gao Quianhui from Shenyang (China) could not play her favourite online game. Angry, she used her webcam to record a rant in which she blamed and insulted the earthquake victims, and uploaded it to YouTube, apparently unaware that the video could be viewed all over the world. Many Chinese internet users were outraged about the rant and, in protest, spread the offending video all over the internet. Subtitles were added, copies made, and thousands of people commented on it in forums. In all several million people have watched the video to date. Numerous rumours about Quianhui's identity circulated on the web, including her address and her passport number. Just one day after posting the video online, Quianhui was arrested by the police.
Case 8: **YouTube divorce** **(2008)**	Playwright and actress Tricia Walsh-Smith produced two semi-professional YouTube videos showing herself in the flat of her soon-to-be ex-husband Philip J. Smith, president of the Shubert organisation, who had announced that he was going to divorce her and that he wanted her to move out of the flat. Walsh-Smith's videos were an attempt to make a scandal out of her husband's behaviour towards her, and also disclosed intimate details about him. Almost 4 million people have watched the first video. Ultimately, a Manhattan judge awarded Philip Smith a divorce from his wife, and described her YouTube videos as a calculated and callous campaign to embarrass and humiliate her husband.
Case 9: **China-Tibet** **(2008)**	In the year of the Olympic Games in Beijing, a small group of students at Duke University, Durham, NC, organised a 'Free Tibet Picket' for Tibetan human rights on the occasion of the Olympic torch relay. About 100 Chinese mounted a counter-protest. Chinese student Wang Qianyuan tried to mediate between the two groups because she knew people from both sides and assumed that there were communication problems – but without success. The Chinese students became angry and threatened Wang, who had also written 'Free Tibet' on the back of a fellow student. The same evening, Wang wrote a letter explaining her actions and posted it on the website of the Duke Chinese Students and Scholars Association – prompting an online witch-hunt of the student. The next

Cases	Short descriptions of the cases
	day, information, photos, and videos showing her behaviour during the demonstration were available on the internet. On the one hand, she received numerous death threats and people threw faeces in front of her parent's apartment in China and wrote on the wall: 'Kill the whole family! Kill traitor of her country!' On the other hand, she was supported by many Americans who were outraged by the attempts (mainly by Chinese people) to turn her behaviour into a scandal. For instance, Wang was able to publish an essay about her point of view in the *Washington Post*.
Case 10: **Jürgen Rüttgers** **(2009)**	During an election campaign in August 2009, the former minster-president of the German *Land* North Rhine-Westphalia, Jürgen Rüttgers, visited several cities in the area. In one of his speeches, in Duisburg, he criticised Nokia for having closed their plant in nearby Bochum. The company had moved the factory to Romania in order to lower manufacturing costs. During his speech Rüttgers used xenophobic language to back his arguments. According to the politician, Romanian labourers worked less well than German ones. Moreover, they came and went whenever they wanted. None of the journalists present reported the xenophobic remarks, but Rüttgers's speech was filmed by members of the German Social Democratic Party's youth organisation, and they then posted parts of the video on YouTube. Bloggers and journalists criticised Rüttgers's comments. However, anonymous commentators on the internet were divided, with about half being highly indignant, and the other half supporting Rüttgers. A criminal complaint was made against the politician and Romanian politicians expressed disapproval.
Case 11: **The whistle-blower (2010)**	In late May 2010, Private Bradley Manning, an intelligence analyst with the US Army stationed near Baghdad, was arrested. He was suspected of leaking to WikiLeaks the 'Collateral Murder' video showing a US helicopter attack that killed 11 men, as well as 700,000 mostly secret documents – which contained a good deal of potentially scandalous material. His arrest was based on incautious confessions which he made in an online chat with ex-hacker and journalist Adrian Lamo, who duly informed the FBI and Army Counterintelligence. Manning conceded in the chat that he had burned the documents to a rewritable Lady Gaga CD. Manning faces court-martial on 22 charges, including aiding the enemy. If convicted he could face life imprisonment.

Cases	Short descriptions of the cases
Case 12: **Arrest in class** **(2010)**	During an anthropology class at the University of Wisconsin-Milwaukee, a noisy dispute emerged between the professor and 24-year-old student Robyn Foster. The lecturer asked the student to leave the classroom several times, but Foster refused. Eventually the campus police arrived, pushed the student to the ground and handcuffed her. A fellow student filmed the whole scene with her smart phone and uploaded it to YouTube. Internet users' opinions were divided on this issue. One group of people was outraged by Foster's behaviour and insulted her loudly, the other was scandalised by the behaviour of the police. Almost no comments criticising the fellow student for posting the video online can be found. The video was copied several times, and numerous bloggers and journalists reported about it. Foster's online reputation remains damaged. Search results for her name (or similarly named women) lead to various stories and videos about her arrest.
Case 13: **Plagiariser (2011)**	In February 2011, the *Süddeutsche Zeitung* reported that a law professor had found plagiarised passages in the doctoral thesis of Karl-Theodor zu Guttenberg, who was then the minister of defence. He denied the allegations, but apologised for 'possible mistakes'. In the following days several internet users collaborated in a wiki called GuttenPlag and revealed that at least 371 out of 393 pages of his thesis contained plagiarised passages. Moreover, in their wiki they reproduced the particular passages as well as the original texts. Guttenberg came under further pressure and eventually had to resign. This case showed how digital technologies and the internet make those in power even more visible than before – not only to journalists but also to ordinary people, enabling them rapidly and effectively to translate transgressions into scandals (Pörksen and Detel, 2011).
Case 14: **Mis-sent photo** **(2011)**	With one click, Democrat US Representative Anthony Weiner disclosed a photograph showing him in underpants. Instead of sending the picture to a student from Seattle via Twitter, Weiner revealed it to his some 56,000 followers. Before he could delete the photograph, it was shared with other users. Weiner first claimed that his account had been hacked, but, soon afterwards, other sexually suggestive pictures and conversations were brought to light, and, at a tearful press conference, he had to confess to lying. Several politicians, including Barack Obama, demanded that Weiner step down, and almost three weeks after his accidental self-disclosure, Weiner resigned his seat in Congress.

Two separate modes of disclosure can be differentiated (see Table 5.2). First, there are external revelations, which are made either by strangers who are outraged at a transgression, or by people who want to harm a certain person whom they know. For instance, Tricia Walsh-Smith made a scandal out of the behaviour of her soon-to-be ex-husband and revealed intimate information about his sexual life in order to take revenge for his announcement of divorce. In certain cases, shaming content is uploaded only for friends to see but then spreads on the internet unintentionally (Case 12: arrest in class). Second, self-disclosure can be found in several of the case studies. One example is Bradley Manning, who confessed in an internet chat with ex-hacker Adrian Lamo that he had leaked secret information and videos to WikiLeaks. The case studies lead to the conclusion that self-disclosure is mostly a result of either incautiousness or lack of knowledge about the medium used.

Based on the findings, three contributing factors could be identified: prominence, intimacy/sexuality, and ludicrousness. Alleged transgression, combined with these amplifying factors, seemed to have a greater potential to receive abundant attention because users relate to such cases in different ways. Prominent people are already the focus of media attention. Thus, when a transgression by such a person is revealed, it is very likely that many people will be interested in it anyway (Case 1: Clinton-Lewinsky, or Case 14: mis-sent photo). Furthermore, it was noticeable that transgressions linked with intimate or sexual information (Case 5: mis-sent email), as well as ludicrousness (Case 8: YouTube divorce), attracted wide interest from internet users.

In order to make the original disclosures, a wide range of different platforms or services were used. From email and blogs through to microblogging services such as Twitter, chats, and wikis, several modalities could be found within the cases studied. The video-sharing website YouTube was involved in a particularly high number of cases.

The cases suggest that audiovisual material is better fitted for shaming purposes than purely written evidence. In most of the cases examined, videos or photos functioned as proof of norm transgressions. There was one exception: the mis-sent email. However, many users assumed that the email conversation between the two employees was a fake. In other cases this kind of suspicion was less frequently expressed in the user comments. Therefore, it can be presumed that audiovisual material is seen as more credible by users, who assume less often than in the case of written material that it has been manipulated.

Table 5.2   Subject, Amplifying Factors, and Mode of Disclosure

Subject of disclosure + amplifying factors	Mode of disclosure	
	External disclosure	Self-disclosure
(Alleged) transgression	Clinton-Lewinsky	Washingtonienne
	Broken laptop	Abu Ghraib
	Bus uncle	Mis-sent e-mail
	YouTube divorce	Rant on earthquake victims
	China-Tibet	China-Tibet
	Jürgen Rüttgers	The whistle-blower
	Arrest in class	Mis-sent photo
	Plagiariser	
Amplifying factor:	Clinton-Lewinsky	Washingtonienne
Intimacy and sexuality	Broken laptop	Mis-sent e-mail
	YouTube divorce	Mis-sent photo
Amplifying factor:	Broken laptop	Mis-sent e-mail
Ludicrousness	Bus uncle	Mis-sent photo
	YouTube divorce	
Amplifying factor:	Clinton-Lewinsky	Mis-sent photo
Prominence	YouTube divorce	
	Jürgen Rüttgers	
	Plagiariser	

Finally, it is important to point out that it is not necessary for the object of the scandal to have actually violated a norm. Digital evidence of supposed transgressions can easily be faked on the internet: images can be manipulated, written text can be changed and accounts hacked. For example, there is no conclusive proof that it was actually Amir Tofangsazan who sold Thomas Sawyer the broken laptop with his data on it, and the odds are that Thomas Sawyer shamed the wrong person.

The findings above throw more light on the factors involving revelation in the case of internet scandals and show how internet scandals are typically disclosed.

The diffusion of the shaming material

All the case studies manifest an 'epidemiological' diffusion of the shaming content. Within days – in some cases hours – of its original appearance, thousands of internet users know about the shaming material.

As previously stated, digitised content loses its physical and material limitations, and can be easily shifted or copied into other contexts. This makes the dissemination of shaming content very simple compared to former times. In order to explain this rapid spread, the comparative case study allows for three principles of diffusion on the web to be distinguished:

1. Prominent connectors (Gladwell, 2002) are highly linked to many other internet users and spread information in a short period of time. In the case of Jessica Cutler, Wonkette played the role of such a prominent connector. After this widely read blog established a link to Cutler's hitherto unknown blog 'Washingtonienne', the latter received a high number of page views within minutes, and before Cutler could delete her blog.

2. Forwarded emails, retweets on Twitter, or recommendations on social media sites function on the snowball principle. Small connectors work effectively together to spread shaming material. Case 5 (mis-sent email) can be cited as an example of that mechanism, because the disclosed intimate email conversation between the two employment agency staff employees was disseminated by numerous people forwarding the text to their friends, colleagues, or merely acquaintances.

3. Social media sites often work with a self-energising mechanism, the so-called 'the rich get richer' principle (Schmidt, 2009). For instance, the most viewed YouTube videos within a certain time period are watched even more often because they are top-rated in the rankings. In the case of bus uncle Roger Chan Yuet-tung, the video showing his rant made it onto the list of the most watched videos of the month. This attracted even more people to the video and, furthermore, the traditional media also took notice and reported the rant on the bus.

A brief example will illustrate the effort that was needed to spread scandalous material in former times compared to today. In 1971, when Daniel Ellsberg, a high-ranking employee of the American Department of Defence, wanted to bring to attention the so-called Pentagon Papers (secret documents revealing that the government was misleading the public about the Vietnam War), he had to copy some thousand pages, which took him several months and involved a high level of risk to himself. It then took several more months until newspapers such as the *New York Times* and the *Washington Post* actually published extracts.

All the cases studied showed that the attention of internet users stagnated after a short period of time, usually a few weeks. In the case of Robyn Foster's arrest in class, nothing new happened, so people lost interest in the scandal. However, this was not the case with stories that developed further in any way – for example, when further revelations of plagiarism were made in the Guttenberg case, which prolonged the attention to the scandal. Another way of keeping the scandal going is to publish follow-up information – for example, about the management of the scandal or the consequences of the case. Third, dealing ironically with a case can call the scandal repeatedly to mind. Within the cases studied mashups, remixes, and the invention of jokes related to the initial scandal all occurred (e.g. Case 6: bus uncle; Case 14: mis-sent photo).

The formation of the cyber mob

Another feature common to all the cases is the formation of a 'cyber mob' united by the same emotion: moral outrage as a reaction to norm transgressions. When contributing factors such as ludicrousness and intimate issues are also involved, mocking and voyeuristic comments can also be found within the reactions.

Usually, moral outrage is expressed in comments or blog posts. This possibility for interaction makes people more powerful than when the audience could only be largely passive and when scandal mongering was in the hands of journalists. It was noticeable that many of the comments on the scandals in the case studies were extremely aggressive and used insulting or threatening phrases. Indeed, even death threats could be found amongst the reactions. In some extreme cases the outrage was expressed in real life and those who were the object of the scandal were attacked (Case 6: bus uncle). One possible explanation for the uninhibited nature of these comments could be that their writers usually employed pseudonyms, which may make them feel less personally responsible for their words. Moreover, it can also be assumed that people feel distant from the person targeted when commenting on the internet.

In most of the case studies, the majority of those who commented shared the same view on the transgression (Case 4: broken laptop; Case 7: rant about earthquake victims). The comments of the few dissidents were met with disapproval or even intimidatory remarks. Certain internet scandals, however, showed that this moral outrage can form into two contradictory threads: in such cases, one side shared the view of the person who had disclosed the alleged transgression, while the other side turned on this person and expressed outrage about the revelation itself. That happened either when the revelation of the norm violation was seen as even worse than the original transgression (e.g. the American side in Case 9: China-Tibet), or when the person who made the original disclosure imparted a good deal of information about himself or herself, as well as about his/her intention in making the disclosure public, and so provided the audience with a target (e.g. Tricia Walsh-Smith in Case 8: YouTube divorce).

Apart from commenting on and spreading the evidence of transgression, internet users also make use of the so-called 'wisdom of crowds' (Surowiecki, 2005) to search for details about the person who has allegedly committed the norm violation. Incorrect or imprecise information is all too frequently circulated as a result of this process. For instance, in the case of Gao Quianhui's rant against the victims of the Sichuan earthquake, internet users at first confused her with a Chinese woman Zhang Ya, whose appearance is similar. Other details about her, however, turned out to be true – such as her passport number, for example.

These findings reveal that so-called 'cyber mobs' have brought shaming processes to a level at which they are much more difficult to control than hitherto.

The intervention of the traditional media

The traditional media are not redundant within these new forms of scandal. Once a case is well known in the social media or the blogosphere, it is likely to spill over into the traditional media. Frequently, shaming content is published for a second time under the guise of serving the public interest – thus involving a process of 'second-order voyeurism' (Bergmann and Pörksen, 2009: 25) for the person concerned.

In particular, the online outlets of the traditional media play a major role in spreading the evidence of a transgression. By linking to a blog or by embedding a video, they increase the number of people watching the video or visiting the blog. For instance, in the case of Jürgen Rüttgers, half of the 145,000 views originated from an article published on Spiegel Online, the online version of German weekly news magazine *Der Spiegel*. However, the online presences of the traditional media are not the only entities playing the role of 'prominent connectors': newspaper articles and broadcast reports make the scandal better known beyond the internet.

This coverage can happen in various ways. First, the traditional media play the role of 'chroniclers' who report the scandal in a relatively factual way. There are also journalists who analyse the scandal and discuss the new form of scandal and its social meaning on a meta-level. For example, in the case of Gao Quianhui's rant against the earthquake victims, a number of articles dealt with the new phenomenon of the so-called 'human flesh search'. Third, there are journalists who carry out follow-up research and disclose further information regarding the person targeted. This happened, for instance, in the case of bus uncle Roger Chan Yuet-tung. Journalists identified the ranting man and wrote about him in a magazine. In summary, it can be said that traditional old media intensify the impact of shaming by reporting on it.

The consequences of internet scandals

Internet scandals can damage the digital reputation of the targeted person globally and permanently. With the help of search engines, shaming content can be retrieved from anywhere in the world – even many years after it was initially uploaded. Once spread throughout the internet, it is almost impossible to remove information completely. Legal steps have failed in most of the cases examined here, and indeed can lead to even more attention being paid to the object of the scandal.

For example, when searching for the name 'Amir Tofangsazan' (Case 4: broken laptop), the first results link to Thomas Sawyer's revenge site where shaming material about Tofangsazan can be found. Other results lead to articles or blog posts about the case. The same pattern can be observed with most of the other cases. This can make it very difficult for the object of the scandal to find a job, make friends, or rent a flat, because more and more people use search engines in order to get a first impression of a person.

Another difficulty for most people in this position is the fact that they can never be really sure about who in their social environment knows about the shaming material and who does not. Thus, for Robyn Foster (Case 12: arrest in class) it was very hard for her to come back to university after her arrest because she could safely assume that many of her fellow students knew about it.

In some extreme cases the aggression in response to a person's transgression has gone beyond the virtual world and had consequences in real life. Certain disclosures such as Case 11 (the whistle-blower) have resulted in criminal proceedings or criminal sanctions. Other real-life consequences such as threats and assaults were found in certain of the cases of internet scandals examined. For example, persons unknown assaulted bus uncle Roger Chan Yuet-tung at his new job, and Wang Qianyuan's intervention in the China/Tibet affair led to people throwing faeces in front of her parent's apartment in China and writing on its wall: 'Kill the whole family! Kill traitor of her country!'

It can thus be concluded that in the digital age global and persistent damage to reputation, and not only digital reputation, is one of the most common results of internet scandals.

Conclusion

This study shows that under the conditions of a new form of mediated visibility, the features of shaming processes and scandals have been significantly transformed. The findings of the study give preliminary insights into typical patterns of how scandals in the digital age usually develop. Five overlapping phases have been differentiated in most of the cases: the original disclosure of the transgression; the diffusion of the shaming material; the formation of a cyber mob; the intervention of the traditional media; and the consequences of internet scandals. All phases of internet scandals are characterised by these new features.

In summary, several main differences are apparent between gate-keeper scandals and the new forms of scandal generation. First, a wider range of people are able to disclose transgressions, as well as to determine who and what behaviours are susceptible to shaming. Not only journalists – the former gatekeepers – are able to invoke a scandal, but now every internet user can do so. For this a variety of internet platforms and services are available. In addition to famous or powerful people, ordinary people too can now become the object of shaming. Moreover, in the new media even small transgressions can be sufficient to trigger a scandal.

Second, the diffusion of scandal-inducing content evolves as an interplay between the traditional and the new media. Although the former have lost the monopoly on invoking and controlling scandals, they still play a major role by intensifying the impact of the transgressions first disclosed on the internet.

Third, the audience is no longer passive, but can intervene by expressing moral outrage directly. Their influence is no longer limited to writing letters to the editor or giving a vox pop. Instead, they – alone or in groups – can impinge on the shaming process by commenting, by spreading or sharing the shaming content, and even by revealing further information.

Finally, compared to scandals in the traditional media, the scope of shaming processes has become less predictable and the potential damage to reputation more extensive. This is because shaming content can be accessed from anywhere in the world, and can be spread and shared extremely rapidly. In extreme cases, it reaches a global audience. Moreover, because this kind of material can remain indefinitely on the internet, transgressions revealed there can ruin reputations for years. All these factors make the shaming processes in the new media even less controllable than were the previous gatekeeper scandals.

References

Allgöwer, Kristina von (2006) 'Der Rächer der Betrogenen', Der Spiegel, 26: www.spiegel.de/spiegel/print/d-47360728.html (accessed May 2013).

Bergmann, Jens, and Pörksen, Bernhard (2009) Skandal! Die Macht öffentlicher Empörung (Cologne: von Halem).

Bigge, Ryan (2006) 'Wearing the digital dunce cap': www.macleans.ca/culture/entertainment/article.jsp?content=20061002_133913_133913 (accessed May 2013).

Burkhardt, Steffen (2006) Medienskandale: Zur moralischen Sprengkraft öffentlicher Diskurse (Cologne: von Halem).

Döring, Nicola (2003) Sozialpsychologie des Internet (Göttingen: Hogrefe).

Eisenhardt, Kathleen M. (1989) 'Building Theories from Case Study Research', Academy of Management Review, 14(4): 532–50.

Gladwell, Malcolm (2002) The Tipping Point: How Little Things Can Make a Big Difference (New York: Black Bay Books).

Glaser, Barney G., and Strauss, Anselm (1967/98) Grounded Theory: Strategien qualitativer Forschung (Bern: Huber).

Goffman, Erving (1963/86) Stigma: Notes on the Management of Spoiled Identity (New York: Simon & Schuster).

Gross, Johannes (1965) 'Phänomenologie des Skandals', Merkur: Deutsche Zeitschrift für europäisches Denken, 19(205): 398–400.

Hondrich, Karl O. (2002) Enthüllung und Entrüstung: Eine Phänomenologie des politischen Skandals (Frankfurt am Main: Suhrkamp).

Kepplinger, Hans M. (2005) *Die Mechanismen der Skandalierung: Die Macht der Medien und die Möglichkeiten der Betroffenen,* 2nd edn (Munich: Olzog).

Mayring, Philipp (2002) *Einführung in die qualitative Sozialforschung: Eine Anleitung zu qualitativem Denken* (Weinheim: Beltz).

Pörksen, Bernhard, and Detel, Hanne (2011) 'Evidenzerfahrungen für alle: Das kontraproduktive Krisenmanagement des Verteidigungsministers und die Logik der Skandalisierung im digitalen Zeitalter', in Oliver Lepsius and Reinhart Meyer-Kalkus (eds), *Inszenierung als Beruf: Der Fall Guttenberg* (Berlin: Suhrkamp), 56–70.

Schmidt, Jan (2009) *Das neue Netz: Merkmale, Praktiken und Folgen des Web 2.0* (Konstanz: UVK Verlagsgesellschaft).

Surowiecki, James (2005) *The Wisdom of Crowds* (New York: Anchor Books).

Thompson, John B. (1995) *The Media and Modernity: A Social Theory of the Media* (Cambridge: Polity Press).

Thompson, John B. (2000) *Political Scandal: Power and Visibility in the Media Age* (Cambridge: Polity Press).

Thompson, John B. (2005) 'The New Visibility', *Theory, Culture and Society*, 22(6): 31–51.

Wesch, Michael (2009) 'YouTube and You: Experiences of Self-Awareness in the Context Collapse of the Recording Webcam', *Explorations in Media Ecology*, 8(2): 19–34.

Yin, Robert K. (2009) *Case Study Research: Design and Methods,* 4th edn (London: Sage).

6

Cultural and Gender Differences in Self-Disclosure on Social Networking Sites

Jingwei Wu and Heng Lu[1]

Introduction

Self-disclosure is defined as what individuals reveal about themselves to others, including thoughts, feelings, and experiences. Computer-mediated communication (CMC) has changed the communication environment and the way people interact with each other. Unlike face-to-face (FtF) communication, CMC can lower barriers of interaction and encourage more self-disclosure (Joinson, 2001; Tidwell and Walther, 2002). The users of particular social web applications tend to reveal many personal details.

The prevalence of Social Network Sites (SNSs) has focused considerable public attention on the threat to privacy brought about by self-disclosure on SNSs. SNS users desire to present themselves, express feelings, and develop relationships (Derlega and Grzelak, 1979), as well as to erase the feeling of loneliness (Morahan-Martin and Schumacher, 2003). However, the protection of privacy is somewhat overlooked. In July 2010, privacy concerns swirled around Facebook after an individual compiled and released personal data on more than 100 million Facebook users, about a fifth of the site's membership (Figueroa, 2010). Although many SNSs have elaborated their systems of privacy settings, peers and even strangers still can access certain personal information. Media coverage also increases concerns about the privacy and information security of SNS users.

The privacy settings of SNS users have captured the attention of researchers. Gender and cultural differences in self-disclosure are two research foci central to the tradition of self-disclosure studies. A meta-analysis of studies of the gender differences in self-disclosure in offline settings has found that women disclose more than men (Dindia and Allen, 1992). However, the results of existing studies of online self-disclosure are unexpectedly inconsistent. These find significant differences in self-disclosure in SNSs (Dominick, 1999; Tufekci, 2008) and evidence that women have more online privacy settings than men (Lewis et al., 2008). Nonetheless, other studies indicate that there are no gender differences in levels of self-disclosure in online forums (Barak and Gluck-Ofri, 2007) or online chatting (Cho, 2007).

There are also differences in self-disclosure between people with different cultural backgrounds. The framework of Hofstede's (1980) cultural dimensions (in particular, the dimension of individualism versus collectivism) is widely adopted to investigate and explain cultural differences. In offline settings, Americans (individualistic) usually have higher levels of self-disclosure than Chinese (collectivist) (Chen, 1995). In SNSs, members of individualistic cultures exhibit higher levels of self-disclosure than do members of collectivist cultures (Cho, 2010). However, cultural context is a country-level variable and most of such comparison studies involve users in only two countries, one collectivist and the other individualistic. Thus, the potential inconsistency within certain cultural polarities (e.g. individualistic versus collectivist) is overlooked in comparisons of only two countries. That is to say, what has been found in certain previous studies could be differences between the cultures of different countries rather than between idealised polar dichotomies. Controlling the differences among countries that tend towards the same poles of the dichotomy is necessary for validating cultural differences in self-disclosure.

SNSs are the rising star of Web 2.0 applications. Facebook-like SNSs have local versions in many countries, especially in non-English-language countries. Only very few studies have investigated both gender and cultural differences in self-disclosure in SNSs. For example, Kim and Dindia (2008) found that culture is a significant predictor of self-disclosure in SNSs, whereas there are no significant gender differences. What is interesting here is not limited to the question of whether or not there are cultural or gender differences in the self-disclosure of SNS users. What we can learn from the offline experiences is that people with different genders or cultural origins have different senses of privacy and exhibit different degrees of self-disclosure. Gender differences may not be identical across different cultural settings. Men's traditional roles generally do not encourage the expression of feelings (Thompson and Pleck, 1986), and may constrain self-disclosure for men more in collectivist cultures than in individualistic ones (Marshall, 2008). Evidence suggests that, even in a collectivist culture (such as that of China), women exhibit a higher degree of self-disclosure than men (Cozby, 1973).

In this study, we use quantitative content analysis to investigate self-disclosure in SNSs. On the one hand, we examine how self-disclosure varies among cultures and genders respectively. On the other, we examine the interaction between gender and cultural effects on self-disclosure. Specifically, we would like to investigate whether or not gender differences in self-disclosure, if there are any, vary across different cultural contexts.

Cultural differences in self-disclosure

The notion of privacy governs ideas of how much information should be disclosed to others. Privacy is conceptualised as a culturally universal process, but also as a culturally specific mechanism used to regulate social interaction (Altman, 1977).

The Individualism-Collectivism (I-C) framework is used by Hofstede (1980) to explain social and behavioural differences among cultures, and is also used to interpret intercultural communication and relationships. The I-C framework can be used to explain the differences in self-disclosure among people with varying cultural origins. Members of individualistic cultures are more active-oriented, and are more inclined to talk and to request information more directly than are members of collectivist cultures (Gudykunst et al., 1996). There is also evidence to suggest that individualistic cultures place greater emphasis on self-disclosure than do collectivist ones (Adams et al., 2004).

There is accumulating evidence to support cultural differences in self-disclosure. Compared with people in individualistic cultures, those in collectivist ones have lower levels of self-disclosure (Marshall, 2008). Chen (1995) points out that American students disclose more than Chinese students, and that this difference may be the consequence of different cultural values. As for self-disclosure to close friends, East Asians (e.g. Japanese) disclose less personal information to other people than do Westerners (e.g. Americans) (Schug et al., 2010).

Studies of self-disclosure in SNSs are limited compared to those conducted in the offline world. As in studies of offline communication, a few indicate salient differences of self-disclosure online between individualistic and collectivist cultures. Several studies of Americans and Koreans find that culture is a significant predictor of self-disclosure in SNSs. For example, Americans disclose more than Koreans, whilst Koreans disclose more photos and blog entries than do Americans on their profile pages (Kim and Dindia, 2008). In addition, Americans are more likely to provide information about their origins, present residence, and self-ascribed identity on personal web pages (Kim and Papacharissi, 2003).

These results suggest that cultural differences significantly affect self-disclosure. However, there are two common flaws shared by several previous studies. The first flaw concerns inter-cultural allegiances. Some studies include Asians who have lived in Western countries for a long time. Such participants could bring 'noise' into the results of studies of cultural differences. In Chen's (1995) study, 144 selected Taiwanese students who studied in American colleges could have been influenced by Western culture and therefore may not have accurately represented members of Asian cultures. Therefore, investigations of cultural differences should carefully avoid the intercultural allegiances brought in by participants who have long resided in other cultures. The second flaw is that certain studies draw conclusions concerning cultural differences based on results of comparisons of only two countries. Such studies ignore the intra-cultural differences among countries which share the same generalised individualistic/collectivist cultural orientation. Thus conclusions drawn from comparisons of two countries might be country differences rather than differences between overall individualistic or collectivist cultural orientations. To reach more accurate conclusions concerning cultural differences, we should include at least three countries in order to control the differences among national cultures.

We have chosen Americans and Chinese to represent people from individualistic and collectivist cultures respectively. The US is usually the standard or default choice to represent individualistic culture in previous studies. However, there are differences between countries with individualistic cultures (e.g. the US and Germany). Americans are highly mobile geographically, socially, and economically, and by necessity have developed strategies for interacting with strangers. On the contrary, Germans are regarded as not used to meeting and interacting with strangers. The sense of privacy of Germans is much stronger than that of Americans, and Germans respect each other's privacy to a degree far beyond anything known in the US (Hall and Hall, 1990). Clackworthy

(1996) also indicates that Germans tend to be more direct and confrontational than Americans. Thus, in this study, we include German culture to control for the differences within individualistic culture.

Hypothesis 1: The privacy settings of Americans, Germans, and Chinese are different.

Gender differences in self-disclosure

Gender differences are significant in self-disclosure: females are reported to disclose more than males in offline settings (Hacker, 1981). Gender role is associated with self-disclosure in relationships (Marshall, 2008). Male–female differences in self-disclosure are found as a function of gender stereotyping of topic content (Derlega et al., 1981). Men disclose less than women (Derlega et al., 1981; Dindia and Allen, 1992; Parker and Parrott, 1995), because men's traditional roles do not encourage them to reveal feelings or to engage in self-disclosure (Thompson and Pleck, 1986). However, self-disclosure varies with the relationship targets. When the target has a relationship with the discloser (e.g. as a friend, parent, or spouse), women disclose more than men; when the target is a stranger, men have been reported to disclose to a similar degree as women (Dindia and Allen, 1992).

Gender differences also exist in the online environment (Dominick, 1999). Gender is a significant predictor of privacy settings of SNS users. Women are more likely to have private profiles than men (Lewis et al., 2008). In general, according to Dominick's (1999) findings, women include more intimate information than men in SNSs. What is interesting here is that men and women are likely to disclose different types of personal information online. Men are more likely to disclose their phone numbers; women are more likely to display their favourite music and books, as well as their religion (Tufekci, 2008). Women tended to provide a record of the day, to discuss a memory, and to communicate feelings or thoughts more often than men, whereas men discuss hobbies or interests more often than do women (Trammell et al., 2006).

Not all studies find gender differences in online self-disclosure. Certain studies argue that the relationship between gender and self-disclosure in the online environment is different from that in the off-line environment. Gender is not a significant variable for explaining self-disclosure in online chatting (Cho, 2007). Huffaker and Calvert (2005) also argue that there are more gender similarities than differences in self-disclosure, and that no significant differences are found in the frequency of using expressive emotions between males and females. These inconsistent results in studies of SNSs explain the necessity of comparing self-disclosure between genders.

Hypothesis 2: Women in SNSs have different privacy settings from men.

Interaction of gender and cultural contexts

Furthermore, gender differences may not be identical across different cultural contexts and cultural differences may not be identical across different genders. In different cultural contexts, gender is associated with different social roles. Thus gender-role ideology varies across different cultures and societies. Within Chinese culture, a more traditional gender-role ideology is endorsed than within Western cultures (Loscocco and Bose, 1998). The Chinese traditional gender-role ideology may be deeply rooted in Confucian social norms, which imbue women with 'self-silence' concerning certain wishes, emotions, or grievances, in order to maintain harmony within close relationships (Jack, 1991).

This interpretation has been examined by international studies of romantic relationships. Disclosure of intimate information has been used to interpret gender differences in two individualistic societies (Canada and the US) and three collectivist societies (China, India, and Japan) (Dion and Dion, 1993). North American women have higher self-disclosure than North American men, while such gender difference is not significant in Japan. However, Seamon (2003) finds that gender has a major effect on self-disclosure and that females are more likely to disclose than males.

Little research has been devoted to the interaction between gender and cultural influence on online self-disclosure, especially in the context of SNSs. We speculate that gender differences may affect cross-cultural differences in online self-disclosure.

Hypothesis 3: Gender difference in self-disclosure is not identical across individualistic and collectivist cultural contexts.

Methods

Data

Three popular SNS platforms were selected: from the US (Facebook), China (Kaixin001), and Germany (StudiVZ). The US and Germany are considered individualistic cultures, while China is regarded as a collectivist culture. Facebook is the biggest social network site, both in the US and worldwide. In 2010, the number of users of Facebook rose to 500 million (Zuckerberg, 2010). StudiVZ is one of the most successful online media in Germany, and by 2010 had 2.9 million users (Compass Heading, 2010). In the same year, the Chinese social network website Kaixin001 had 86 million users (Xin, 2010). Due to the similarity of their web structures, these three websites are more easily comparable than are other online social networks in the US, Germany, and China.

Generally, we searched certain user names in each SNS platform and included them as qualified for our study. To make sure that the sampled SNS users from different websites were comparable, we drew probability samples from these three websites using the following procedures. First, five provinces/states were randomly sampled in each country. The results of search queries could be affected by the IP addresses of the computer involved in the searches. The websites recommend users with IP addresses in particular neighbourhoods by listing them at the top of the results list. In order to avoid the influence of IP address (of the computer doing the searching), we randomly selected five provinces/states as filters. Second, we chose the ten most common surnames for each country as our search queries for qualified users. Third, we searched for the users who live in the five provinces/states under the ten most common surnames in each SNS. The first eight users returned for each surname through each query are included in this study. Therefore, our study includes a sample of 1,200 users (three websites × five provinces/states × ten surnames × eight returned top-listed users of SNSs). There are 13 and seven duplicated cases in Facebook and StudiVZ, respectively. Therefore, there were 1,180 valid cases (i.e. Facebook 387, Kaixin001 400, StudiVZ 393) in this study.

Measures of self-disclosure

The variable which is most relevant to self-disclosure in SNSs is that of the viewing-status of the user profile. SNS users can set the viewing-status of their profiles. If this is set as public, a profile can be viewed by anybody, without restriction. If it is set as limited or private, a profile can be viewed only by friends and the person who established the profile. SNS users can disclose their personal information under many topics, such as education, employment, residence, and favourite books. Due to the different settings of the websites, only those items which are available on all three social network sites were selected for further comparisons. The demographic information, profile photos, and information about groups, activities, interests, as well as entertainment (e.g. favourite book/music/film/TV), are measured as 'yes' or 'no' according to the absence or presence of the relevant information. After a four-hour training session, two undergraduate students were made responsible for the coding. The mother language of the two coders was Chinese, but both of them speak fluent English, and one of them also speaks fluent German. The intercoder reliability (namely Cohen's Kappa) for each variable ranges from 0.861 to 1.000 (see Table 6.1).

Table 6.1   Intercoder Reliability of Variables

Variables	Intercoder reliability (kappa)
Website	1.000
Privacy	1.000
Picture	0.941
Gender	0.895
Hometown	0.928
Residence	0.947
High school	0.980
University	1.000
Employer	0.993
Class year	0.912
Friend	0.949
Activity	0.890
Interest	0.979
Music	0.928
TV	0.946
Movie	0.970
Book	0.861
Photo	0.969
Activity	0.890
Interest	0.979

Results

Of the sampled SNS users, 77.4% set the viewing-status of their profiles as limited or private, while 22.6% of users set it as public. That is to say, a large proportion of SNS users were not willing to share their personal information with the public. They were willing to share it only under certain conditions (namely, with their permission). The gender distribution of the sampled profiles is as follows: missing 237 (20.1%), male 542 (45.9%), and female 401 (34.0%).

Culture and self-disclosure in SNSs

There is a significant difference in the privacy settings of profiles among users in the three countries, χ^2 (2, N = 1,180) = 92.02, p = 0.000. The percentages of users who set the viewing-status of their profiles as public were 34.1%, 27.5%, and 6.8% for Facebook, StudiVZ, and Kaixin001 users respectively. The result indicates that self-disclosure differs among cultural contexts (see Table 6.2).

Americans and Germans, who belong to individualistic cultures, disclose more than Chinese, who come from a collectivist culture. We further tested the differences between American and German SNS users. Within this individualistic cultural context, the percentage of German SNS users who set their profiles to be public is significantly less than that of American users, χ^2 (1, N = 780) = 4.02, p = 0.045. Therefore, Hypothesis 1 is fully supported.

As depicted in Table 6.3, the difference of profile-picture among the three countries is salient: χ^2 (6, N = 1,180) = 340.33, p = 0.000. In general, most members (60.4%) in all countries prefer to present their

Table 6.2 Privacy Settings of Users of Different SNSs

	Facebook	Kaixin001	StudiVZ	Total
Public-viewing profile	34.10%	6.80%	27.50%	22.60%
Private- or limited-viewing profile	65.90%	93.30%	72.50%	77.40%
Total	100.00%	100.00%	100.00%	100.00%
	N=387	N=400	N=393	N=1,180

χ^2 (2, N=1,180) = 92.02, p = 0.000.

Table 6.3 Picture Types on Profiles of Users of Different SNSs

	Facebook	Kaixin001	StudiVZ	Total
Blank	2.10%	1.50%	3.80%	2.50%
Avatar	11.60%	48.30%	10.70%	23.80%
With others	31.80%	1.50%	7.40%	13.40%
Self	54.50%	48.80%	78.10%	60.40%
Total	100.00%	100.00%	100.00%	100.00%
	N=387	N=400	N=393	N=1,180

χ^2 (6, N=1,180) = 340.33, p = 0.000.

own portraits, 23.8% and 13.4% of users present Avatars and pictures with others, and 2.5% of users leave their profile-picture blank. We further tested the differences between the two individualistic cultures – the US and Germany. The difference of self-disclosure was statistically significant: χ^2 (3, N = 780) = 78.11, p = 0.000.

We zoomed in on the differences between the three countries. Germans are the most willing to post their own portraits – 78.1% of StudiVZ users present themselves in this way. Many users of Facebook (31.8%) prefer to present themselves in pictures with others, while only 7.4% of users of StudiVZ and 1.5% of users of Kaixin001 did so. More Chinese prefer to use Avatars (48.3%) than do Americans (11.6%) or Germans (10.7%).

We further found that users in these three countries disclosed themselves in different ways. Most users of Kaixin001 (94.5%) prefer to disclose the information of 'Home and Residence'; figures for users of Facebook (72.6%) and StudiVZ (47.8%) are lower. The percentage of Chinese SNS users who post photos online is higher (74.3%) than that of Americans (62.8%) and Germans (18.8%). German users are more likely to share information concerning 'Education and Employment' – 86% of the StudiVZ users make such information public. The Americans are more likely to share their hobbies: 76.3% and 66.7% of Facebook users publish their interests and activities, and entertainment (namely favourite movie, TV programme, book, and music) information, respectively.

Gender and self-disclosure in SNSs

As shown in Table 6.4, generally speaking, women are more conservative than men when setting the viewing-status of their SNS profiles: 78.3% of

Table 6.4   Privacy Settings of SNS Users of Different Genders

	Male	Female	Total
Public-viewing profile	31.40%	21.70%	27.30%
Private- or limited-viewing profile	68.67%	78.37%	72.70%
Total	100.00%	100.00%	100.00%
	N=542	N=401	N=943

$\chi^2 (2, N = 943)$, $p = 0.001$.

women users have private- or limited-viewing profiles, while 68.6% of men users had the same. The gender difference in setting public-viewing profiles is significant: $\chi^2 (2, N = 943)$, $p = 0.001$. Therefore, Hypothesis 2 is supported.

We further found that females are more likely to disclose information concerning home and residence, whereas males are more likely to disclose information concerning education, employment, interests, activities, and entertainment. Male users put more photos on personal profiles than did female users, but the results show no significant difference of types of profile-picture between genders.

The interplay of gender and cultural effects on self-disclosure in SNSs

Now we turn our spotlight onto the interplay between gender and cultural effects with regard to self-disclosure. Although we confirmed that (1) people from individualistic cultures are more willing to share their profiles with the public than are people from collectivist cultures, and that (2) men are more willing, in general, to do so than women, we were still not sure about whether or not men from both individualistic and collectivist cultures are more willing to do so than women. Therefore, we conducted a two-way ANOVA analysis to test the interaction between gender and cultural effects for self-disclosure. As we can tell from Table 6.5, the main effect of gender on self-disclosure is significant – $F (5,937) = 6.9$, $p = 0.009$ – as is that of culture – $F (5,937) = 68.8$, $p = 0.000$. The results of the ANOVA analysis also indicate that gender differences in self-disclosure are not identical across different cultural settings. There is a significant interaction between the effects of gender and of cultural context on self-disclosure: $F (5,937) = 4.75$, $p = 0.009$.

Table 6.5   Two-Way Analysis of Variables for Self-Disclosure in Different Cultural Contexts

Source	Sum of squares	Df	Mean square	F	Sig
Corrected model	27.66	5	5.53	32.53	0.000
Intercept	72.29	1	72.29	425.20	0.000
Gender	1.17	1	1.17	6.88	0.009
Website	23.41	2	11.71	68.85	0.000
Gender × website	1.62	2	0.81	4.75	0.009
Error	159.30	937	0.17		
Total	257.00	943			
Corrected total	186.96	942			

Figure 6.1 demonstrates the above-mentioned interaction effects. In the individualistic cultural contexts (i.e. Facebook and StudiVZ), there are more male users who have public-viewing profiles than there are female users, while there are more female users in the collectivist cultural context (i.e. Kaixin001). The results of the ANOVA test confirm that the gender differences in online self-disclosure vary across different cultural contexts.

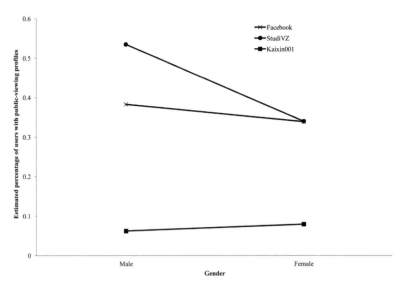

Figure 6.1   Estimated percentages of users with public-viewing profiles on Facebook, StudiVZ, and Kaixin001.

Table 6.6   Two-Way Analysis of Variables for Self-Disclosure within Individualistic Cultural Contexts

Source	Sum of squares	Df	Mean square	F	Sig
Corrected model	3.19	3	1.06	4.50	0.004
Intercept	82.58	1	82.58	349.43	0.000
Gender	1.84	1	1.84	7.80	0.005
Website	0.75	1	0.75	3.18	0.075
Gender × website	0.74	1	0.74	3.15	0.077
Error	135.17	572	0.24		
Total	231.00	576			
Corrected total	138.36	575			

As we discussed earlier, one of the possible flaws of certain previous studies is that they failed to control for the intra-cultural differences (i.e. individualistic versus collectivist) when they were investigating cultural differences in self-disclosure. We further examined the main effects of gender and country on self-disclosure within individualistic cultural contexts. Two-way ANOVA analysis was applied in order to test this. As we can learn from Table 6.6, gender differences in self-disclosure are significant and identical across two countries – the US and Germany: $F(3,572) = 7.80$, $p = 0.005$. The country differences in self-disclosure within the individualistic cultural contexts are not statistically significant: $F(3,572) = 3.18$, $p > 0.05$. Therefore, we can further conclude that the cultural differences (namely, individualistic versus collectivist) in self-disclosure found in this study are not merely a reflection of country differences. Therefore, Hypothesis 3 is supported.

Discussion

The topic of gender and cultural differences in self-disclosure is not new. Nevertheless, few studies have been conducted in the context of SNSs using a probability sample with a comparative perspective. Our study is based on three independent probability samples of SNS users in three different countries.

We found that the users from individualistic cultures are more willing to disclose themselves to the public in SNSs than are users from collectivist cultures. We further found that American users are more willing to disclose than are German ones. This cannot be attributed simply to certain cultural differences. However, future cross-country comparisons should not overlook the inconsistency within certain cultural polarities (e.g. individualistic versus collectivist). More perspectives and variables should be brought in to investigate and explain such differences.

We also found that men are more willing to disclose themselves in SNSs than are women. This contradicts what has been found in offline settings (e.g. Dindia and Allen, 1992), but echoes certain previous studies conducted in online settings (such as Lewis et al., 2008). It seems that people behave differently online and offline. The online environment is complicated. In cyberspace, females show more concern about the privacy of their profiles than do males, thus challenging gender-role ideology. One of the limitations of this study is that we failed to bring in the users' perceived risks of self-disclosure. Men and women may have different perceptions about risks of online self-disclosure, which should be correlated with their self-disclosure behaviours.

We further found that the gender differences in online self-disclosure vary across different cultural contexts. Within individualistic cultures, men are more willing to disclose themselves; within collectivist cultures, women are more willing to do so. This is interesting and very likely to have been overlooked in previous studies. Men and women have been assigned different social roles in different cultural contexts. Their behaviours are guided by such social roles. Although Americans have a higher level of online self-disclosure than Germans, men are more willing than women to disclose in both countries. The gender differences in self-disclosure do not significantly vary between users in these two countries with individualistic cultures.

We also found that Avatar is the second favourite photo type (the photo of oneself is the favourite) for SNS users to present themselves. Moreover, the preference for Avatar differs among the three countries. Compared with Americans and Germans, Chinese are more likely to use Avatars as their profile-pictures.

This study has several limitations. Due to the difference of the website structures, the comparable personal information is limited. For example, there is no 'interested in women/men' in Kaixin001 and StudiVZ. Another limitation is that the structure of the website can affect the result. Although we tried to find three comparable websites which have a similar structure and users, most users of StudiVZ in Germany are college students and only a minority of them are in careers, which may result in the fact that the Germans in StudiVZ prefer to disclose more about their education and employment. Because on Kaixin001 so many data are missing (which means that the limited and private-viewing profiles cannot be measured), the coders could not access such profiles and carry out further analysis. Such limitations also result in the lack of analysis of the 'interest and activities' and 'entertainment (Favourite movie, TV programme, book and music)' on Kaixin001 (0% and 0%).

Despite these limitations, our results have important implications for the study of self-disclosure in SNSs and for our understanding of privacy in the context of gender and cultural differences generally. The comparison is not only between individualistic and collectivist cultures, but also includes a comparison between individualistic countries (namely, the US and Germany). The differences between Germans and Americans are statistically significant. This could be interpreted as cultural difference, and not merely that of individualism versus collectivism. There are cultural differences between individualistic cultures. Such differences can be attributed to factors other than that of individualism versus collectivism. Further studies could usefully explore the nature of these factors.

Note

1   The authors would like to thank Prof. Dr Klaus Beck and the editors for their comments and suggestions.

References

Adams, G., Anderson, S. L., and Adonu, J. K. (2004) 'The Cultural Grounding of Closeness and Intimacy', in D. J. Mashek and A. P. Aron (eds), *The Handbook of Closeness and Intimacy* (Mahwah, NJ: Lawrence Erlbaum Associates), 321–39.

Altman, I. (1977) 'Privacy Regulation: Culturally Universal or Culturally Specific', *Journal of Social Issues*, 33(3): 67–83.

Barak, A., and Gluck-Ofri, O. (2007) 'Degree and Reciprocity of Self-Disclosure in Online Forums', *Cyberpsychology and Behavior*, 10(3): 407–17.

Chen, Guo-Ming (1995) 'Differences in Self-Disclosure Patterns among Americans versus Chinese: A Comparative Study', *Journal of Cross-Cultural Psychology*, 26(1): 84–91.

Cho, Seong Eun (2010) *Cross-Cultural Comparison of Korean and American Social Network Sites: Exploring Cultural Differences in Social Relationships and Self-Presentation* (New Brunswick, NJ: Rutgers University).

Cho, Seung Ho (2007) 'Effects of Motivations and Gender on Adolescents' Self-Disclosure in Online Chatting', *Cyberpsychology and Behavior*, 10(3): 339–45.

Clackworthy, D. (1996) 'Training Germans and Americans in Conflict Management', in M. Berger (ed.), *Cross-Cultural Team Building: Guidelines for More Effective Communication and Negotiation* (London: McGraw-Hill), 91–100.

Compass Heading (2010) http://www.compass-heading.de/cms/2010-hat-nur-einen-gewinner-facebook/#more-1255 (accessed Sept. 2011).

Cozby, P. C. (1973) 'Self-Disclosure: A Literature Review', *Psychological Bulletin*, 79(2): 73–91.

Derlega, Valeria J., and Grzelak, A. L. (1979) 'Appropriate Self-Disclosure', in G. J. Chelune (ed.), *Self-Disclosure: Origins, Patterns, and Implications of Openness in Interpersonal Relationships* (San Francisco, CA: Jossey-Bass), 151–76.

Derlega, V. J., Durham, B., Goekel, B., and Sholis, D. (1981) 'Sex Differences in Self-Disclosure: Effects of Topic Content, Friendship, and Partner's Sex', *Sex Roles*, 7(4): 433–47.

Dindia, K., and Allen, M. (1992) 'Sex Differences in Self-Disclosure: A Meta-Analysis', *Psychological Bulletin*, 112(1): 106–24.

Dion, K. K., and Dion, K. L. (1993) 'Individualistic and Collectivistic Perspectives on Gender and the Cultural Context of Love and Intimacy', *Journal of Social Issues*, 49(3): 53–69.

Dominick, J. R. (1999) 'Who do you Think you Are? Personal Home Pages and Self-Representation on the World Wide Web', *Journalism and Mass Communication Quarterly*, 76(4): 646–58.

Figueroa, A. (2010) 'Privacy Issues Hit Facebook Again: Privacy Issues are Again at the Center of Debate over Whether Facebook is Doing Enough to Protect its Users': http://www.csmonitor.com/Business/new-economy/2010/0730/Privacy-issues-hit-Facebook-again (accessed Sept. 2011).

Gudykunst, W. B., Matsumoto, Y., Ting-Toomy, S., Nishida, T., Kim, K., and Heyman, S. (1996) 'The Influence of Cultural Individualism-Collectivism, Self Construals, and Individual Values on Communication Styles across Cultures', *Human Communication Research*, 22(4): 510–43.

Hacker, H. M. (1981) 'Blabbermouths and Clams: Sex Differences in Self-Disclosure in Same-Sex and Cross-Sex Friendship Dyads', *Psychology of Women Quarterly*, 5(3): 385–401.

Hall, E. T., and Hall, M. R. (1990) *Understanding Cultural Differences: Germans, French, and Americans* (Yarmouth, ME: Intercultural Press).

Hofstede, G. H. (1980) *Culture's Consequences: International Differences in Work-Related Values* (London: Sage).

Huffaker, D. A., and Calvert, S. L. (2005) 'Gender, Identity, and Language Use in Teenage Blogs', *Journal of Computer-Mediated Communication*, 10(2): http://onlinelibrary.wiley.com/doi/10.1111/j.1083-6101.2005.tb00238.x/full (accessed Sept. 2011).

Jack, D. C. (1991) *Silencing the Self: Women and Depression* (Cambridge, MA: Harvard University Press).

Joinson, A. N. (2001) 'Self-Disclosure in Computer-Mediated Communication: The Role of Self Awareness and Visual Anonymity', *European Journal of Social Psychology*, 31(2): 177–92.

Kim, H., and Papacharissi, Z. (2003) 'Cross-Cultural Differences in On-Line Self-Presentation: A Content Analysis of Personal Korean and US Homepages', *Asian Journal of Communication*, 13(1): 100–19.

Kim, J., and Dindia, K. (2008) 'Gender, Culture, and Self-Disclosure in Cyberspace: A Study of Korean and American Social Network Websites', paper presented at the annual conference of the International Communication Association, Communication and Technology Division, Montreal: https://perswww.kuleuven.be/~u0041092/Facebook%20resources/Kim%20and%20Dindia_gender%20culture%20and%20selfdisclosure%20in%20cyberspace_a%20study%20of%20korean%20and%20american%20SNS.pdf (accessed Sept. 2011).

Lewis, K., Kaufman, J., and Christakis, N. (2008) 'The Taste for Privacy: An Analysis of College Student Privacy Settings in an Online Social Network', *Journal of Computer-Mediated Communication*, 14(1): 79–100.

Loscocco, K. A., and Bose, C. E. (1998) 'Gender and Job Satisfaction in Urban China: The Early Post-Mao Period', *Social Science Quarterly*, 79(1): 91–109.

Marshall, T. C. (2008) 'Cultural differences in Intimacy: The Influence of Gender-Role Ideology and Individualism-Collectivism', *Journal of Social and Personal Relationships*, 25(1): 143–68.

Morahan-Martin, J., and Schumacher, P. (2003) 'Loneliness and Social Uses of the Internet', *Computers in Human Behavior*, 19(6): 659–71.

Parker, R., and Parrott, R. (1995) 'Patterns of Self-Disclosure across Social Support Networks: Elderly, Middle-Aged, and Young Adults', *International Journal of Aging und Human Development*, 41(4): 281–97.

Schug, J., Yuki, M., and Maddux, W. (2010) 'Relational Mobility Explains between- and within-Culture Differences in Self-Disclosure to Close Friends', *Psychological Science*, 21(10): 1471–8.

Seamon, C. M. (2003) 'Self-Esteem, Sex Differences, and Self-Disclosure: A Study of the Closeness of Relationships', *Osprey Journal of Ideas and Inquiry*, 3: 153–67: http://digitalcommons.unf.edu/ojii_volumes/99 (accessed June 2011).

Thompson, E. H., and Pleck, J. H. (1986) 'The Structure of Male Role Norms', *American Behavioral Scientist*, 29(5): 531–43.

Tidwell, L. C., and Walther, J. B. (2002) 'Computer-Mediated Communication Effects on Disclosure, Impressions, and Interpersonal Evaluations: Getting to Know one Another a Bit at a Time', *Human Communication Research*, 28(3): 317–48.

Trammell, K. D., Tarkowski, A., Hofmokl, J., and Sapp, A. M. (2006) 'Rzeczpospolita blogów [Republic of Blog]: Examining Polish Bloggers through Content Analysis', *Journal of Computer-Mediated Communication*, 11(3): 702–22.

Tufekci, Z. (2008) 'Can you See me Now? Audience and Disclosure Regulation in Online Social Network Sites', *Bulletin of Science, Technology and Society*, 28(1): 20–36.

Xin, Yuanwei (2010) 'Kaixin001's Happy Growth with Network Trouble': http://www.21cbh.com/HTML/2010-8-16/0NMDAwMDE5MjA0Ng.html (accessed Sept. 2011).

Zuckerberg, Mark (2010) '500 Million Stories': http://blog.facebook.com/blog.php?post=409753352130 (accessed June 2011).

7

Crime News and Privacy: Comparing Crime Reporting in Sweden, the Netherlands, and the United Kingdom

Romayne Smith Fullerton and Maggie Jones Patterson

> *Social attitudes [in England] are horrible and fuelled all the time by this rampant press that this 'Other' is being convicted. ... In Holland and Scandinavia, committing an offence is seen as a temporary blip that all of us might be prone to, but in our country, it's seen as something completely unforgivable and the person is not redeemable and the most severe possible punishment must be brought against this person. (Yvonne Jewkes, Professor of Criminology, University of Leicester[1])*

> *I'm not involved in justice. I'm not a cop. I'm not a judge. I'm not a barrister. If I thought about the impact of what I do – and I do have thoughts and a soul – but look, I report. And I check it for accuracy. If I put my moral code into every story I did how could I possibly write about a story of a car crash where a child is killed? How could I do that? (Michael O'Toole, crime reporter for the Irish Daily Star)*

> *I say give the facts and let the people decide. But here in Holland we were part of these pillars and the propaganda and our aim in Holland was to raise the people up. We are also trying to emancipate journalism from these pillars. Hard to stray too far away from the society. The question of decency is a commercial question and one I take into account. (Arendo Joustra, Dutch editor of the weekly Elsevier)*

Joanna Yeates had been missing for six days when a man stumbled upon her body near a quarry in Bristol on Christmas Day, 2010. While the crime was horrific, it presented British tabloids with a perfect storm: a pretty, blonde landscape architect from a 'good' family, killed during a slack news time. All the story needed was a villain. Within a few days, Yeates's landlord, retired boarding school teacher Christopher Jefferies, unwittingly stepped into the role. These types of crimes, which run in a bizarre parallel to royal weddings or Olympic medals, unite a nation across seemingly irreconcilable differences: income, ethnic background, education, and class. As Yvonne Jewkes has put it:

> *In our increasingly individualized culture where offending is regarded as the inflicting of harms by some individuals onto other individuals, mediated articulations of crime and punishment can still be seen as vehicles for connecting people. (2011: 267)*

Albeit in this particular instance, connecting people in a most disconcerting and unethical manner. On 31 December, police arrested – that is, detained for questioning under British law – but did not charge Jefferies, and the tabloids spiralled into what the Attorney General for England and Wales, Dominic Grieve, later dubbed a 'feeding frenzy'.

The popular press had crossed both legal and moral lines. In summer 2011, English courts imposed libel damages and costs on eight tabloids and, additionally, found two of them in contempt of court. All were required to apologise to Jefferies, although at the time of writing he has received no written apology from any of the editors of the newspapers involved.[2] But while this case is extreme, news consumers in Great Britain are accustomed to this 'tell-all-and-then-some' style of crime coverage. In this instance, it 'convicted' an innocent man of 'offences' ranging from being odd and eccentric to being a peeping tom and possibly a paedophile, in addition to assuming he was a murderer. For example, the *Sun*, 31 December 2010, in an article headed 'The Strange Mr Jefferies', called him 'weird', 'posh', 'lewd', and 'creepy'. And so on, and on.

In England and other developed, predominantly English-speaking countries, news media routinely probe an accused person's private life in search of villainous elements, to explain alleged wickedness – but also to entertain. This story-telling style appeals to what Anderson (1983) called the consensual values of an imagined community and sets up an 'us' versus 'the accused' mentality. So when Vincent Tabak, a Dutch national living in Bristol, confessed to Yeates's murder three weeks after Jefferies was arrested, the tabloids mined Tabak's Facebook page for photos with his girlfriend and speculated about her involvement. There was none.

Broadsheets and broadcasters in Great Britain adopt different tones from those of the tabloids, but in Jewkes's view, the effect of their reporting is similar, with the tabloids simply doing the dirty work for the rest. While the primary mission of the tabloids is to entertain and the quality press is to inform, the quality press, so-called, will report what the tabloids report one step removed, and they will say: 'Isn't it terrible how this has been reported?' But then report pages and pages of it. On 13 July 2011, the Prime Minister, David Cameron, announced an inquiry into the role of the press and the police in the *News of the World* phone-hacking scandal, and Sir Brian Henry Leveson, Lord Justice of Appeal of England and Wales, was put in charge of it. The formal hearings began on 14 November 2011. Until the Leveson Inquiry into the culture, practices, and ethics of the British press, journalists in England have mostly clucked their tongues and shrugged their shoulders about the seemingly inevitable aggressive behaviour of sections of the press. They have shown little or no awareness that colleagues in other European countries follow very different codes of practice, other than to sneer at the French press for not exposing the private lives of its politicians. The Dutch media, for example, picked up the Yeates murder story once the Dutch national Tabak's confession became public, but many outlets did so without identifying him. In contrast to their British counterparts, Dutch journalists routinely shield the privacy of persons accused and even convicted of crimes, as do their colleagues in much of Northern and Central Europe. Indeed, in April 2009, when Karst Tates made news worldwide after trying to kill Queen Beatrix by crashing his car into the royal family, killing himself and seven bystanders in the process, an event carried live on national television, the Dutch national news agency ANP and most other 'quality' Dutch media withheld his name and identifying details. Even when ANP obtained exclusive interviews with Tates's family at the funeral, its editors agreed to the parents' request to withhold their names. Doubtless the English press would regard them simply as wimps. But the Dutch are not alone in their default position of not naming. In Sweden in 2004, Foreign Minister Anna Lindh was stabbed while shopping in Stockholm; she died in hospital the next day. While the Swedish press routinely protect the identity of criminal defendants, in this particular instance journalists decided that public interest in the case was sufficient to warrant overcoming their usual practice, and most news outlets chose to identify the suspect, Mijailo Mijailovic, who later confessed and was convicted, born in Sweden to Serbian parents. It was a decision that still generates discussion amongst Swedish journalists and academics several years after the fact.

The study

These crimes exemplify what Martin Innes has called 'signal crimes', stories about 'the seeming encroachment of the forces of disorder, drawing upon diffuse and inchoate existential anxieties about the state of contemporary society' (2003: 52). Each is accompanied by what Innes claims is the 'widespread popular concern' that something is wrong with society, and that this 'requires some form of corrective response' (ibid. 51). Such fears are not uncommon in modern societies, and are liable to become more intense as technological change, globalised competition, and immigration remake the world in often disturbing ways. News media play a central role in shaping public attitudes towards these changes and anxieties. Their reporting of crime and deviance is capable of both fanning and quelling public fears. Crime coverage, and especially coverage of violent crime, speaks in particular to readers' fears for their own safety and that of their community, as well as reinforcing socially constructed definitions of what is acceptable and unacceptable behaviour.

However, despite the social significance of these stories, research shows that most reporters select their story frames and details based on long-standing habits, rather than on considerations of social consequence or underlying ethical principles. (See in particular Ericson et al., 1987: 95–138.) On both sides of the Atlantic, distinctive crime-reporting practices have a taken-for-granted quality, in part because journalistic rituals are deeply embedded in the culture in which they exist. As Tuchman put it, news stories 'take social and cultural resources and transform them into public property' (1978: 5).

Inevitably, then, these stories take measure of a society's cultural values and are an index of how they are changing. This chapter is part of a larger project that is attempting to measure those cultural and value shifts because crime stories play an important role in shaping culture, ideas of citizenship, and empowerment. As Katz noted:

> As members of society continuously confront issues of personal and collective competence, they develop an appetite for crime news. Worrying

about miscalculating their own and others' personal abilities, people find interesting the questioning of personal moral competence that is often intensely dramatized in crime stories. Repeatedly assessing whether, how, and how effectively certain people, organizations and places represent collective identity, members of society consume tales about the vulnerable integrity of personages, institutions, and sites. (1987: 69)

Details in crime stories help readers to monitor new wrinkles in their world, a process which Katz called 'a daily moral workout' (ibid. 50).

Swedish and Dutch journalists seek to protect the identity of accused criminals, their innocent family members, and convicted criminals' ability to rehabilitate. On the other hand, news organisations in the UK and North America value informing the public more highly than protecting the accused. Such differences, however, are endangered as the internet carries news across borders, globalisation means more non-indigenous media owners, competition for scarce revenues becomes ever fiercer, and movement of people across borders creates divisions within nations that once conceived of themselves as homogeneous. These forces are pushing countries that have cared about and valued privacy and the presumed innocence of criminal suspects to yield to the practices of English-speaking journalistic cultures.

The goal of our ongoing study is to understand and analyse ritualised journalistic practices within various democracies of Western Europe and North America through a four-fold approach: (1) a close reading and semiotic analysis of the reporting of 'signal crimes' by news organisations in these countries; (2) in-depth interviews, codified using a grounded theory approach, with journalists and scholars about press practices and cultural values; (3) an analysis of prevailing ethics codes and accountability practices of national professional organisations, press councils, and journalists' unions; (4) an exploration via the interviews and already-existing literature of the pressures that appear to be minimising national story-telling differences and leading to a default tell-all style. We completed data collection in the Netherlands and Sweden in 2010, and conducted a study of England and Ireland in 2011 and 2012. In this chapter, we compare practices in England with those in Sweden and the Netherlands.

Our sample countries so far allow us to begin a comparison of practices in two of the three media systems which Hallin and Mancini (2004) identified in Western Europe and North America. These loosely configured media models are distinguished by their historic relationships with government, political parties, and major institutions, such as churches:

1. the North Atlantic liberal model (Britain, the US, Canada, Ireland), where the press has largely been politically independent and privately owned;
2. the North/Central European corporatist model (Scandinavia, Germany, Austria, Switzerland, the Netherlands, and Belgium), where news organisations were historically affiliated with churches and social/political interest groups;
3. the Mediterranean or polarised pluralist model found in France, Greece, Italy, Portugal, and Spain, in which media are associated with political parties and the state has influence.

Hallin and Mancini's work does not touch upon journalistic practices. We borrow their comparative model in anticipating that these practices follow the media structures they identify, but we do so without assuming what those patterns will reveal. The value of such an approach, Hallin and Mancini argue, is that 'comparative analysis makes it possible to notice things we did not notice and therefore had not conceptualized, and it forces us to clarify the scope and applicability of the concepts we do employ' (ibid. 3).

The ethics of care and responsibility in journalistic practice

Protecting the identity of a person accused of a crime – especially a crime that makes news of national significance – is virtually unheard of in the US, Great Britain, and Canada. In these locales, an obligation to provide information and sometimes entertainment about criminals and their deviance is paramount. In our interviews, journalists said that they felt obliged to serve as the public's eyes and ears on the criminal justice system in order to ensure that justice was not only done but seen to be done. In these countries, journalists follow a moral theory of justice which leads to an epistemological blindness to the concrete other (Benhabib, 1987: 91). In the classical image, Justice weighs her scales while blindfolded. If these journalists expressed a sense of community or an ethic of care, it was in their sympathy for the victim of a crime rather than for the alleged perpetrator, whom they defined entirely in terms of the crime committed.

Journalists in Sweden and the Netherlands speak of crime coverage in terms that more closely resemble 'communitarianism' (see, for example, Christians et al., 1993; Craig, 1996) or a feminist ethic of care and responsibility (as outlined by feminist scholars like Gilligan, 1982; Noddings, 1984). By describing this ethic as 'feminist', we are not claiming that journalism practices are directly influenced by feminism. Rather, we are suggesting that studies carried out largely by and about Western women over the past 30 years have identified an epistemology that locates a person's primary moral obligations in his or her relationships, and in the care and responsibility owed in those relationships. Carol Gilligan found this form of moral reasoning more frequently in US women than men, and in the private rather than public sphere. She labelled it 'the ethics of care', and it became known as 'feminist ethics', but it shares characteristics with communitarianism in its political applications and with the Christian tradition of agape.

The ability of journalists to incorporate care and responsibility considerations into their practices can be witnessed in attitudes to crime coverage articulated by those working in the Dutch and Swedish media. Daphne Koene, secretary for the Netherlands Press Council, spoke for most other journalists we interviewed there:

> We have the idea to protect every person and every person has the right to protection of privacy including criminals and criminal suspects, and this should be kept in balance. ... As a journalist, you weigh if it's more necessary for publication to mention a name or if the protection of privacy of people is higher in weight. ... For criminals, a suspect should not be convicted in the media before he or she goes to court, and we have this value that the court decides the punishment and [there] shouldn't be extra punishment by publication. When a criminal has done time, he or she has the right to be reintegrated into society, and it shouldn't be harder for him. Also, his family shouldn't be harmed, which is possible to do when publishing the name of an accused or convicted person.

Morgan Olofsson, head of Swedish Public Television, used almost identical language, adding that the Swedish government makes almost all information public – even salaries and licence plate registrations.

Consequently, Olofsson said, journalists shoulder a great ethical responsibility: 'Whoever is strong has to be kind as well'. In every crime story, his network strives for balance, asking: 'How important is the information to the audience compared to how much we affect the family?' Journalists exercise special caution if the suspect has school-age children. These responses echo the ethical guidelines set by the Netherlands Press Council, which outline four separate instances in which journalists must be cautious in identifying persons accused or convicted of serious crimes. These include a directive to weigh public interest against potential harm of publication, and a specific proscription against identifying suspected criminals in section 2.4.5, under the heading 'Privacy':

> *A journalist refrains from publishing details in pictures and text as a result of which suspects and accused can be easily identified and traced by persons other than the circle of people that already know about them. A journalist does not have to observe this rule when the name forms an important part of the report, not mentioning the name because of the general reputation of the person involved does not serve any purpose, not mentioning the name could cause a mix-up with others who might be harmed as a result of this, his name is mentioned within the framework of investigative reporting, or the person himself seeks publicity.*[3]

To name or not to name

In this study, interviews with journalists were open-ended. After a brief introduction, we asked journalists to describe decisions they and their news organisations made about covering signal crimes that we were studying in the case of their country (namely the Yeates murder in England, the Karst Tates drama in the Netherlands, and the assassination of foreign minister Anna Lindh in Sweden). Thus journalists framed their own narratives of what they did and why. Afterwards, as we combed the interview transcripts, we found remarkable consistency within the latter two countries. Dutch and Swedish journalists cited first and most frequently their concern for the privacy and protection of innocent family members as the reason for their practice of withholding names of accused and convicted criminals. Next, in short order, they expressed their belief in the presumed innocence of the accused and the right of the convicted to be folded back into their communities without their reputations being irreparably damaged. While the journalists themselves do not locate their practices and attitudes within the perspective of an ethics of care, it is clear that there is a relation: they see the criminal as a part of, not apart from, the rest of society. They view crime (the occurrence, the judicial process, the verdict, the outcome, and the reports of the foregoing) as relational, a situation in which everyone – accused, convicted, and ordinary citizen – is bound within a web that connects all members of society.

Dutch and Swedish journalists seek to protect the ability of the accused and of convicted criminals to rehabilitate their lives once their debt to society has been paid. This contrasts with attitudes in the English-speaking world. As the Secretary of the Dutch Union of Journalists, Thomas Bruning, put it: 'In America, everyone has the right to make a million dollars. In Holland, everyone has the right to start again.'

England: the press as prosecutor

Such thinking differs radically from British attitudes towards those who unwittingly enter the public sphere, like Christopher Jefferies, who detailed at the Leveson Inquiry, in the *Financial Times,* 8 October 2011, and in a talk in Bristol, his and his family's sufferings as a result of the way in which he was treated by certain newspapers. Despite his successful libel suit against the eight most egregious offenders, he argued that

> the libel actions have by no means addressed all the damage done to my
> personal and professional reputation, which I spent over 30 years building.
> … I doubt the damage done can ever be repaired. Had I not been retired,
> I think the effect on my career would have been catastrophic.

The press harassed his friends and relatives, and in particular an elderly aunt who said the ordeal aged her 'a hundred years'. Of his own treatment, he stated: 'The incalculable effect of what was written about me by these highly influential tabloid newspapers is something from which it would be difficult ever to escape.'[4] And at a talk organised by the National Union of Journalists in Bristol, Jefferies said that he was 'repeatedly amazed by the insensitivity of journalists and the lack of awareness of the damage they cause.'[5]

England, Sweden, and the Netherlands all value a free press and the individual's right to a fair trial. All their regulatory codes mention the importance of accuracy, unfettered pursuit of truth, and the pursuit of stories in the public interest. Yet, in spite of these common features, the way in which British newspapers write about crime differs sharply from the manner adopted by the Dutch and Swedish newspapers. We would argue that the most profound differences in press practices with respect to crime coverage result from ritualised, largely unexamined habits and from voluntary ethics policies – not from laws and formal regulations.

The watchdog function

As Professor Chris Frost, Head of Journalism at Liverpool John Moores University and chair of the Ethics Council for the National Union of Journalists, noted:

> *I think the big key difference in the way we approach things [in England] and perhaps the approach in Holland and Sweden is that we think it's much more important that we're aware who's been arrested, why they've been arrested, and we see that justice is done than whether or not that risks damaging any particular individual in the process. I accept that it's a balancing act, but if you start to say we'll give them this privacy protection, you probably end up giving it partly to some who don't deserve it because there're probably more people guilty of something than the other way around.*

This sentiment, expressed by virtually all British journalists to whom we spoke, is at odds with the perspective articulated by the general secretary of the Dutch Union of Journalists, Thomas Bruning, who stated: 'You should have the presumption of innocence and that should be the basis of media coverage before someone is convicted.' And Tim Overdiek, former deputy editor at NOS, Netherlands public TV and radio, made the point that 'even when people are convicted, they will come out of prison. They deserve their privacy even more because they have done their dues.'

Frost additionally drew certain connections between press practices and wider cultural attitudes towards public authorities:

> *It seems to me that America typifies something that we don't feel as strongly or as clearly about in Britain but we still feel it more than they do in Sweden: that we must hold the authorities to account, that we don't trust the police, we don't trust the government as a matter of course. ... Europeans have a higher system of trust in the authorities.*

Similarly, Benedict Brogan, deputy editor of the *Telegraph*, noted in his witness statement to Lord Justice Leveson:

> *I believe that the proper functioning of our democracy requires the closest possible scrutiny of those who are elected or employed to act in our name. There may at times be reason to extend that scrutiny to their private lives if, for example, what they are doing is illegal or, when their public pronouncements are taken into account, would alter significantly how they are perceived by those they represent.*[6]

Members of the Dutch and Swedish press would draw the public/private line in a different place. In those countries, public officials' wrongdoing is usually exposed only if it directly involves official business.

In the 1960s, press associations negotiated with the Swedish parliament about what should be subject to law and what should be left to ethical considerations. Ethical policies regarding withholding the names of suspected and convicted criminals were strictly observed until Prime Minister Olof Palme was assassinated in 1986, and journalists came to believe that they might be able to publish a name if the person concerned was a public figure involved in a public event, but not in the case of a private person and a private event, according to Lennart Weibull, senior researcher at the SOM Institute and professor in the Department of Journalism, Media and Communication at Gothenburg University (see Figure 7.1). Although social forces could precipitate a further change in this policy, in Weibull's view, the prevailing sentiment among journalists is that criminal events in quadrant one (a private person committing a private crime, such as domestic violence) should not be published, but those in quadrant four (a public person committing a public crime, such as a public official engaged in fraud with public monies) should be named.

1 Private person Private event	3 Public person Private event
2 Private person Public event	4 Public person Public event

Figure 7.1 Factors determining whether an accused person should be named in public.

More difficult questions arise in situations that fit into quadrants two and three. The press is more likely to publish the name of a private person involved in a public event, such as the assassination of a public official, than the name of a public person involved in a private event, such as a public official involved in a domestic dispute.

Playing games with police

Hallin and Mancini (2004) identify the media's function as a watchdog in Great Britain and North America. In our interviews, some members of the British media have gestured towards distrust of government to explain the compromising coverage of Christopher Jefferies. But Brunel University journalism professor and chair of the Campaign for Press and Broadcasting Freedom, Julian Petley, offers a different view. He argues that, had the press been acting as a watchdog, it would have immediately smelled a rat in the police treatment of Jefferies, and painted the police as the real villains of this story:

> In the UK, much of the national press behaves rather more frequently as an attack dog, savaging politicians simply because they are politicians. … The real problem here [in the Jefferies case] is actually the quite remarkably credulous attitude on the part of journalists towards police sources.

Roy Greenslade, journalism professor at City University London and media commentator/blogger for the *Guardian*, said the lack of trust and sharing of information between police and press led to reporters' piecing together bits of an apparently plausible story: 'It's a jigsaw: the police arrested Jefferies on suspicion. They put out a brief saying they're not looking for anyone else. Reporters ask the neighbours, who say "Oh, he had strange hair" and "He resigned under mysterious circumstances". The police, because they are engaged in an ongoing investigation, can withhold puzzle pieces about certain aspects of the investigation, or leak material if they believe they already have a guilty suspect. But even silence can fuel speculation by reporters – some of whom, especially in Jefferies's case, need absolutely no encouragement, as media commentator Brian Cathcart and Jefferies's lawyer, Louis Charalambous, both noted in separate posts on the International Forum for Responsible Media (Inforrm) blog.[7]

Mike Norton, editor for the *Bristol Evening Post*, also pointed out how the silence functioned. He said that reporters, acting as amateur sleuths, would cook up a theory:

> *Someone would speculate on why Jo [Yeates] wasn't wearing any shoes, that perhaps she went to post a letter in the letterbox outside and that's when she was grabbed and taken away. So they'd ring the [police] press office in relation to this theory and all they'd get is 'no comment, nothing to say'. And away [the reporters] went.*

To Petley, this all takes on a much more sinister tone. He calls the relationship between much of the press and the police 'collusive and corrupt':

> *As the events which gave rise to the Leveson Inquiry show, the really significant information sharing which takes place between the police and journalists happens at an informal and invisible level, with journalists paying individual police officers for the information which is passed to them. In the case of criminal investigations, this is a win-win situation. The police are able, publicly but invisibly, to blacken the name of a suspect whom they have decided is guilty and the sensational titbits they feed to the newspapers help the latter to build circulation on the back of the investigation of a high-profile crime.*

Bob Satchwell, executive director of the Society of Editors, moved the discussion to a more abstract realm, and blamed the rumour-chasing game on the opaque British criminal justice system and compared it to the more transparent North American one: 'Because the U.S. is far more open and up-front and accountable, a lot of the speculation goes away. ... Secrecy breeds suspicion and contempt, and openness breeds trust and respect. When police are not talking openly, it's then that rumours start running.'

On a more day-to-day level for members of the public, blurred distinctions between 'arrest' and 'charge' in British law might further confuse the matter. Police can arrest a person for an indictable offence, and they can be held for questioning without charge for up to 72 hours, or longer if a magistrate grants an extension. As Greenslade explains, 'arrest' actually means little but can imply much: 'It legitimizes – even in the minds of the press who should know better – a headline that reads: "On Suspicion of Murder". The person might never be charged, but they have been made to look guilty. While it is possible that members of the public do not understand these distinctions, Petley agrees with Greenslade and argues that such cannot be the case for practising journalists.

> There is absolutely no excuse whatsoever for journalists blurring the distinction between arrest and charge. If they have taken a course validated by the National Council for the Training of Journalists, this distinction will have been drummed into them from the earliest days of their module on media law. It is also perfectly clearly explained in what the newspaper industry repeatedly tells us is the journalists' bible – NcNae's Essential Law for Journalists.

Christopher Jefferies was never charged but was held on bail for almost six weeks, even after Vincent Tabak had confessed to manslaughter and was charged on 22 January with Yeates's murder. As Jefferies himself told the Leveson Inquiry, he was 'essentially under house arrest' until Tabak was charged, and felt that he had to remain in hiding, because he was afraid that some would still think him guilty of murder. It was not until 4 March that the police lifted his bail conditions and formally confirmed that he was no longer a suspect. Indeed, at the Bristol meeting noted earlier, Jefferies stated that he thought that one of the reasons why the police believed that they had captured the right man was because of what they were reading about him in the press.

Cut-throat competition

But neither press credulity towards the police nor their watchdog role can entirely explain behaviour the courts found illegal and so many at the Leveson hearings labelled as unethical. Cut-throat competition played a key role here. Always intense at the popular end of the market, it has become even more so with the arrival of new forms of communication, which tabloid newspapers regard as unfair (because relatively unregulated) competition. This may indeed result in what Roy Greenslade calls 'wacko jacko journalism', but as Yvonne Jewkes puts it:

> It's all about a good story, about novelty and about how to make a story quirky. ... it's all about selling the papers and circulation figures. A story so bizarre that Kate McCann[8] could possibly have killed her own daughter was really irresponsible coverage, but it was all about the drama and titillation. The same is true in the Joanna Yeates story.

Changing cultural values and news practices/attitudes

While the cut-throat practices of the British tabloids seem, at times, devoid of anything save desire for profit, the community responsibility attitude that the ethics of care stance espouses did at one time permeate the practices of at least certain sections of the press in England. In particular, the hardships of the Second World War forged the English, and indeed the British, in common cause. The outcome of the war laid the basis for the welfare state, and the sense of 'we're all in this together', which was engendered by the war, lasted to an extent into peacetime, and imbued elements of popular culture, such as the more liberal elements of the popular press. As Professor of Criminology at the London School of Economics, Robert Reiner said of such papers' crime coverage in the 1950s and 1960s:

> *That these crimes were heinous acts was not what stories pointed out. The real mystery in the stories was how come someone – and this is a tacit assumption: that defendants are not a different species of being; they are the same stock as we are – so how could they do this? ... There is no representation that [criminals] are heinous beasts from somewhere else. The question is what tragic circumstances led someone into this? Generally crime is seen as related to social deprivation, and the hope was that as conditions improved, so crime would come under control.*

However, the popular left-of-centre press either disappeared (*Daily Herald, News Chronicle, Reynold's News*) or changed with the ideological tenor of the times (the *Mirror*), Brunel journalism professor Julian Petley noted. In the 1970s, the dominant political and economic model started to shift from that of the welfare state and social-democratic consensus to one of neoliberalism, Petley pointed out, and the values of the market and consumer capitalism came to permeate social life and to replace the attitude of an ethics of care in many areas of social life. The new prevailing ideology could be summed up by John Major's remark about crime that 'society needs to condemn a little more, and understand a little less'.

The majority of the national daily and Sunday press did not merely reflect the political, economic, and ideological shifts that began in the late 1970s, but played a major role in propagandising them as authoritarian-populist 'common sense', according to Petley. Their accent is not on explaining the social causes of crime, but rather on blaming individuals for being criminals and demanding that they are punished as harshly as possible, Petley added. The criminal is thus seen as the irredeemable other, as Yvonne Jewkes claimed, and as a modern folk devil (witness the treatment handed out to Jefferies and those like him, which is popularly referred to as 'monstering').

The public sphere, press councils, and the ethic of care

The taken-for-granted habits of British journalists have received a public airing at the Leveson Inquiry and recent Select Committee inquiries into the British press; however, the British journalists we interviewed were mostly concerned with the duties to inform the public and beat the competition. They knew little about their continental counterparts in Sweden and the Netherlands, but our comparison has revealed three significant points:

- The ethic of care in journalism practice correlates with its presence in the public sphere and in the discourse about journalism. (Social welfare states with consensus forms of government often call upon communitarian values in public and journalistic discourse – see, for example, Green 2008a, 2008b.)
- An active press council plays a normative role in shaping discourse about journalistic practice.
- Without the normative effect of the first two factors reminding the press of its primary mission of public service, press practices risk becoming unethical.

We do not claim to establish cause and effect, only the correlations that our cross-cultural comparisons bring into relief.

A public ethic of care

By reference to Hallin and Mancini's above-mentioned models, we can see the importance of examining the historic relationship between a country's political system and its media economy. The democratic corporatist media model that prevails in central and northern Europe is characterised by a commercial media system that coexists with one tied to social and political groups. These news media historically have played a normative role of collaborating with the state and encouraging deliberation among citizens (Christians et al., 2009). For Froukje Sanling, a member of the Dutch Press Council, the central questions about the role of the press in a democracy are: 'What is the role of the press in a decent society? So what are the pillars of a decent society or do they want to go with the flow – like the internet? How do you want to treat people in a decent society? We are caught in a discussion of what is decent.' Sanling, fellow Dutch Press Council members, and Dutch journalists themselves have all expressed concern about how the press should treat people, including criminals, with decency and respect when they become newsworthy. And although disagreement is widespread about the Council's and Dutch Journalists Union's codes and their enforcement, they provide the framework within which debate takes place.

On the other hand, the British press has historically practised primarily within Hallin and Mancini's (2004) liberal model in which the press is, formally, politically independent and is supported by market mechanisms. Under this model, journalists tend to see the role of the press as a monitor on power or a watchdog on authority, with an adversarial rather than cooperative posture towards the state. In theory, the press keeps the public informed, and citizens then determine the best course of action. According to Bob Satchwell, head of the Society of Editors in the UK, ethical judgements should be kept at a minimum:

> *I believe ethical judgments are best if kept narrow as possible. In media, our job is to inform the public of what's happening without fear or favour and recognize that sometimes in doing that someone may get hurt. But what's very important is that the public does have a right to know, and it should know.*

In our research, when Dutch journalists reported on how they had wrestled with whether to withhold the late Karst Tates's name from their coverage out of deference to his family, they readily applied what we see as an ethic of care. Even if they had published Tates's name or disagreed with the principle of anonymity in this case, they justified their convictions by reference to notions of caring and responsibility, which was the default position. Swedes also called upon aspects of this perspective when they ultimately decided that the public's need to know outweighed their consideration for Anna Lindh's accused assassin. We suggest that an unarticulated but nonetheless present ethic of care shaped their practice and the culture in which that ethic is embedded. However, for the most part, English journalists did not refer to an ethical framework or foreground ethical concerns when they talked to us about how they covered the Yeates murder – or crime in general. Instead, they framed their concerns in terms of what the law permitted or forbade, or what they perceived that their audience wanted.

But British journalism academics, and certain journalists, do lament the absence in contemporary British journalism of concern for community, and criticise the 'othering' by the press of those accused of crimes. We have already noted the comments to this effect by Frost and Greenslade, and Jewkes regretted that England 'has become a much more divided society where it is us, the great moral majority, against the amoral, the unruly, those with no respect for authority'. Others have focused on this concern by comparing the press coverage of two cases of childhood murders, one in England and the other in Norway. (See in particular Franklin and Petley, 1996; Green, 2008b; Haydon and Scraton, 2000; Jewkes, 2011; Kehily and Montgomery, 2003; Morrison, 1998; Muncie, 2001.) The handling of these two events by both the news media and the criminal justice system displays the stark contrast between British and Scandinavian practices in both fields.

Two-year-old James Bulger was abducted and killed by ten-year-olds Robert Thompson and Jon Venables in Liverpool in 1993. British tabloids quickly labelled the boys 'monsters', 'freaks', 'animals', and 'evil'. As Bob Franklin and Julian Petley noted of press coverage of the conclusion of their trial for murder: 'Even by the skewed standards of the British press, the "normal" requirements of reporting were abandoned in favour of undiluted, vitriolic editorializing' (1996: 134). The boys were tried in an adult criminal court, and the press covered the story largely in a punitive 'criminal justice' frame that focused primarily on the boys' responsibility for wilful kidnapping and murder (Green, 2008a: 203).

Twenty months later, outside Trondheim, Norway, three six-year-old boys killed five-year-old Silje Marie Redergård. The boys were identified briefly before their parents withdrew their consent. Child welfare handled the case, and the boys were never punished. Instead, they were placed in a kindergarten, partly so that teachers and psychologists could monitor them and assist them in coming to grips with what they had done. Thus in England the case was dealt with predominantly within a criminal justice framework in contrast to the child welfare one within which it was placed in Norway. Furthermore, as Green puts it:

> Domestic coverage of the English case of James Bulger presented it as alarmingly symptomatic of deep-seated moral decline in Britain that only tough, remoralizing strategies could address. Coverage of the Norwegian case of Silje Redergård constructed it as a tragic one-off, requiring expert intervention to facilitate the speedy reintegration of the boys responsible. (2008a: 197)

Admittedly the cases differed: the British boys were older and the murder more brutal. But these differences do not fully explain the contrast between the press coverage of the two. Following the lengthy and sensational coverage of the Bulger murder, concern about crime in Britain doubled (ibid.), and the case ushered in an era in which the press routinely vilified children whom they perceived as 'deviant'. The Bulger case became a law-and-order touchstone, the Tory and Labour parties began vying for the toughest law-and-order stance (John Major's remark quoted above was made in the wake of the Bulger murder), and in the 14 years following the boys' convictions, the prison population in England and Wales rose by 80% (ibid.). By contrast, during a 2008 visit, Green found that the Redergård case had largely faded from Norwegian collective memory. In fact, most Norwegians remembered the Bulger case more clearly. But in Britain, the press kept the Bulger case alive in collective memory, its indelible place encouraged by ongoing coverage of Thompson and Venables, who were released from prison in 2001 and given new identities, while the tabloids protested. Venables was rearrested in 2010, having blown his own cover, and immediately became the target of negative press coverage. But Norwegians, Green found, felt little need to label the children from Trondheim as dangerous anomalies, or even as murderers, let alone to expel them from their communities as freaks. Instead, they preferred to follow a path toward reintegration. In fact, the act that left Silje Marie Redergård dead was always referred to in the Norwegian press as an 'accident'. As Green puts it:

> It is impossible to account for the differences in responses to the Bulger and Redergård homicides without considering the political-cultural context in each jurisdiction. Whether or not a particular crime event becomes a suitable vehicle to which late-modern anxieties can be attached appears to be conditioned not only by the levels of confidence that members of the public have in their institutions and in those charged with responding to that event, but also by the incentives that particular ways of doing politics create to politicize such events and to magnify their significance. (2008a: 215)

133

In our interviews, reporters in Sweden and the Netherlands frequently mentioned confidence in the government and official agencies as a factor affecting the way in which they covered certain stories. By contrast, those in England were more likely to mention a lack of any such faith. These divergent attitudes correlate with differences between political and economic systems, and with their respective models as outlined in Hallin and Mancini. In the United Kingdom, government is shaped by a majoritarian or Westminster model and a highly adversarial political culture. This system has traditionally been dominated by two parties, with each party having a strong incentive to politicise issues and tilt the majority in its direction. Hence, politicians are more likely to use volatile issues like crime to wedge the population into mutually exclusive camps. And journalists are more likely to see their role as one defined by the watchdog function.

Sweden and the Netherlands, on the other hand, govern primarily by consensus. Because multiple parties share power in a broad coalition, these governments tend to bargain and compromise in an inclusive manner that embraces the broadest possible consensus. Therefore, politicians have little incentive to use the issue of crime to set sections of society against each other and to paint criminals as wicked outsiders. In short, their political system, not just their journalistic style, has elements of an ethics of care. In addition, these corporatist welfare states

> have lower cultural appetites for punishment, inclusionary penal inter-
> vention and low imprisonment rates. They also generally tend be more
> egalitarian, have narrower income disparities, broad and strong welfare
> systems, low levels of social exclusion and left-wing political ideologies.
> (Cavadino and Dignan, quoted in Green, 2008a: 214)

An active press council

The most provocative point we noted in our British interviews and in the Leveson witness statements that we read was that ethics, as a form of active behaviour in which one might choose to engage, figured only minimally in English newsroom decisions. The so-called 'grey area' where right versus wrong might be debated seemed not to be a priority in Britain. In contrast, such concerns were prominent in Dutch and Swedish journalists' accounts of what drives their practices. British journalists discussed only what legal rights they possess and what legal restrictions they feared. US Supreme

Court Chief Justice Earl Warren once remarked: 'In civilized life, law floats on a sea of ethics. Each is indispensable to civilization. Without law we should be at the mercy of the least scrupulous; without ethics, law could not exist.' But many journalists we spoke with in England defined their boundaries by law alone.

Far out beyond the concerns of ethics, however, were the eight newspapers found guilty of libel in the Jefferies case. They apparently decided breaking the law and being sued was worth the risk of publishing what they did. In fact, certain newspapers revealed that they have a 'risk committee' that assesses the likelihood of being sued. The Press Complaints Commission offers an alternative to the law for those unhappy with press coverage in one way or another, and its Editors' Code includes respect for privacy and respect for criminals' family members. But the PCC is widely – though not uniformly – derided as toothless. The National Union of Journalists (NUJ) also operates under a code of practice, but the organisation has been greatly weakened by union-busting activities ever since Rupert Murdoch de-recognised it during the 1980s, with other press owners following suit.

Unlike the press councils and journalists' unions in Sweden and Holland, in England, no strong and respected system exists that allows newspapers to moderate and mediate each other. As Michelle Stanistreet, general secretary of the NUJ, told the Leveson Inquiry:

> *We strongly believe that the union-busting that has taken place at News International [Murdoch's UK news empire] and the barrier that exists for NUJ at the titles is linked to the moral vacuum that has been allowed to proliferate at the News of the World … The action has directly in our view impacted upon the approach to journalistic ethics and standards in the broader newspaper industry.*[9]

Some NUJ members, Stanistreet said, told her that they were bullied by editors who demanded that they write stories the journalists knew to be false. She thus supported a conscience clause that would protect journalists if they refused an assignment that they felt violates the NUJ code.

In his expert testimony to the Leveson Inquiry, Steven Barnett, Professor of Communications at Westminster University, noted the problem is less with the contents of the Editors' Code than with its implementation:

> *The Press Complaints Commission has neither the powers nor the institutional will to investigate breaches, to provide remedies, or to promote high standards of professional practice. As the creature of newspaper interests, it cannot (and would not) impose fines, and appears to be mainly concerned to ensure that complaints are assessed with minimal fuss, minimal publicity, minimal transparency and minimal redress.*

While he was keen to make it clear that he was 'categorically not [making] an argument for statutory regulation of the press, for the imposition of impartiality rules … or for licensing of newspapers', he held up British television as a model that print journalism might emulate, pointing out that television is respected because of its independent practices *and* its ethical standards, both of which are underpinned by regulation:

> *This comparison is to help us understand that an independent regulatory framework can not only protect but actively promote the kind of intelligent, accessible, information-rich, and watchdog journalism which most professionals crave and on which democracy thrives.*[10]

The print media in Britain's European neighbours have built such structures in the form of press councils and fully recognised journalist unions. Ireland adopted such a model in 2008, which witnesses at the Leveson Inquiry frequently cited as suitable for the UK. This introduced elements of social responsibility, which journalists themselves largely fashioned and now enforce with government and citizen participation.

The point of our comparisons is not to advocate uniformity nor necessarily to suggest a privileging of the Dutch and Swedish attitude over that espoused by the British. The UN Declaration of Human Rights and the European Convention on Human Rights both make provisions for privacy, but their interpretation is mediated by each nation's cultural assumptions and sensibilities, which the press of each nation both reflects and helps to shape. What privacy means in Holland or Sweden differs from what it means in England. The application of journalism ethics is specific to each culture and is thus difficult to subject to overarching, cross-cultural diktats. But while standards and practices may vary from one country to another, without the moderating influence of the attitudes encouraged by an ethic of care and its emphasis on the fragile threads that connect citizens to each other, journalism can easily lose sight of its primary democratic mission: to serve the public. Strong press councils and effective journalist unions strengthen public trust in journalism and institutions.

The Swedish press enjoys immense freedom. But journalists there believe that this freedom imposes strong ethical obligations and realise that it is under constant threat of legislation. As a result, they engage in vigilant self-policing. Journalists there sometimes disagree with press council policies and procedures and vigorously debate them. Certain news organisations even refuse to participate. But most profess an ethical commitment, not simply to reporting crime accurately, but to protecting the accused from being damaged by that reporting. They back this commitment by endorsing the power wielded jointly by the judiciary and the press council. While a press council's power to make and enforce rules is clearly a valuable contribution, it is not the only benefit this model offers; also important is the platform that press councils provide for journalists and the public to discuss the mission of the press mission within a democracy and the ethical practices that best suit the particular cultural/political climate.

Claude-Jean Bertrand (2008) mapped 100 different press accountability systems worldwide and considered press councils to be 'potentially the most useful press accountability system and the greatest weapon in the fight for quality news media' (quoted in Koene, 2009: 5). Calling press councils the 'watchdogs of democracy', Daphne Koene, secretary of the Netherlands Press Council, found that their importance is growing in Western Europe and especially in her native country:

> As a body that can easily be approached by private persons and organizations alike with complaints about journalistic conduct, the council is pre-eminently suited to deliver self-regulation in the media. For each case, it can investigate whether reporters have abided by professional ethics. In addition, the council is also the institute responsible for shaping opinions and developing journalistic norms, since its rulings establish general principles (for example, about granting the right to reply). The amalgamation of all the rulings ever made – considering several hundreds of cases have been dealt with over the years – create a good picture of the journalistic ethics of our country. (Ibid. 1)

Journalism and penal populism

Comparing journalistic modes of reporting signal crimes points out how an overwrought 'mean world' framing helps to make newspaper readers fearful, and encourages a belief that violent crime is more widespread than it actually is, a stance probably embraced by the neoliberal 'tough on crime' governments. But the result of this style of coverage, as Martin Innes points out, is often a frightened population that demands harsher anti-crime measures:

> *Understanding how particular incidents are construed as signal crimes and form the basis for collective memories may then be particularly consequential in a cultural context where there is a pervasive feeling of malaise and a concern with the efficacy of traditional social ordering mechanisms. Under such conditions, the signals that incidents past and present convey may be vitally important in encouraging an expansion of social control. (2003: 66)*

In such a situation, discussion of crime at the political level becomes framed in terms of what has been called 'penal populism' or 'populist punitiveness', which John Pratt (2007: 3) argues 'consists of the pursuit of a set of penal policies to win votes rather than to reduce crime or promote justice'. Such populism thrives on the impression routinely given by the press that crime rates are inexorably rising, but it also draws on the sense that 'modern society is changing in ways that are threatening and unwanted by many ... as if the pillars on which the security and stability of modern life had been built are fragmenting' (ibid. 4). This too is a particular trope of Britain's press.

Britain's press isn't exactly short of critics who accuse it of sensationalising stories in ways that are distinctly harmful to social harmony and damaging to democratic processes. But despite being repeatedly warned of the negative and destructive power such stories wield, British journalists, including most of those to whom we spoke or who testified at the Leveson Inquiry, focused on their own freedom and desire to compete, with little mention of concern for harmful consequences, social responsibility, or the common good.

Journalism's mission: looking forward

Towards the end of the last century in the US, the Committee of Concerned Journalists gathered together some of America's most influential newspaper people to ask the absolutely fundamental question: what is journalism for? The result was a book by Bill Kovach and Tom Rosenstiel called *The*

Elements of Journalism (2001). Their conclusion was that 'the primary purpose of journalism is to provide people with the information they need to be free and self governing' (2001: 12). This mission provides a guiding light for journalists and for the self-determining society. Conversely, if the press puts other interests, such as profit or individual ambition, before this primary one, it will behave in a way that betrays its mission and breaches its faith with the public.

As James Carey put it, the 'scales between quality journalism and schlock sensationalism are in precarious balance', lamenting the fact that the public cannot locate its own interests at the heart of a 'money-grubbing enterprise, barren of anything but self-serving values' (2002: 80). In Carey's view, journalism needs to steer itself away from what he describes as 'an independence that has freed itself of the duties of citizenship', one that has helped to shape a thin democracy of passive spectatorship, and instead follow practices that support 'a thick democracy of participation' (ibid. 81).

We have seen that journalists in the Netherlands and Sweden are more concerned about protecting the privacy of the subjects of their articles than are their British counterparts, who focus instead on transparency and the watchdog function. But even the Dutch and the Swedish have begun to wonder whether their ethical standard of privacy protection for accused persons or convicted criminals might become futile as their countries face two major challenges. Globalised ownership and new forms of communications technology threaten to standardise commercial values across borders, and to bring with them a tell-all journalistic style that will make quaint relics of the concerns for privacy that are currently observed in much of Central and Northern Europe. Independent bloggers and news organisations from neighbouring countries can now distribute information that journalists in Sweden and the Netherlands protect, as do certain publications within their borders. Although readers always had access to information via public records that the press held back, it now springs forth electronically at their fingertips. At the same time, British-style tabloids and tabloid-style broadcast news are penetrating their countries and encouraging the indigenous media to compete with them on their terms. But some journalists argue such a process is not inevitable.

'I still have the feeling that it's about the right to know versus the need to know – do you *need* to know? That's the question reporters in Holland ask themselves,' said Tom Meens, ombudsman for *De Vokskrant.* 'I never get letters from readers that say "why didn't you inform us of this or that?", so they must think we give them the news they need to know.'

In 2011, the British people began asking the same question that Meens suggested, as the press found itself part of a larger self-examination of civil society. In *The Exclusive Society*, Jock Young (1999) documented the numerous ways in which the social contract of post-war Britain had broken down. He also stressed that there is no going back. The world has changed too much, and new contracts of citizenship must now emphasise diversity rather than absolute values. As he put it: the new social contract must negotiate a 'plethora of cultures, ever changing, ever developing, transforming themselves and each other' (Young, 1999: 198). He continued:

> *Crime and intolerance occur when citizenship is thwarted; their causes lie in injustice, yet their effect is, inevitably, further injustice and violation of citizenship. The solution is to be found not in the resurrection of past abilities, based on nostalgia and a world that will never return, but on a new citizenship, a reflexive modernity which will tackle the problems of justice and community, of reward and individualism, which dwell at the heart of liberal democracy. (Ibid. 199)*

In this transformation, the demise of social-democratic traditions, the dominance of market forces, and the essentialising of the 'other' all have the potential to push liberal democracies in the direction of oppression. But Young makes a strong case against such a dystopia, arguing that new technologies and market forces can broaden and strengthen the social contract, that certain traditions, especially those based in patriarchy and homogeneity, are better pushed aside, and blaming or othering of 'foreigners' for crime or social displacement is ultimately irrational and a dead end for social policy.

The negotiation of public and private is particularly difficult in the case of crime coverage, and guiding ethical journalistic principles are needed to navigate it. Whether Swedish and Dutch journalists can manage to retain such principles in a rapidly changing media environment, and whether British ones can learn to develop them in a post-Leveson world, remains to be seen.

Notes

1   Quotations from otherwise unreferenced sources are taken from interviews with the authors.

2   http://www.guardian.co.uk/uk/2012/nov/24/christopher-jefferies-leveson-press-inquiry (accessed Dec. 2012).

3   http://ethicnet.uta.fi.

4   http://www.levesoninquiry.org.uk/wp-content/uploads/2011/11/Witness-Statement-of-Christopher-Jefferies.pdf.

5   http://www.thisisbristol.co.uk/Chris-Jefferies-speaks-debate-press/story-15541952-detail/story.html (accessed Dec. 2012).

6   http://www.levesoninquiry.org.uk/wp-content/uploads/2012/01/Witness-Statement-of-Benedict-Brogan1.pdf.

7   See http://inforrm.wordpress.com/2011/09/04/opinion-courts-and-controversy-consequences-of-the-jeffries-contempt-case-brian-cathcart/#more-11175 and http://inforrm.wordpress.com/2011/08/05/opinion-christopher-jefferies-case-delivers-wake-up-call-to-the-tabloids-louis-charalambous/#more-10788 (both accessed Dec. 2012).

8   In May 2007, three-year-old Madeleine McCann disappeared from her parents' hotel room in Portugal while she and her twin siblings were on a family vacation. Kate and Gerry McCann had left the children unsupervised in a ground-floor bedroom while they themselves ate dinner nearby. The parents were initially suspects. The child has never been found. Kate McCann testified at the Leveson Inquiry about how emotionally difficult the tabloids' methods and coverage were for her.

9   http://www.levesoninquiry.org.uk/wp-content/uploads/2012/02/Witness-Statement-of-Michelle-Stanistreet.pdf.

10 http://www.levesoninquiry.org.uk/wp-content/uploads/2011/12/Witness-Statement-of-Professor-Steven-Barnett.pdf.

References

Anderson, Benedict (1983) *Imagined Communities: Reflections on the Origins and Spread of Nationalism* (London: Verso).

Benhabib, Seyla (1987) 'The Generalized and the Concrete Other: The Kohlberg-Gilligan Controversy and Feminist Theory', in Seyla Benhabib and Drucilla Cornell (eds), *Feminism as Critique* (Minneapolis: University of Minnesota Press).

Bertrand, Claude-Jean (2008) 'Watching the Watchdog-Watching Dog: A Call for Active Press Councils', in Torbjörn von Krogh (ed.), *Media Accountability Today … and Tomorrow: Updating the Concept in Theory and Practice* (Göteborg: Nordicom), 115–18.

Carey, James (2002) 'What does "Good Work" in Journalism Look Like?', *Neiman Reports* (Spring): 79–81.

Cavadino, Michael, and Dignan, James (2006) 'Penal Policy and Political Economy', *Criminology and Criminal Justice*, 6(4): 435–56.

Christians, Clifford, Ferre, John, and Fackler, Mark (1993) *Good News: Social Ethics and the Press* (New York: Oxford University Press).

Christians, Clifford G., Glasser, Theodore L., McQuail, Dennis, Nordenstreng, Kaarle, and White, Robert A. (2009) *Normative Theories of the Media: Journalism in Democratic Societies* (Urbana, IL: University of Illinois Press).

Craig, David (1996) 'Communitarian Journalism(s): Clearing Conceptual Landscapes', *Journal of Mass Media Ethics*, 11(2): 107–18.

Ericson, Richard V., Baranek, Patricia M., and Chan, Janet B. L. (1987) *Visualizing Deviance: A Study of News Organization* (Toronto: University of Toronto Press).

Franklin, Bob, and Petley, Julian (1996) 'Killing the Age of Innocence: Newspaper Reporting of the Death of James Bulger', in Jane Pilcher and Stephen Wagg (eds), *Thatcher's Children? Politics, Childhood and Society in the 1980s and 1990s* (London: Falmer Press), 134–54.

Gilligan, Carol (1982) *In a Different Voice: Psychological Theory and Women's Development* (Cambridge, MA: Harvard University Press).

Green, David A. (2008a) 'Suitable Vehicles: Framing Blame and Justice When Children Kill a Child', *Crime Media and Justice*, 4: 197–220.

Green, David A. (2008b) *When Children Kill Children* (Oxford: Oxford University Press).

Hallin, Daniel, and Mancini, Paolo (2004) *Comparing Media Systems: Three Models of Media and Politics* (Cambridge: Cambridge University Press).

Haydon, Deena, and Scraton, Phil (2000) 'Condemn a Little More, Understand a Little Less? The Political Context and Rights Implications of the Domestic and European Rulings in the Venables–Thompson Case', *Journal of Law and Society*, 27(3): 416–48.

Innes, Martin (2003) '"Signal Crimes": Detective Work, Mass Media and Constructing Collective Memory', in Paul Mason (ed.) *Criminal Visions: Media Representations of Crime and Justice* (Cullompton: Willan Publishing), 51–69.

Jewkes, Yvonne (2011) *Media and Crime*, 2nd edn (London: Sage).

Katz, Jack (1987) 'What Makes Crime "News"?', *Media, Culture and Society*, 9: 47–75.

Kehily, Mary Jane, and Montgomery, Heather (2003) 'Innocence and Experience', in Martin Woodhead and Heather Montgomery (eds), *Understanding*

Childhood: An Interdisciplinary Approach (Milton Keynes: Open University Press), 221–65.

Koene, Daphne C. (2009) *Press Councils in Western Europe* (Amsterdam: The Netherlands Press Council/The Hague: The Netherlands Press Fund).

Kovach, Bill, and Rosenstiel, Tom (2001) *The Elements of Journalism: What News People Know and the Public Should Expect* (New York: Crown Publishers).

Morrison, Blake (1998) *As if* (London: Granta).

Muncie, John (2001) 'Policy Transfers and "What Works": Some Reflections on Comparative Youth Justice', *Youth Justice*, 1(3): 27–35.

Noddings, Nel (1984) *Caring: A Feminine Approach to Ethics and Moral Education* (Berkeley, CA: University of California Press).

Pratt, John (2007) *Penal Populism* (London: Routledge).

Tuchman, Gaye (1978) *Making News: A Study in the Construction of Reality* (New York: Free Press).

Young, Jock (1999) *The Exclusive Society: Social Exclusion, Crime and Difference in Late Modernity* (London: Sage).

8

The Dominique Strauss-Kahn Scandal: Mediating Authenticity in *Le Monde* and the *New York Times*[1]

Julia Lefkowitz

Examination of news media coverage of the Dominique Strauss-Kahn scandal in the US and in France reveals differences in national cultural ideologies and journalistic norms. To provide a brief overview of the affair, Strauss-Kahn was arrested in New York on 14 May, following charges that he had sexually assaulted an immigrant maid in his midtown Manhattan hotel suite. The story quickly became the subject of an international news media frenzy, and in the wake of these events, Strauss-Kahn, who was considered a potential presidential front runner in France, resigned from his post as managing director of the International Monetary Fund. Roughly three months later, criminal charges against Strauss-Kahn were dismissed and doubts were raised about the credibility of the Guinean maid, who was found to have told lies about her past.

As a French politician was arrested on US soil, mediation of the scandal played into trans-Atlantic clichés of one kind or another. Such clichés have largely been engendered and perpetuated by historical transnational disagreements and disputes which can in turn be related to the competing versions of democracy, modernity, and universalism fostered by each country. As such, and as frequently noted, the US and France offer a fruitful case study for cross-national research. More specifically, mediation of the Strauss-Kahn scandal reflects core complexities of modernity, and comparing US and French media coverage of the scandal helps us to pinpoint complex sets of values and differences in the contemporary media landscape.

Media and images have, in recent years, come to exist in increasingly complex and pervasive forms. Through the internet, we now have instant access to a virtually infinite number of news articles and images of people, places, and stories that are outside our immediate locality. The rise of citizen journalism has also transformed the current mediascape, with proponents arguing that citizen journalism is more transparent and democratic than stories produced by traditional news organisations.

Accordingly, in the context of a cross-national media scandal, in which global flows, the growing influence of the media, and national ideologies each serve as principle axes, the concept of authenticity can serve as a framework by means of which to identify complex sets of differences, as well as shared values and sensibilities. The concept of authenticity is of particular relevance as it is a term whose meaning varies from national culture to national culture according to culturally rooted norms. In the context of a modern landscape characterised by hybridity and global flows, news publications can also deploy culturally rooted concepts of authenticity to provide readers with a sense of national self-identity, frequently 'othering' foreign national cultures in the process.

This chapter demonstrates differences between French and US national cultural ideologies and journalistic norms manifest in the coverage of the DSK scandal in *Le Monde* and the *New York Times*, ultimately identifying the culturally rooted concepts of authenticity reflected in each publication, and evaluating the authenticity of each newspaper's discourse. In the first part, I will provide an overview of the relevant US and French national cultural ideologies and journalistic norms, and then examine pertinent concepts of authenticity. Before I analyse articles featured in *Le Monde* and the *NYT*, I will also briefly discuss my methodology, critical discourse analysis. After the analysis itself, in the final part of this chapter, I will identify the national ideologies and culturally rooted concepts of authenticity mediated by the two publications, and then evaluate the authenticity of each newspaper's discourse. As this chapter will demonstrate, in today's globalised context, awareness of authenticity as it relates to news media discourse is crucial in understanding the engagement of citizens in democratic societies.

National cultural ideologies and journalistic norms in France and the US

In France, politics and media have historically been intertwined. Until 1967, the government set cover prices of newspapers and state monopolies were established in newsprint, newspaper distribution, and the sale of advertising space. Corruption in the French press predating the Second World War is well-documented and did not decline substantially until the 1980s (Chalaby, 2004). Throughout this time, newspapers were highly reliant on state subsidies for funding.

When broadcasting was liberalised in 1982, the press was also affected by the new phenomenon of competition between broadcasting organisations, and newspapers became increasingly reliant on non-government parties such as advertisers for revenue. Competition between newspapers forces publications to distinguish themselves one from another by means such as publishing 'exclusives'. But while investigative journalism became more prevalent in post-1982 France, it is still not as widespread or pronounced as it is in the US or UK, and this can be attributed partly to the fact that the French press is still less commercialised (Benson, 2009).

French privacy laws are also notoriously stringent, and France's political class has continued to use privacy regulations in order to suppress the disclosure of damaging information prior to publication. As newspapers can face substantial damages through potential legal suits, the power of the press is limited considerably by fear of prosecution. In a study comparing culturally rooted concepts of privacy in the US and a number of European countries, Whitman (2004) argues that notions of privacy in France reflect a broader cultural emphasis on personal dignity, honour, and the individual's right to maintain their public image. He also attests that this last notion in particular stemmed from early modern aristocrats, demonstrating in turn the lasting influence of an upper class that views the media as its most significant threat to privacy.

In his work on early modern and contemporary French history, Sowerwine (2001) discusses the high reliance of a privileged elite on state institutions that in turn maintain the class's elevated status. This phenomenon reflects a European class structure that is, in contrast to the US, older and more autonomous from financial markets. As French ideologies place a greater value on cultural capital, a broader range of intellectuals enjoy a higher status in France than in the US. French appreciation of cultural capital and emphasis on refinement and humanist culture is also reflected in the nation's journalistic norms. Chalaby states that 'literary values and literary capital had a tremendous importance in the journalistic field, and many journalists courted these honors rather than journalistic prizes' (2004: 1200). Literary sensibilities and skill continue to infuse French journalism, also linking to the prevalence of the debate-style approach that is common amongst French newspapers. While US news stories focus more heavily on information and facts, articles in French press tend to be more polemical. The debate-style format frequently entails the inclusion of multiple viewpoints and, in the national cultural context of France, opinion expressed in news articles can serve as a stepping-stone for a wider public debate. As such, while French news articles may generally be more partisan, they can ultimately be more thoroughly informative.

Journalistic norms that more overtly and extensively involve readers also reflect the dominance of a collective, rather than an individualistic, national outlook. As Chalaby notes: 'for a long time, the dominant social theories have focused on the system itself rather than the individual' (2004: 1204). Accordingly, the notion of focusing on a single member of an institution who may be at fault – such as, for example, a corrupt politician – does not cohere with a collectively oriented outlook.

While a certain sense of solidarity is manifest in French cultural ideology, attitudes to multiculturalism reflect a less egalitarian mindset. As Hoffman (1995: 325) has noted, a particular French stereotype of American multiculturalism 'deplores the lack of uniformity and the fragmentation of the United States', in turn reflecting a French fear of the 'tyranny of minorities'.

US and French media represent opposite ideal types: the laissez-faire, liberal model of US news media, and the more state-dominated, pluralist French approach. As US media outlets generally receive minimal government subsidies, newspapers are more dependent on their readership and advertising for revenue. Unlike French publications that operate as an extension of the public sphere, US newspapers operate as purely commercial entities. The role of advertising and commercialisation are thus central to an analysis of US journalistic norms and relevant national cultural ideologies.

In his analysis and critique of contemporary US news journalism, Lance Bennett (1992: 404) cites the detrimental impact of market forces on the country's media:

> *Political consultants tell politicians how to say what, when, where, how, and to whom. News doctors tell media organizations how to select and package news to grab the attention of fickle individuals in competitive markets.*

While strong links between the state, politicians, media, and major French companies have influenced the country's newspapers, it is commercial interests that shape, and indeed have an even stronger impact on, the day-to-day practices of US news publications.

Bennett has also discussed the narrative-driven format of US journalism, identifying four characteristics used by US news media that serve to attract the short-term attention of readers: personalisation, dramatisation, fragmentation, and authority-disorder. The first three practices are of particular relevance to this chapter. Personalisation is 'the journalistic bias that gives preference to individual actors and human-interest angles in events over larger, institutional, social, and political contexts' (Bennett, 2012: 49), frequently using formulas such as 'he/she was a reflection of us' (ibid. 45), thereby missing the bigger picture. Dramatisation similarly hinders meaningful audience engagement by utilising dramatic narrative and qualities deriving from fiction that evoke immediate emotion. Bennett argues that personalisation and dramatisation contribute to a third trend, fragmentation, which involves the isolation of key facets of a news story such as actors, themes, background, and context, whilst obscuring broader, more fundamental aspects of the story.

Whilst, as noted earlier, privacy laws preclude journalists' access to certain kinds of information in France, Benson and Hallin (2007: 3) argue that 'the trend in U.S. federal court interpretations of the First Amendment has been a decrease in the state's capacity to inhibit journalistic investigations of government agencies or politicians' private lives'. Differences in privacy laws and, subsequently, certain journalistic norms reflect broader ideological divergences in national cultural notions of privacy. Whitman (2004) argues that American sensibilities regarding privacy emerge from a national cultural emphasis on an idea of liberty that is derived from two related cultural values: freedom of expression and freedom of property, both of which are perceived as linked to a free market. While French ideology perceives public image as a function of dignity and honour, US ideology views public image as a commodity that can, as such, be sold. Whereas the media are seen as the most substantial threat to privacy in France, it is the state that is viewed with the most suspicion in the US.

In regard to class, US ideologies linked to Puritanism place a substantial emphasis on material prosperity, contrasting with the French system in which class mobility is more limited and is linked to notions of cultural capital. The anti-monarchist sentiments of the Puritans gave rise early on to an American culture that was anti-statist and favoured an ideology of meritocratic individualism. This notion also reflects an individualist US ideology in sharp contrast to the collectively minded French perspective.

As Puritan communities in early American history also gave a central and crucial role to moral law in both private and public spheres, punishing individuals who deviated from the strict moral laws of the Bible, American culture continues to apply moral laws and standards to matters that fall within the realm of the public sphere. Puritan ideologies regarding sex and sexual conduct also contrast with a French tendency to view sexual behaviour as separate from morality (Lamont, 1992).

Authenticity: frameworks of construction

In the context of this chapter, constructions of authenticity should be understood as a function of national ideologies and categorised into two frameworks that distinguish how the term relates to two broader subjects: identity and discourse. My critical discourse analysis of *Le Monde* and the *NYT* will demonstrate how the dynamics of these two frameworks differ across national cultures, and here I will provide a brief account of theories of core relevance to each realm. It should be noted that there is a dearth of academic literature analysing authenticity as a function of national cultural ideologies, and that this is a topic that merits further research.

The notion of 'performance' is key to identity-related considerations of authenticity. The work of sociologists, such as Erving Goffman (1959), who explicitly attest to the constructed and context-sensitive nature of identity, supports the idea that all of our actions are in fact 'performed', subsequently reinforcing the idea that authenticity can exist only as a 'performance'. Conversely, the work of those theorists who posit the existence of a true, inner self contradicts the idea of identity as wholly constructed. Thus, on a broader level, the contested, subjective nature of identity is reflected in different conceptions of authenticity.

Richardson contrasts truth and sincerity to authenticity, stating: 'Authenticity is a different matter, for it has regard to "being" rather than "saying", whereas the former "pertain to the content of spoken or written text"' (Richardson, 2001: 483). This notion taps into the complex role of visual communication in authenticity judgements, which is also famously referenced by Walter Benjamin in the context of art and its reproduction:

as established through such perspectives, authenticity is something both identifiable and elusive, which ultimately makes the term all the more susceptible to the subjectivities of national value sets.

A prominent consideration for authenticity within the framework of discourse is as a form of expanded accuracy. For example, Harwood (2004) argues that the US news media's tendency to reduce complex issues into simplified, sensationalised narratives reflects a lapse in accuracy, and thus a lack of authenticity. Connotations of inauthenticity are also relevant here. Academic literature identifies the term as a 'mismatch' (Richardson, 2001: 483) between words and actions, explaining it as 'revelations of stark contrasts to the professed persona' (Gamson, 2004: 56). As such, inauthenticity can be understood as an implication of 'moral censure' (Richardson, 2001: 482). This association can quite directly be applied to the question of identity, and inauthenticity in contexts of both identity and discourse can be viewed as a lack of honesty or transparency. Conversely, in relation to this notion, authenticity can be understood as being upfront or transparent.

Methodology

Critical discourse analysis (CDA) is a key methodology in identifying the national cultural ideologies that play a role in *Le Monde*'s and the *NYT*'s mediation of the DSK scandal, and in determining nationally rooted concepts of authenticity reflected in the publications' discourse. This methodology enables analysis of media discourse by exploring the link between language and ideology. CDA is especially useful in determining the relationship between a text (micro-level) and socio-cultural practices (macro-level), and in showing how discursive practices operate as a mediator between the two. Particularly important in CDA is Van Dijk's discourse–cognition–society model (2009), which analyses the links between discourse, cognition, and society, substantiating the ability of language to tie into and reflect the cultural and socio-economic beliefs of a particular community. As McGregor (2003) puts it:

> *The objective of CDA is to uncover the ideological assumptions that are hidden in the words of our written text or oral speech in order to resist and overcome various forms of 'power over' or to gain an appreciation that we are exercising power over, unbeknownst to us.*

There is no one, single way of carrying out CDA. Rather, any number of means can be deployed in order to pinpoint the various subjectivities manifest in a text. These might include consideration of a piece's lexis, grammar, attribution of agency, headlines, images, photographs, layout, and so on.

Methods

While an extensive number of publications in the US and France have reported on the Strauss-Kahn scandal, in order to conduct an intensive analysis, I have chosen to analyse *Le Monde* and the *New York Times*. As the two publications operate from a similar position of cultural and economic capital, or habitus, a cross-comparison of the two can yield valid results that are substantially controlled, although a limitation of this approach is that intra-organisational factors – such as, for example, newsroom hierarchies or time pressures – can vary between the two publications. However, more broadly speaking, and relevant to this project, is the argument that when it comes to the organisation of newsrooms, 'the most significant differences seem to be cross-national', as Benson (2004: 280) puts it.

Furthermore, as the quantity of articles published in *Le Monde* and the *NYT* on the DSK scandal is vast, I have opted to focus on coverage of two key events in the US criminal case against Strauss-Kahn: DSK's arrest and the dismissal of charges against him. While the two publications ran numerous articles on these two stories, in order to conduct an intensive analysis, I have analysed the first news article to report on each event. An analysis of these two events, which are also arguably the key developments in the scandal, encapsulates the timeline of the US criminal proceeding against DSK, providing a temporally thorough overview of the scandal and its coverage.

I selected three aspects of the articles to which to apply CDA: headlines, agency, and word choice. A limitation of this approach is that each of these three criteria can overlap. But despite the inevitable crossovers, analysis of these aspects of the articles can be used to reveal the national ideological frameworks and values of journalists at *Le Monde* and the *NYT*. Again, as mentioned in the introductory section of this chapter, it is textually coded and culturally rooted concepts of authenticity that produce a broad sense of national self-identity.

The analysis

Headlines

While headlines in the *NYT* use words that are subjective to describe the Strauss-Kahn affair, *Le Monde*'s headlines either refrain from referring to the affair directly or use language that is technical in order to do so. For example, in the headline of the first article run in the *NYT* on 14 May, 'I.M.F. Chief, Apprehended at Airport, Is Accused of Sexual Attack', the incident that has led to the story is referred to as a 'sexual attack' (Baker and Erlanger, 2011). Furthermore, agency is not attributed to the 'I.M.F. Chief' who 'is accused' of this activity. The headline does not explain who has directed this accusation at Strauss-Kahn. Similarly, in the lead article published on 23 August, 'Strauss-Kahn Drama Ends With Short Final Scene', the case is referred to as a 'drama', and the court session that resulted in the case's dismissal is conveyed as the 'final scene' (Eligon, 2011).

In contrast, *Le Monde*'s headlines are of greater length, providing a wider breadth of background information. The newspaper's 17 May headline reads: 'Dominique Strauss-Kahn devait être présenté devant un juge à New York, lundi 16 mai. Le patron du FMI rejette les accusations et plaide non coupable: Les 36 heures où tout a basculé' (*Dominique Strauss-Kahn had to be presented before a judge in New York on Monday, May 16. The head of the IMF rejects accusations and pleads not guilty: the 36 hours in which everything has shifted*) (Bacqué and Cypel, 2011). Where the *NYT* refers to a 'sexual attack', *Le Monde* refers to 'les accusations'. Furthermore, while the *NYT* states that Strauss-Kahn 'is accused' of specific actions, *Le Monde* states that he 'rejects' these charges; in the latter case, Strauss-Kahn has the stronger agency. Readers of *Le Monde* are also told who produced these charges, namely 'a judge in New York'. Although it is possible that *Le Monde* felt it necessary to provide more extensive information in order to inform a French audience not familiar with US legal procedures, readers of *Le Monde* are assumed to be thoroughly informed of the event that is the subject of the article's coverage.

The headline of the 24 August article in *Le Monde* is similarly extensive in its provision of context. Technical terms are used to describe the events covered in the story, and the parties involved with entailed activities are clearly identified: 'Le procureur recommande au juge l'abandon des poursuites contre M. Strauss-Kahn: Cyrus Vance affirme que "l'accusé a eu un rapport précipité avec la plaignante" sans que l'on puisse établir qu'il ait été "non consenti".' (*The prosecutor recommended to the judge to drop the charges against Strauss-Kahn: Cyrus Vance affirms that 'the accused precipitated a relationship with the complainant,' and no one can establish that it was 'non-consensual.'*) (Lesnes, 2011). The headline quotes the content of the verdict against Strauss-Kahn, whereas the *NYT* does not incorporate any quotations in its corresponding headline on 23 August (Eligon, 2011). However, it should also be noted that this is not necessarily different from practices deployed by the *NYT* in other types of coverage: rather, in the US, it is rare for prestige press publications to incorporate quotations in headlines. Such differences between practices exhibited by the two newspapers can be said to reflect a broader US emphasis on ostensible neutrality and a French emphasis on transparency.

The disparity of factual information and objectivity between the headlines featured in *Le Monde* and the *NYT* highlights the relative fragmentation and subjectivity of the *NYT* headlines. Although headlines are by nature reductive fragments, the *NYT*'s represent greater deviations from accuracy and objectivity than do those of *Le Monde*.

Agency

Agency refers to how activity referenced in a text is or is not attributed to the actors involved. As it can convey who has power and who is passive and powerless, agency is a means of identifying how the author of a text has chosen to depict power relations. In this particular cross-national context, agency is a key tool through which to identify the views and values of French versus US journalists.

Strauss-Kahn is the main subject of the articles run in the first series of stories in *Le Monde* and the *NYT*. *Le Monde*, however, gives Strauss-Kahn agency more often, underscoring actions he has taken in reaction to the charges against him. Again, the 17 May article's headline states (Bacqué and Cypel, 2011): 'Le patron du FMI rejette les accusations et plaide non coupable' (*The head of the IMF rejects accusations and pleads not guilty*), and: 'Il dispose des avocats les plus renommés de New York, William Taylor et Benjamin Brafman' (*He has the most renowned lawyers in New York, William Taylor and Benjamin Brafman*). Within the article itself, Strauss-Kahn's alleged actions in room 2820 are conveyed as hypothetical. The article states: 'Selon les versions policières – dont la chronologie a parfois divergé' (*According to the police versions, whose chronology has sometimes diverged*); and subsequently uses the conditional tense to convey what supposedly happened in room 2820: 'Sortant nu de la salle de bain,

Dominique Strauss-Kahn se serait approché "par derrière" de la jeune femme' (*Leaving the bathroom naked, Dominique Strauss-Kahn would have approached the woman 'from behind'*). *Le Monde*'s use of agency thus conveys the journalist's scepticism of the veracity of the charges against Strauss-Kahn and, as such, agency reflects the journalist's opinion.

The *NYT*'s use of agency portrays Strauss-Kahn in passive terms, instead placing emphasis on descriptions of him that serve to inform a US demographic that is less familiar with him. The article also undermines Strauss-Kahn's credibility through mention of his sophisticated, expensive tastes. For example: 'The couple are known to enjoy the finer things in life, and Mr. Strauss-Kahn has sometimes been attacked for being a "caviar leftist"'; and: 'Recently, Mr. Strauss-Kahn and his wife were photographed entering an expensive Porsche in Paris belonging to one of their friends.' The *NYT* conveys Strauss-Kahn's expensive tastes through third parties – in the first instance, an unspecified party, and in the second, those who photographed Strauss-Kahn entering the Porsche. Through these means, the *NYT* distances itself from the production of judgement, instead referencing the role of outside parties, who are probably based in France: although judgement is conveyed, the *NYT* employs agency in order to retain an impression of neutrality and accuracy.

Furthermore, this discourse identifies DSK as representative of a French other that is described by third parties who are presumably more familiar with the other's socialist, collectively oriented mentality. Agency and language also underscore a mismatch between DSK's image as a socialist and his private life as a wealthy individual who enjoys an extravagant lifestyle. This focus on the gap between Strauss-Kahn's public and private life reflects an ideologically rooted American mistrust of politicians as representatives of a state that is perceived as the most significant threat to the privacy and independence of US citizens.

On 23 August, the *NYT* gives the strongest agency to DSK, his lawyers, and those of Diallo. While Diallo is linked directly to her own actions, a distance between these actions and the results of the case is emphasised, making Diallo seem more removed from the article's central focus. For example:

> *For the accuser, Nafissatou Diallo, a 33-year-old immigrant, the result caps a precipitous fall. Prosecutors initially portrayed her as a credible and powerful witness, but then said that her myriad lies about her past – including a convincing, emotional but ultimately fraudulent account of*

> *being gang-raped by soldiers in Guinea – ended up undermining the case.*
> *(Eligon, 2011)*

The article also states: 'Ms. Diallo, who has made her identity public, still has a civil suit pending against Mr. Strauss-Kahn for unspecified damages.' Diallo is never directly quoted, whereas quotes from the prosecutors, lawyers for both sides, and Strauss-Kahn are featured throughout the article.

Le Monde gives Diallo agency, but this agency links Diallo to actions that undermine her credibility. For example (Lesnes, 2011): 'Elle a manifesté beaucoup d'émotion et de conviction et affirmé que sa fille de 2 ans avait été arrachée de ses bras' (*She showed a lot of emotion and conviction and affirmed that her 2-year-old daughter was torn from her arms*), and 'L'employée guinéenne n'a pas declaré toute sa paie pour pouvoir bénéficier d'un logement social. Elle a menti aux services de l'immigration' (*The Guinean employee did not declare all of her pay in order to benefit from social housing. She lied to the immigration services*). In this way, *Le Monde*'s use of agency overtly adopts a perspective that assigns blame to Diallo as an alleged victim who has lied to authorities throughout her life. In this way, *Le Monde* transparently portrays Diallo as a deceitful performer, someone whose actions contradict their words.

The newspaper's use of agency more broadly portrays Diallo as a 'guinéenne' or a member of a minority who has taken advantage of the American immigration services that provide immigrants with financial benefits. Diallo is thus represented not as an American other, but rather as a member of a minority who has been enabled by the US to operate within its culture, which embraces multiculturalism and fosters greedy individualism.

Word choice

Differences between the first set of articles run in the *NYT* and *Le Monde* underlie the latter's more critical view of DSK's lawyers and the American legal system. While the *NYT* refers to Benjamin Brafman as 'a lawyer', *Le Monde* describes him as 'une star du barreau new-yorkaise' (*a star of the New York bar*), 'l'ancien défenseur de Michael Jackson' (*the former defender of Michael Jackson*), and states of the judicial proceedings: 'La machine judiciaire est effectivement enclenchée' (*The judicial machinery is effectively engaged*). *Le Monde*'s word choice thus makes its disapproving view of the US legal system quite apparent: it is portrayed as a machine, something industrial that is a means to a commodified end, and Brafman is described as an attorney in the service of celebrities, emphasising a certain commodification and mediatisation of the US legal system. Again, *Le Monde* exhibits a more transparent perspective that highlights the mismatch between the image and the reality of Brafman and the US legal system.

Both the *NYT* and *Le Monde* reference the high price of DSK's room at the Sofitel, and, as previously mentioned, the *NYT* provides further information that attests to Strauss-Kahn's reputation as a 'caviar socialist'. Again, the latter states: 'The couple [Strauss-Kahn and Sinclair] are known to enjoy the finer things in life' and:

> *Recently, Mr. Strauss-Kahn and his wife were photographed entering an expensive Porsche in Paris belonging to one of their friends. The image of a Socialist with Porsche tastes was quickly picked up by the news media, especially the newspapers that generally support Mr. Sarkozy. (Baker and Erlanger, 2011)*

While both publications refer to the $3,000 price tag of Strauss-Kahn's hotel suite, the *NYT* includes more information that serves more explicitly to suggest the gap between DSK's political platforms and his personal actions.

The articles that break the news of the case's dismissal both reference qualities of fiction and drama within the scandal. Again, the *NYT* article on this event demonstrates a reflexive awareness of tendencies common to the scandal's mediation. As mentioned in this chapter's section on headlines, the *NYT*'s headline for this story, 'Strauss-Kahn Drama Ends With Short Final Scene', overtly likens the scandal to a drama. This comparison is continued in the first sentence of the article, which refers to the case as 'one of New York's most gripping and erratic criminal dramas'. A similar reference is again made in the article's fourth paragraph, which refers to:

> *A three-month episodic criminal investigation, each chapter offering a sensational twist on the underlying storyline: Mr. Strauss-Kahn, a man of international power and prestige, was accused of sexually assaulting an immigrant hotel housekeeper after she entered his suite to clean it. (Eligon, 2011)*

The placement of these statements at the beginning of the article makes readers aware of the dramatic, narrative qualities of the scandal that are described in the rest of the article.

In this way, the article's choice of words demonstrates its reflexive awareness of the media's role in constructing the DSK scandal. For as it reflects, it is through the media's words and coverage that the case has become a drama. At one point, a quote is even included from DSK's lawyer, William Taylor, stating: 'There was a collective rush to judgment, not only by law enforcement, but also by the media.'

Through reflexively referencing the media's role in turning this alleged assault into a scandal, the author thus acknowledges the constructions made by journalists such as himself. The words used in this article underline the author's awareness of the singular ideological standpoint and subjectivities commonly used by journalists who have turned an international news event into an international media scandal. It is this reflexive awareness that shapes his mediation of the case's dismissal and leads to the production of a news piece that subtly demonstrates how the media have come to shape the news events that they cover.

In comparison to the *NYT*, *Le Monde*'s coverage is more intensively and extensively focused on the reasons for the case's dismissal, and provides a broad overview of the case's trajectory. The contrast between the two headlines encapsulates rather well the differences between each publication's mediation of the case. Again, *Le Monde*'s headline reads: 'Le procureur recommande au juge l'abandon des poursuites contre M. Strauss-Kahn: Cyrus Vance affirme que "l'accusé a eu un rapport précipité avec la plaignante" sans que l'on puisse établir qu'il ait été "non consenti".' (*The prosecutor recommended to the judge to drop the charges against Strauss-Kahn: Cyrus Vance affirms that 'the accused precipitated a relationship with the complainant', and no one can establish that it was 'non-consensual'*). The extensive factual information conveyed through this headline starkly contrasts with the brevity of the *NYT* headline and its reference to the 'drama's' 'final scene'. As previously mentioned, a number of verbatim quotes from the verdict's text are also included in the article, thus providing a substantial fact base of relevant information.

In addition to its extensive provision of factual data, *Le Monde*'s article again draws negative attention to a number of Diallo's actions relevant to the case. For example: 'L'employée guinéenne n'a pas declaré toute sa paie pour pouvoir bénéficier d'un logement social. Elle a menti aux services de l'immigration' (*The Guinean employee did not declare all of her pay in order to benefit from social housing. She lied to immigration services*); 'les procureurs ont eu la surprise de la voir revenir en arrière le 8 juin, et reconnaître qu'elle avait fabriqué l'histoire' (*prosecutors were surprised to see her come back on 8 June, and recognise that she had fabricated the story*); and '[elle] a raconté cette fiction comme un fait avec conviction totale' (*she had recounted this fiction as fact with total conviction*). Through language used to relay accounts and accusations proffered by Diallo, *Le Monde* depicts her as a deceitful performer with financial motives. In this way, the publication portrays Diallo as connected to an American ideological framework in which minorities manipulate the law in order to obtain money for themselves.

Authenticity, national ideologies, and 'the other' in the *NYT* and *Le Monde*

Within the framework of discourse, it can be concluded that the *NYT*'s claims to authenticity are based on the appearance of accurate and neutral reporting. For example, the newspaper makes use of numerous fragmented quotes, or conveys a view through those of third parties, in order to create an impression of authenticity that is actually quite misleading. The authenticity which the *NYT* purports to offer is one which is in fact very much in line with the dominant cultural values of its US audience. Accordingly, within the framework of identity, it, by contrast, repeatedly depicts DSK as inauthentic, drawing attention to mismatches between surface and reality, or words and actions, so that he comes across as not only a hypocritical socialist who is linked with acts of sexual misconduct, but a French other.

In the context of discourse, *Le Monde*'s claims to authenticity are based on accuracy and transparency, traits that correlate directly with a French ideological emphasis on intellectual quality and cultural capital. Accuracy, as a reflection of intellectual quality, in particular reflects a French ideological appreciation of intellectual achievement, and transparency more broadly ties into a broader emphasis on cultural capital: the views conveyed through *Le Monde*'s transparency force readers to engage intellectually with the subject of DSK, thus appealing to a French audience that appreciates intellectual endeavours and possesses and values cultural capital.

Authenticity and national identity: figments of contemporary disillusionment?

The *NYT*'s tendency to disguise its high levels of fragmentation and dramatisation through giving an impression of accuracy and neutrality highlights the substantial degree of inauthenticity in the publication's coverage of the scandal. The appearance of neutrality constructed by the *NYT* is particularly problematic. One source of tension that arises is in the disjuncture between the journalist's personal point of view and that which is apparently reflected, but is in fact hidden, in the articles published. As few individuals or journalists themselves possess a viewpoint that is entirely neutral, such neutrality is almost purely constructed and inauthentic. Tactics of fragmentation and dramatisation that serve to encourage an impression of authenticity actually serve to disguise these very constructions.

Furthermore, the views of the *NYT* journalists end up subtly infusing the publication's articles, creating a narrative whose subjective qualities are more or less imperceptible to many readers. In this way, the *NYT*'s apparent neutrality is a constructed facade that can easily mislead the paper's readers. As Bennett (1992) has argued, the top–down structure of the US news media precludes the democratic engagement of audiences who are provided with information that is coded and one-sided. It can thus be said that an appearance of authenticity is deliberately used by the *NYT* as a means of mediating this one-way process.

The article run in the *NYT* on 23 August acknowledges and as such confirms the problematic presence and nature of the media's role in morphing the Strauss-Kahn case into a scandal. However, this piece does not directly pinpoint or campaign against the inauthenticity that it references, nor does it allude to specific media institutions or frameworks that can be identified as culprits: rather, the author merely attests to his own personal awareness of these factors, which serves to exempt the piece from appearing itself to contribute to the media's sensationalism and inauthenticity (Eligon, 2011). In this way, the article references the inauthenticity prevalent in the mediation of the scandal in a manner that aligns itself with authenticity. But while the article is, by acknowledging this inauthenticity, a step in the right direction towards authenticity, it also, paradoxically, attests to the impossibility of authenticity as something real in the sense that it is not constructed or contrived, particularly in a broader context in which inauthenticity is so predominant.

In the matter of authenticity, *Le Monde* is less of a paradox. The publication exhibits substantially less fragmentation than the *NYT*, and while its coverage is polemical and, in this sense, subjective and somewhat dramatised, these qualities are transparently conveyed and thus apparent to any reader. Whereas the *NYT* uses language in such a way as to disguise its various subjectivities and viewpoints, *Le Monde* encourages audience engagement through presenting opinions that, in their overtness, can serve as a stepping stone for wider public debate. The publication's use of elevated literary skills also forces readers to engage intellectually and, in these ways, *Le Monde* puts authenticity to an end that is more democratic, ultimately encouraging readers to come up with their own (and, in this sense, authentic) viewpoints. In fact, the change that ultimately took place in French public opinion (at least as reflected in opinion polls) should be seen as evidence relevant to this point: whereas initial data indicated majority views of DSK as a victim (a view exhibited by *Le Monde*), eventually polls and debates reflected public criticism of this initial response as representing a knee-jerk elitist protectionism of the politician.

The sense of nationality that is constructed via the *NYT*'s and *Le Monde*'s reporting of this case should be called into question as well. The national sense of self communicated by both publications is, in these articles, highly vague and generalised, as it consists largely of inferred differences between a national self and a national other. This actually leads us to question the validity of the notion of national identity and boundaries in an increasingly post-national, postmodern, global landscape. Strauss-Kahn was himself a global figure whose decisions as the head of the IMF affected people from the US, France, and around the world. As Strauss-Kahn's resignation from the IMF undoubtedly affected global economic policies at a crucial time in history, coverage that focuses on stereotypical depictions of the other, aiming to induce feelings of national identity and belonging, ultimately obscures matters that are of utmost global significance.

While news stories that centre on the sexual misconduct and alleged hypocrisy of a high-powered politician might, today, very well sell more newspapers than pieces that more directly cover the increasingly dire predicament of the global economy, it is the responsibility of news publications to communicate news that meaningfully informs and subsequently enables media audiences to engage as democratic, global citizens. Although authenticity and a sense of national self might play to illusions that appeal to the public in a time of change and instability, newspapers should not disseminate information which merely interests the public. Rather, news publications should operate in line with a broader vision of and commitment to the public interest, placing a more central emphasis on problems that are urgent and real.

The ways in which the two publications fall short of mediating news fully and responsibly is largely in line with the notions conveyed through this chapter's opening sections on the contemporary landscapes and national ideologies relevant to journalistic norms. However, a matter that engages related expectations and merits further discussion is, perhaps, the French public's second wave of responses, in which it rejected the more traditional, protectionist views exhibited through the likes of *Le Monde*. If one looks to similar cases in the past, such as, in particular, the Roman Polanski scandal, an initial tide of protectionist and anti-American public sentiments remained in the long term. This disjuncture could even suggest the possibility that, amidst the broader changes mentioned, French society has become more open to the positive potential of transnational exposure, whereas, conversely, an American public functioning within the context of the journalistic tendencies discussed in this chapter has, perhaps, sustained a viewpoint that is more insular and US-centric. Again, this is a matter that merits further qualitative and quantitative research.

Note

1   Differences in dates between articles covering corresponding events in *Le Monde* and the *NYT* reflect the time difference between France and the US, as well as differences in the print schedules of the two papers. Of particular note, *Le Monde* publishes a weekend edition that combines Sundays and Mondays into one newspaper.

References

Bacqué, Raphaelle, and Cypel, Sylvain (2011) 'Dominique Strauss-Kahn devait être présenté devant un juge à New York, lundi 16 mai. Le patron du FMI rejette les accusations et plaide non coupable: Les 36 heures où tout a basculé', *Le Monde*, 17 May.

Baker, Al, and Erlanger, Steven (2011) 'I.M.F. Chief, Apprehended at Airport, Is Accused of Sexual Attack', *New York Times*, 14 May.

Bennett, Lance W. (1992) 'White Noise: The Perils of Mass Mediated Democracy', *Communication Monographs*, 59: 401–6.

Bennett, Lance W. (2012) *News: The Politics of Illusion*, 9th edn (Glenview, IL: Pearson).

Benson, Rodney (2004) 'Bringing the Sociology of Media Back In', *Political Communication*, 21: 275–92.

Benson, Rodney (2009) 'What Makes News More Multiperspectival? A Field Analysis', *Journal of Empirical Research on Culture, the Media and the Arts*, 37(5–6): 402–18.

Benson, Rodney, and Hallin, Daniel C. (2007) 'How States, Markets and Globalization Shape the News: The French and American National Press, 1965–1997', *European Journal of Communication*, 22(1): 27–48.

Chalaby, Jean K. (2004) 'Scandal and the Rise of Investigative Reporting in France', *American Behavioral Scientist*, 47(9): 1194–1207.

Eligon, John (2011) 'Strauss-Kahn Drama Ends With Short Final Scene', *New York Times*, 23 Aug.

Gamson, Joshua (2004) 'Normal Sins: Sex Scandal Narratives as Institutional Morality Tales', in Paul Apostolidis and Juliet A. Williams (eds), *Public Affairs: Politics in the Age of Sex Scandals* (Durham, NC: Duke University Press), 39–68.

Goffman, Erving (1959) *The Presentation of Self in Everyday Life* (Garden City, NY: Doubleday).

Harwood, Richard C. (2004) 'In Search of Authenticity: Public Trust and the News Media', *National Civic Review*, 93(3): 1–15.

Hoffmann, Stanley (1995) 'Battling Clichés', *French Historical Studies*, 19(2): 321–9.

Lamont, Michèle (1992) *Money, Morals, and Manners: The Culture of the French and American Upper-Middle Class* (Chicago: University of Chicago Press).

Lesnes, Corine (2011) 'Le procurer recommande au juge l'abandon des poursuites contre M. Strauss-Kahn: Cyrus Vance affirme que "l'accusé a eu un rapport précipté avec la plaignant" sans que l'on puisse établis qu'il ait été "non consenti"', *Le Monde*, 24 Aug.

McGregor, Sue L. T. (2003) 'Critical Discourse Analysis: A Primer', *Kappa Omicron Nu Forum*, 15: 1: http://www.kon.org/archives/forum/15-1/mcgregorcda.html (accessed Sept. 2012).

Richardson, Kay (2001) 'Broadcast Political Talk: A Discourse of Licensed Inauthenticity?', *Communication Review*, 4(4): 481–98.

Sowerwine, Charles (2001) *France since 1870: Culture, Politics and Society* (New York: Palgrave).

Van Djik, Teun A. (2009) 'Critical Discourse Studies: A Sociocognitive Approach', in Ruth Wodak and Michael Meyer (eds), *Methods of Critical Discourse Analysis* (London: Sage), 62–85.

Whitman, James Q. (2004) 'Two Western Cultures of Privacy: Dignity versus Liberty', *Yale Law Journal*, 113(6): 1151–1221.

9

Public Interest and Individual Taste in Disclosing an Irish Minister's Illness

Kevin Rafter

The media's changed approach to disclosing political illness is very clearly evident from the coverage of the illnesses of two British prime ministers: Winston Churchill and Tony Blair. Churchill's stroke in June 1953 went unreported. The absence of media comment was achieved not simply because the illness was kept secret within a close political circle. Three newspaper proprietors actively agreed to withhold the truth about Churchill's health from the British public. Given the scale of this collusion between members of the political and media elites, it is little wonder that the episode has been described as 'one of the most audacious cover-ups in modern political history' (Price, 2010: 146–7). It would be difficult to argue that Churchill's illness was a private matter, as the stroke prevented him from adequately doing his job – a key point in this chapter that considers the right of media organisations to disclose the private health matters of politicians. Peter Hennessy has written about the 'near senility' of Churchill a year following his stroke, whilst also quoting Harold Macmillan's alarming description of the Prime Minister:

> Churchill is now often speechless in Cabinet, alternatively, he rambles about nothing. Sometimes he looks as if he is going to have another stroke … He was always an egoist, but a magnanimous one. Now he has become almost a monomaniac. (2000: 196)

In his diary, Macmillan also wrote about 'a kind of conspiracy we were all in' (Hennessy, 2000: 196) – half a century later this type of concealment is no longer possible in Britain. There is now an acceptance that medical

165

information about senior politicians should not be withheld from the public – in part due to greater openness with the public and in part due to the advance of communications methods which make keeping secrets much more difficult. In the latter regard, when Tony Blair was taken ill in 2003 there was widespread coverage to the effect that the Prime Minister had suffered a heart scare.

There has been longer acceptance in the US of the public's right to know about the health of their elected representatives. Revelations about the level of concealment of the medical condition of President Woodrow Wilson, who suffered a stroke in 1919, was an influencing factor. The extent and seriousness of Wilson's health problems were withheld not just from the American public but also from members of his cabinet. Indeed, documents released in December 2006 led one authority to conclude: 'This is the worst instance of presidential disability we've ever had. We stumbled along … [for eighteen months] without a fully functioning president' (Milton Cooper, 2007). Three decades after Wilson's illness was withheld, news that Dwight Eisenhower had suffered a heart attack was widely reported in September 1955. It should be noted, however, that White House staff still sought to manage information about the President's condition so as to miminise political damage to his position.

Disclosure in the US extends beyond elected representatives to incorporate the principle that the public has a right to know about the health of a candidate seeking political office. Many well-known figures have been questioned in public about their medical history. Examples in recent times include Senator John McCain in his White House bid in 2008. Had he been successful, McCain would have been the oldest first-term president in American history. On 14 May 2008, *Time* magazine published an article under the headline, 'How Healthy is John McCain?', which detailed the Republican candidate's recent medical history including specifics about surgery for skin cancer. Readers were informed that the McCain campaign 'says it expects to offer enough documents and medical opinions to lay to rest any concerns about the candidate's condition'. Others who have faced similar levels of scrutiny include Dick Cheney as vice-president to George W. Bush, and Rudy Giuliani when he was mayor of New York.

Medical information that reaches the public domain can obviously be damaging for the individual concerned, as was the case for Thomas Eagleton in the 1972 presidential contest. The career of the Democratic vice-presidential candidate ended with release of information that he had undergone electroshock therapy. In American politics, however, a candidate's health is not only an issue in determining their electability, but once in office holders of political positions are now obliged to accept that their medical records are a matter of public information. In this regard, the results of the 'first routine periodic physical examination' of President Barack Obama was published on the White House website in February 2010.[1] A subsequent report from his physician – which included specific detail on Obama's cholesterol and blood pressure – declared him 'fit for duty and predicted he would remain so for the remainder of his presidency'.[2]

Controversy over the issue of placing a politician's medical history in the public domain versus their right to keep their health private has not just been a British or American dilemma. For example, the suppression of information concerning the well-being of François Mitterrand when he was president of France ultimately made its way to the European Court of Human Rights. The Court concluded that it is the duty of the media to report on the health of political figures in certain circumstances (*Plon (Société) v France*, EHRR 2004). Similar debates have featured in several countries in more recent times including in Canada (Smith, 2011) and India (Jagannathan, 2011).

There was considerable debate in India in August 2011 when the Congress party confirmed that Sonia Gandhi had been diagnosed with a medical condition requiring surgery abroad. The lack of information about the nature of Gandhi's medical diagnosis led one commentator to ask a question that has universal application: 'How can the nation's most powerful political leader, virtual chief executive of the ruling party, not let us know that there was something for us to be concerned about?' (Jagannathan, 2011). Providing an answer to such a question in the US or in the United Kingdom – to go by recent cases mentioned previously – would seem fairly straightforward. The public right to know overrides the individual politician's personal privacy. A more nuanced debate, however, arose in Canada in the case of NDP leader Jack Layton who, while ill, sought election as Prime Minister in May 2011. While revealing that he had been treated for cancer, Layton refused to discuss the nature of his illness, and as the *Vancouver Sun* noted on 22 August 2012: 'A year after his death Canadians are still in the dark about what actually killed Jack Layton, who mere weeks before dying had asked voters to let him lead Canada.'

Cultural differences alongside specific media systems and political contexts obviously influence attitudes towards public disclosure of a political leader's health matters. The availability of the internet has made concealment more difficult even for repressive regimes. For example, in late July 2012 it was revealed that the Ethiopian leader Meles Zenawi was taking 'sick leave' to deal with an unspecified illness. The official line from the Ethiopian government was that Zenawi was recovering and would be returning to work in a short space of time, but rumours quickly spread on dissident websites that Zenawi had cancer. He died in a Belgian hospital some weeks later.

These different national experiences raise the issue of why and when health matters are considered suitable matters for public disclosure. Many news organisations subscribe to the view that private lives should remain private unless public trust is broken because certain standards of behaviour have not been met (integrity) or because private actions have conflicted with public positions (hypocrisy) (Sanders, 2008: 86). More often than not, controversy emerges over exposure of marital infidelities, but, in the area of health, there remains a contested dividing line between the public's right to know and a politician's right to privacy.

Providing answers is not straightforward – and raises editorial and ethical challenges for news journalists. Developing 'a coherent expectation as to what represents appropriate ethical journalistic performance' (Starck, 2001: 145) involves ethical considerations beyond legislation and regulatory codes. The difficulty for journalists and news organisations is that wider public consideration of these issues is generally framed within the context of discussions of privacy laws and restrictions on reporting. But unlike in the case of other public figures – celebrities, for example – politicians, with their ability to make decisions over people's lives, are in a different space. It is hard not to accept that voters should be aware of the medical condition of candidates who seek to run their country, or should be reassured that an elected office holder is healthy enough to undertake the duties of that office.

The following sections of this chapter offer a specific case study that addresses many of the questions concerning the news media, politicians, and medical information. It does so by examining in detail the experience in Ireland in late 2009 when the broadcasting of information about the health of the country's Finance Minister, Brian Lenihan, became a matter of public debate. In particular, the chapter examines the television news broadcast at the source of the controversy. Unlike examples from other countries, this Irish case was examined by the regulatory authorities.

Case study: TV3 in Ireland

Brian Lenihan, who died on 10 June 2011 from pancreatic cancer at the age of 52, had in the post-2008 period achieved international recognition well beyond that normally received by a public office holder who was neither a head of government nor a head of state. This strong recognition factor was largely on account of Lenihan's role as Ireland's Finance Minister at the time of the dramatic collapse of the Irish economy. Lenihan was appointed Finance Minister in May 2008 at a time when the economic troubles of Ireland's national fiscal position and banking system were first emerging into the public domain (Rafter, 2011). Under his stewardship, a state-supported scheme for the Irish banking system was introduced which guaranteed the assets and liabilities of the six main financial institutions to the order of €440bn.

This controversial policy intervention did not, however, stave off ongoing difficulties. By late 2010 the banking and fiscal situation in Ireland was judged to have reached the point at which external intervention was necessary, and the increasingly beleaguered Irish government agreed a €85bn bailout deal with the International Monetary Fund and the European institutions. Set against this background it was not unsurprising that the incumbent coalition government was swept from power in parliamentary elections in February 2011. Lenihan's Fianna Fail party suffered dramatic seat losses. The outgoing Finance Minister was returned as his party's sole representative in the Dublin region although it was clear that he was seriously ill during the campaign. Despite the government's record – and the austerity policies implemented – there remained considerable public sympathy for a popular politician, coupled with widespread acknowledgement of the fortitude with which he was battling his illness.

The first public indication that Lenihan had medical issues emerged on 16 December 2009. The Finance Minister was absent from a parliamentary debate on a draconian budget that he had announced the previous week. The limited information released – and published initially online and reported by the broadcast media – was repeated the following day, 17 December 2009, when the *Irish Times* reported that the Minister was undergoing a minor medical procedure which 'had been brought forward' – he had been due to go into hospital for 'an elective treatment' – although the spokesperson declined to comment on the condition. Other newspaper articles contained greater detail. The *Irish Independent* reported on 17 December 2009 that Lenihan had admitted himself to hospital early 'after suffering discomfort and missing out on sleep with a suspected hernia problem', but that 'government officials and aides stressed … there was no great concern over his medical condition'. In subsequent days it was reported that Lenihan had returned home from hospital.

On 24 December 2009, TV3, the national commercial television service in Ireland, learned from a source that Lenihan's illness was far more serious than had previously been acknowledged. It was subsequently reported, for example in the *Sunday Business Post*, 3 January 2010, that rumours had been circulating in media and political circles in the days prior to Christmas to the effect that Lenihan was more seriously ill than previously reported, but that journalists had failed to substantiate these stories. Hanlon and his station's political editor Ursula Halligan were able to confirm that the hernia story was incorrect and that, in fact, the Minister had been diagnosed as suffering from pancreatic cancer. Halligan contacted the Department of Finance, which expressed concern at the broadcasting of the news on Christmas Eve. In light of this concern, TV3 decided to hold the story until 26 December 2009. Lenihan had already informed certain people about his diagnosis, including Taoiseach (Prime Minister) Brian Cowen and businessman Peter Sutherland. But, as he subsequently explained, he had decided not to tell some members of his immediate family until after Christmas.

On 26 December 2009, TV3 told the Department of Finance it was planning to broadcast the story in its 5.30p.m. news bulletin. The Department indicated that it would prefer the story not to be broadcast, but in light of TV3's decision a holding statement was released to the station which neither confirmed nor denied the story. The story led TV3's main evening news at 5.30p.m. on 26 December 2009. The segment dealing with Minister Lenihan's medical condition lasted seven minutes and four seconds, and was divided into three elements: two live interviews and a prepared package. The bulletin structure had been agreed by senior editorial staff so that 'in each of the packages the tone was serious and within the confines of journalistic objectivity, sympathetic to the issues' (TV3, 2010).

The bulletin opened with the programme presenter Colette Fitzpatrick revealing the dramatic news: 'TV3 News has learned that the Finance Minister Brian Lenihan has been diagnosed with cancer. Our political editor Ursula Halligan is at Government Buildings this evening. Ursula, how serious is this?' Halligan's initial contribution was to acknowledge the question – 'Certainly, Colette, it is very serious' – following which she recalled that Lenihan had been taken to hospital prior to Christmas:

> We all understood it was a minor procedure. It now turns out the problem is much more serious than a hernia. TV3 understands that initial tests revealed that the minister is suffering from a malignant tumor. The precise location, and severity of which, will be assessed in the next few days as he undergoes more tests.

The interview confirmed the nature of the illness, although no additional information was provided about the Minister's condition. Indeed, at no stage during the broadcast did any of the four participants express an opinion on the actual diagnosis. The first interview – between Fitzpatrick and Halligan – avoided speculation about the medical – or political – implications of the revelation. Halligan observed in response to a question about possible political consequences that it was 'far too early to talk about what this means, where it might go, because of course the Minister continues to undergo further tests'.

The interview with Halligan was followed by a second live interview in which Fitzpatrick spoke with Professor John Crown, a consultant oncologist in Dublin. The decision to interview a medical expert was taken, TV3 said later, in line with its normal practice of providing expert background information on complex issues 'to ensure a thorough, objective and impartial report' (TV3, 2010). Crown had been contacted on 24 December 2009 and informed that a story was being prepared about a politician who had been diagnosed with cancer. He agreed to be interviewed so long as he was not asked to comment on the illness of any individual, but was invited to provide only general information about the disease. In explaining his approach, Crown (2010) noted: 'The disclosure that a well-known figure had been diagnosed with cancer can increase public awareness, encouraging people to avoid risk factors to the disease, and highlight the need for greater investment in research and in treatment.'

In linking between the Halligan and Crown interviews, Fitzpatrick confirmed for the first time that the illness was pancreatic cancer:

> Well, TV3 understands that the minister has been diagnosed with pancreatic cancer. John Crown is a consultant in oncology at St. Vincent's Hospital in Dublin. John, what does a diagnosis of pancreatic cancer mean?

Crown provided general and factual medical information on the disease including the implications of both timely and untimely diagnosis. During his interview Crown did not refer to Minister Lenihan, nor did he refer to a prognosis of any specific patient, noting simply:

> Most patients are not candidates for surgery; the disease has spread a little bit. And under those circumstances the aims of the treatment are really about more in the area of control, comfort, survival, prolongation, rather than outright cure.

The final element of the coverage was a prepared package on Lenihan's role as Finance Minister, which included archive footage. The decision to include this report was taken to highlight the central role that the Finance Minister played in national life and to reinforce the public-interest argument for the broadcast. The package was complimentary about Lenihan's performance and concluded with the words: 'Few would disagree with Brian Lenihan's ability to tackle the many economic problems he has encountered over the past eighteen months. The hope now is that the new challenge he is facing can also be overcome.'

Reaction and fallout

In the aftermath of the TV3 broadcast on 26 December 2009, Brian Lenihan maintained silence. On 4 January 2010 his officials issued a media statement, following which he undertook a radio interview and briefed political journalists. He stated that he would not be making a formal complaint to the Irish broadcasting regulator, adding: 'It's an issue on which journalists and media organizations will reflect on themselves. It's a bit like politics, journalism – the only rule appears to be that there are no rules' (quoted in the Irish Times, 5 January 2010). While Lenihan said he was 'not concerned about it [the broadcast] in a personal sense' – which, as discussed below, had implications for the scope of the subsequent regulatory inquiry – he did question the timing of the report:

> It is in the public interest that people know the state of health of the Minister for Finance and I quite accept that. On the other hand, I would question whether there was any real interest served in disclosing it on St Stephen's Day as distinct from January 4th. (Quoted in the Irish Times, 5 January 2010)

The Minister's 400-word statement confirmed the TV3 story that in the week before Christmas 2009 he had received a cancer diagnosis. In the intervening period there had been significant public discussion about Lenihan's illness. The initial reaction was defined by universal sympathy for the Minister and considerable criticism of the broadcaster. It is the latter reaction that is of interest in this chapter.

TV3's main television competitor, the state-owned RTÉ, followed up the initial report of Lenihan's illness later on 26 December. RTÉ did not name the original source of the initial information, nor did it indicate that it had itself confirmed the accuracy of the medical information, stating: 'The Department of Finance had refused to comment on reports that Minister Brian Lenihan has been diagnosed with cancer and would be undergoing further tests' (RTÉ, 26 December 2009). The broadcaster quoted a Department of Finance spokesman who repeated the statement provided to TV3. The Government Press Secretary was also quoted as stating: 'Any Minister's health affairs were a personal matter.' In a report the following day,[3] RTÉ repeated its refusal to comment while also now identifying TV3 as the source for the original story. The report also noted: 'Government sources said the reports represented an unwarranted intrusion.' Interestingly, in initial newspaper reports following up the TV3 story, the nature of source confirmation varied from attributing the information to its own 'authoritative sources' (*Sunday Times*, 27 December 2009) to a reference to the Minister's 'suspected illness' (*Irish Independent*, 28 December 2009).

There was limited on-the-record political reaction. Lenihan's constituency colleagues from two opposition parties (Ireland has a multi-seat electoral system) issued brief statements. They criticised TV3 for 'an appalling invasion of privacy' and coverage that was 'absolutely inappropriate' (quoted in the *Irish Times*, 28 December 2009). The report was met with a barrage of commentator criticism ranging from 'disgraceful' (Tom McGurk, *Sunday Business Post*, 3 January 2010) to 'an insensitive invasion of a popular politician's privacy' (Michael Foley, *Irish Times*, 30 December 2009). The broadcast was discussed in early January 2010 on TV3's nightly current affairs programme. The presenter – veteran journalist Vincent Browne – disagreed with the approach taken by his employer, stating: 'I think the timing was wrong and it should have been delayed' (quoted in the *Sun*, 9 January 2010). As well as hostility from other media organisations, TV3 received hundreds of complaints from viewers. Many critical letters were published in the national newspapers, where the focus was on privacy and the timing of the broadcast. In the words of one letter-writer quoted in the *Irish Times*, 29 December 2009: 'The announcement of a private and personal situation by TV3 ... truly marks a watershed for the fourth estate in the country.'

There were, however, a number of supporting voices. In the *Irish Independent* (5 January 2009), in an article headlined 'The Abyss Beckons After Ignorant Hysterical Lynching of TV3', columnist Kevin Myers congratulated TV3 for 'their courage and their sensitivity in breaking the dreadful news'. He argued that it was a journalistic duty to report such a story – and that suppression of the truth should be considered only when the life of a kidnap victim was at stake or in matters of national security. Taking issue with political figures who had lambasted TV3 on privacy grounds, Myers noted: 'He is a politician; we are in the media. We report on you. No minister is sick in "private", and no-one is taking advantage of anyone.' These differing ethical perspectives highlight the universality of the issues in the Lenihan case and the conflicts that emerge for journalists in fulfilling their multiple roles, including journalists as citizens and journalists as seekers of the truth (Harcup, 2002: 101).

The Compliance Committee of the Broadcasting Authority of Ireland (BAI) has a statutory role in adjudicating complaints against Irish broadcasters. In the Lenihan–TV3 case, they received 88 written complaints, 14 of which were considered by the Compliance Committee in the context of existing broadcasting legislation and the published code of standards. Section 48(1) of Ireland's Broadcasting Act 2009 requires that news reports are fair to all interests concerned and are 'presented in an objective and impartial manner' (Broadcasting Act, 2009). Section 3.5.2 of the BAI's Code of Programme Standards requires: 'Factual programming shall not contain material that could reasonably be expected to cause undue distress or offence unless it is editorially justified and in the public interest' (BAI, 2007).

The complainants objected to the TV3 news broadcast broadly on the grounds that it invaded privacy, that it was inappropriate to report on health matters, and that the timing of the broadcast was ill-judged. The emphasis is similar to the situation in the United Kingdom with press complaints, where privacy cases 'generate most public concern' (Frost, 2004: 101). According to the adjudication of the Compliance Committee (BAI, 2010), complaints labelled the broadcast 'sensationalism at its worst and grossly unethical', 'a brand of cheap and tacky journalism', and 'not in the public interest'. In its submission to the Compliance Committee,

TV3 (2010) acknowledged that the news report had 'caused genuine upset' and accepted that the timing was a 'sensitive and contentious matter'. Nevertheless, the station considered the timing legitimate and noted that, whilst the item was of a sensitive nature, the station itself was not in a position to choose when news emerged. TV3 argued that its motivation 'was entirely driven by its professional obligation to report the news as and when it happens, in an objective, impartial and fair manner as required by Statute and by TV3's license'.

The station further argued that the report was a legitimate news story supported by two essential elements – first, it was in the public interest; and, second, it was professionally sourced. In terms of the public-interest argument, TV3 reasserted its initial view that, as Lenihan held the important public position of Minister for Finance at a time of national financial crisis, 'the diagnosis of a serious condition may relate to Minister Lenihan's performance of his official duties as Minister for Finance either now or in the future'. TV3 argued that the story was 'sourced without impropriety' and was based on a minimum of two sources which were independent of each other. The station asserted that it had dealt only with the appropriate channels in the Department of Finance, adding: 'There was no intrusion into the family life or personal background of the Minister and no filming of the Minister, his family or his home.' The station acknowledged that 'journalism is an imperfect trade and TV3 accepts that others may reasonably have different views as to how the news should be presented'.

In its published judgment, the Compliance Committee found that the report was in the public interest; was factual and accurate; was fair, objective, and impartial; and that the presentation style was professional and respectful of the Minister's role (BAI, 2010). The judgment acknowledged that certain viewers may have disliked the news report and would have found it offensive, but it also noted that 'such reaction in itself cannot determine whether the broadcast was not in compliance with the Codes'. It accepted the 'pivotal role' of the Minister for Finance in government and noted that, 'given the current economic crisis, the significance of the role is further heightened'. In this context, the health of the holder of the office 'was in the public interest'.

The Compliance Committee also considered whether broadcasting about the type of illness and discussing it on air were editorially justified and in the public interest. The Committee acknowledged the views of complainants that the news in the TV3 report was shocking, but concluded nonetheless that the report was in keeping with the legal and regulatory requirements in terms of editorial impartiality. The Committee also noted that the context of the TV3 report was, at all times, the political position of Minister Lenihan, and that he was offered a right-of-reply through his office. The Committee recorded that the Minister's health was in fact an ongoing news story, in that he had been hospitalised before Christmas. It thus concluded: 'Therefore, the news story reported by TV3 was based on the developing facts of the actual illness of the Minister for Finance, an issue which was already in the public domain. It was an on-going news story.'

Two issues were not considered – first, whether the broadcast was an unwarranted invasion of privacy; and, second, the timing of the broadcast. The regulations governing the operation of the Compliance Committee mean that it is able to assess complaints of unwarranted invasion of an individual's privacy only when they are made by the actual individual concerned, or by someone nominated by him/her. As such, the issue of privacy was not considered because neither Lenihan nor his immediate family had complained. The Compliance Committee noted that it had no power, nor should it have the power, to consider the timing of the broadcast in the light of the editorial independence of the broadcaster and its right to freedom of expression. To have done so, the Committee asserted, would have taken its remit into the realm of editorialising. Interestingly, it did acknowledge that there might have been specific circumstances in which it might have set aside considerations of editorial independence, as well as the principle that broadcasters are free to determine the context of news reports. The personal impact of the broadcast's timing could have been considered if Lenihan, a member of his family or somebody nominated by them, had complained, but 'no such complaint was made and therefore there is no other context or legislative basis for the Committee to consider the timing of the report in this instance' (BAI, 2010: 77).

Conclusion

In the aftermath of the TV3 disclosure, one of Brian Lenihan's cabinet colleagues, Mary Hanafin, then Minister for Tourism, Culture and Sport, was quoted in the *Irish Independent*, 1 January 2010, as asserting that: 'Even public people are entitled to their privacy and are entitled to be sick in private.' The former point is certainly true – individuals do not surrender every aspect of their private lives on becoming public figures or elected representatives. Most reasonable media organisations would support the view that private lives should remain private unless public trust is broken or private actions conflict with public positions. But Hanafin's latter point – privacy over medical matters – is more nuanced in the case of politicians who, in this specific aspect of disclosure, are a separate category of public person. This distinction is made because value is placed on having informed citizens and on knowing that those acting on behalf of those same citizens are actually capable of carrying out their job. The hostility heaped upon TV3 in Ireland was driven not just by the timing of the Lenihan broadcast but, more specifically, by a belief in separating the private sphere of public figures from the public domain. This issue features widely in numerous international debates about what is understood by public figures' entitlement to privacy. The individual's right to privacy sits alongside the right to freedom of expression and the right to know about matters of public interest and importance. These are often competing interests – and the rights involved have to be balanced. So, then, at what point does illness require disclosure? In none of the national cases mentioned at the start of this chapter – nor in the detailed case study presented from Ireland – would regulations or ethical codes offer adequate guidance. The balance must lie with the politician and an acceptance that in such cases public interest negates privacy considerations. So, directly addressing Hanafin's assertion – yes, politicians have a right to be sick in private, but politicians, by nature of their role and wider responsibilities to citizens, lose the right to withhold disclosure of their medical condition.

Notes

1   http://www.whitehouse.gov/sites/default/files/rss_viewer/potus_med_exam_feb2010.pdf (accessed Aug. 2011).
2   http://www.thedailybeast.com/articles/2011/10/31/obama-deemed-in-excellent-health-after-latest-physical-exam.html (accessed July 2012).
3   http://www.rte.ie/news/2009/1227/lenihanb.html (accessed July 2011).

References

Broadcasting Act (2009) Available at http://www.irishstatutebook.ie/2009/en/act/pub/0018/index.html (accessed Sept. 2012).

Broadcasting Authority of Ireland (2007) *Code of Programme Standards*: http://www.bai.ie/wordpress/wp-content/uploads/bci_cops_Mar07.pdf (accessed Sept. 2012).

Broadcasting Authority of Ireland (2010) *Compliance Committee: Broadcasting Complaints Decisions* (Dublin: BAI).

Crown, J. (2010) 'The Story behind Brian Lenihan, TV3 and me': www.johncrown.ie (accessed Aug. 2011).

Frost, C. (2004) 'The Press Complaints Commission: A Study of Ten Years of Adjudications on Press Complaints', *Journalism Studies*, 5(1): 101–14.

Harcup, T. (2002) 'Journalists and Ethics: The Quest for a Collective Voice', *Journalism Studies*, 3(1): 101–14.

Hennessy, P. (2000) *The Prime Minister: The Office and its Holder since 1945* (London: Allen Lane).

Jagannathan, R. (2011) 'Sonia Gandhi's Health Can't Be a State Secret: It's Not about Privacy', *First Post*, 5 Aug.

Milton Cooper, J. (2007) 'A President's Illness Kept Under Wraps: Woodrow Wilson's Deteriorating Health Detailed in Doctor's Correspondence': http://www.woodrowwilson.org/a-presidents-illness-kept-under-wraps (accessed July 2012).

Price, L. (2010) *Where Power Lies: Prime Ministers v the Media* (London: Simon & Schuster).

Rafter, K. (2011) *The Road to Power: How Fine Gael won in 2011* (Dublin: New Island).

RTÉ (2009) 'Lenihan Report an '"Unwarranted Intrusion"': http://www.rte.ie/news/2009/1227/lenihanb.html (accessed July 2011).

Sanders, K. (2008) *Ethics and Journalism* (London: Sage).

Smith, J. (2011) 'Questions over Layton's Health: Does the Public Really Need to Know?', *The Star* (24 March): www.thestar.com/news/canada/2011/03/24/questions_over_laytons_health_does_the_public_really_need_to_know.html (accessed Aug. 2011).

Starck, K. (2001) 'What's Right/Wrong with Journalism Ethics Research?', *Journalism Studies*, 2(1): 133–52.

TV3 (2010) 'Submission to Broadcasting Authority of Ireland Compliance Committee' (copy in possession of the author).

10

Visible 'Evidence' in TV News: Regulating Privacy in the Public Interest?

Tim Dwyer

Introduction

As a result of the landmark Leveson Inquiry into the culture, practices, and ethics of the press, it would not be an overly dramatic prognosis to state that a pall has been cast over media and journalism across the world. Indeed, many of the witnesses at the Inquiry have contributed to a general critique of the notion that contemporary commercial news journalism can be expected to unquestioningly act as a fourth estate on behalf of some generic public interest (Fenton, 2012; Freedman, 2012; Kellner, 2012; Leveson, 2012). As Fenton argues:

> *The phone hacking saga shows that a marketised and corporatised media cannot be relied on to deliver the conditions for deliberative democracy to flourish ... when markets fail or come under threat ... ethical journalistic practice is swept aside in pursuit of competitive or financial gain ... we need a whole new framework for news in the public interest. (2012: 3)*

Validating this report card, and in anticipation of being superseded by a new body to be recommended by Justice Leveson's Inquiry, the UK's Press Complaints Commission (PCC) announced in March 2012 that it 'had moved into a transitional phase' pending its replacement by a new regulatory body.[1] But these are not isolated national events; they are part of the global restructuring of the news media industries. At the same time as these events have been taking place in the UK, in the southern hemisphere, Australia's regulatory institutions have been under review, with both the general electronic media regulator, the Australian Communications and Media Authority (ACMA), and the print media regulator, the Australian Press Council (APC), awaiting a government response to separate inquiry processes DBCDE (2012) and the Finkelstein Report (2012).

The concerns discussed in this chapter offer a snapshot of news media conditions and ethical trends that are observable in many contemporary media systems. Indeed, the news narrative in this chapter will be all too familiar to readers around the globe. My suggestion is that privacy-related regulatory problems depend on the medium and the news genre, and that these will vary between media markets in specific national contexts. For example, privacy-intruding sex scandals in the UK's 'red tops' or in US tabloids will be represented differently from the less racy accounts which appear in the broadsheets in these countries, as will their packaging in 24-hour cable channels and other commercial free-to-air television outlets, such as the one that is the focus of this chapter.

As Smith Fullerton and Patterson argue elsewhere in this volume, disclosure of personal facts in news-crime-scandal stories tend to be represented differently across different cultures. They note that British, Dutch, and Swedish reporting of the same crime will diverge in the extent to which the private details of the accused persons are published. Similarly, Solove advocates a cross-cultural understanding of our conceptions of privacy in which different societies 'protect against privacy problems differently' because of the divergent values 'ascribed both to privacy and to the interests that conflict with it' (2008: 184). In a related conception of privacy, Nissenbaum has developed a 'framework of contextual integrity' in which 'context-relative informational norms' apply to 'historical, cultural and even geographic contingencies' (2010: 3) evolving over time in different societies.

The oft-seen practice of media 'outing', the basis of the media practice under the microscope in this chapter, can also be seen to vary across national media cultures. Solove, having reviewed the literature examining the social norms behind sexual outing, concludes that 'the revelation of people's personal secrets often does damage to the individuals without having much effect on changing norms' (2008: 144). And, of course, the assumptions made in this kind of framing are themselves ethically suspect. But whether the motives and meanings are interpreted as being related to the public interest, public shaming, or other normative constructs, we can surmise that the news disclosure practices of the commercial television station in question, and the regulatory response they provoke, will be characteristic of broadly similar media cultures. In this case, a comparison with the UK is likely to be more closely analogous than with, for example, the media cultures and practices in Nordic nations, the Netherlands, or France.

Outing the minister

In May 2010, David Campbell, the transport minister in the former New South Wales Labour government led by then Premier Kristina Keneally, announced that he was resigning as a Minister for 'personal reasons'. His resignation came shortly before an evening news bulletin on the Channel Seven commercial, free-to-air television station outed the minister as leading a 'double life' as a gay man for 25 years. The TV news item included poor-quality video surveillance images, most likely taken by private investigators and later acquired by the Seven Network, of Mr Campbell leaving a gay sauna club, 'Ken's of Kensington', in the darkness.

The incident quickly escalated to become a *cause célèbre* for privacy and gay rights advocates: it served to highlight the fact that Australia has no general tort for breach of privacy either at common law or in statute (continuing to be hotly debated in the wake of the *News of the World* scandal, with a statute under consideration by the Federal Government), and it also pointed to shortcomings in the rather flimsy protections offered under the *Commercial Television Industry Code of Practice* (Free TV, 2010), registered and supervised by ACMA. Most media commentators viewed the TV news story as an attack on the private life of a gay man, one which had nothing to do with journalism 'in the public interest' as understood, for example, in the context of analyses of media governance and citizenship (Feintuck, 2004; Feintuck and Varney, 2006: 117–25).

My argument in this chapter is that the journalist concerned (and Seven Network in broadcasting the item) had acted unethically in assembling a patchwork of assertions and smear in order to carry out a media scalping. However, before the surreptitious footage and the story could be aired, they needed to wait for circumstances that would allow them to use a 'public-interest' justification. Campbell had heard that Seven were intending to air the footage and resigned. But it was two days later, and one hour before the broadcast announcing his resignation, that he was asked to comment. The Minister's announcement of his resignation had provided the trigger, in the station's view, to run the story, as the *Sydney Morning Herald* reported on 11 February 2011.

The wider context of this matter was that the embattled Keneally government had been caught in a series of media scandals, and one more was always going to inflict damage. Ultimately, the regulator found that there had been no breach of the TV industry's codes of practice. For many, though, the *Commercial Television Industry Code of Practice* had clearly failed: the key privacy provision in the code had allowed the broadcaster to defend its actions by way of a specious 'public-interest' claim.

The broader argument is that the regulatory failure evident in this case was enabled through and by discursive conditions in commercial media industries and represented in their co-regulatory code: that is, contemporary moral positions held by certain news media workers in relation to personal privacy, coupled with the prevailing market-based priorities in the competitive free-to-air television sector in Australia (Spence et al., 2011; Whittle and Cooper, 2009).

The regulator investigates

Under the TV sector's co-regulatory framework, complaints lodged by concerned viewers (not by ex-Minister David Campbell) with ACMA were required to be adjudicated, as the complainants were dissatisfied with the first-instance responses that they had received from the broadcaster.

ACMA received two unresolved complaints in relation to the broadcast on *Seven Nightly News*, on 20 May 2010: the first of these three weeks after the broadcast, and the second six months later. The first complainant stated:

> *I feel Channel 7's choice to expose him was a provocative act which was intended to cause severe ridicule to him, on the grounds of his sexual preference ... there has been a homophobic element ... this was a private matter and this type of exposure was likely to force his resignation due to his embarrassment.*

The second complainant said: 'I struggle to comprehend how [the Minister's] sexuality could make him unfit for any of the offices he held during his time as a Minister of the NSW State Parliament' (ACMA, 2010: 1–2).

Applying a common-law, 'ordinary, reasonable viewer' test, ACMA found the words in the broadcast were unlikely to provoke the required threshold of 'intense dislike', 'serious contempt', and 'severe ridicule' specified in section 1.9.6 of the *Commercial Television Industry Code of Practice*. This provides that 'a licensee may not broadcast a program … which is likely in all the circumstances, to: provoke or perpetuate intense dislike, serious contempt or severe ridicule … on the grounds of sexual preference' (Free TV, 2010: 3). ACMA argued that, for the 'ordinary reasonable viewer', the news bulletin would simply convey the fact that the Minister had resigned because of the revelation of his visit to the gay sauna, and that this would be seen as related to his performance of his duties 'in matters of politics, government and public administration', and to certain political incidents in the lead-up to his resignation. Notwithstanding this construction, the regulator noted:

> *Through the detailed description of services offered by that club, and the inference that the Minister had attended it on more than one occasion, the bulletin also strongly implied that he had engaged in extra-marital homosexual activity. In common parlance, it 'outed' the Minister. (ACMA, 2010: 4)*

The regulator found no breach of the code's provision on sexist vilification.

The main privacy regulations, which are contained in the *Commercial Television Industry Code of Practice*, were relied upon to assess whether the Minister's privacy was breached. Clause 4.3.5 states:

> *In broadcasting news and current affairs programs, licensees: must not use material relating to a person's personal or private affairs, or which invades an individual's privacy, other than where there is an identifiable public interest reason for the material to be broadcast. (Free TV, 2010: 22)*

The broadcaster argued in its submission to the regulator that the privacy guidelines accompanying the code envisage a range of circumstances justifying media intrusion into an individual's privacy, including 'matters of politics, government and public administration' (ACMA, 2010: 7). The latter circumstances echo the public-interest 'privilege' defences available at common law for defamation. Seven defended their report using a number of public-interest-style justifications based on the Minister's past actions and behaviour. These include the manner in which he had managed a major train project and motorway incident in his capacity of Transport Minister; the need for the Minister to have 'secrets' as a former

Police Minister, thus making him susceptible to blackmail; his presentation of himself to the electorate as a family man; and the requirement for Ministers to have the highest standards of propriety and discretion. I will not explore the conjectural flavour of each of these assertions, other than to highlight the problems in the 'presentation of himself as a family man' argument. As Simon Longstaff, from the St James Ethics Centre, pointed out on ABC's *The World Today* on 22 May 2010, it was a weak argument (as was inferred in both the broadcast and the licensee's submission) that sending out Christmas cards from his family was hypocritical. Longstaff observed that an individual can have a family and be gay and send out Christmas cards 'because that was part of who he is'.[2] Indeed, Campbell is also on record as supporting gay rights reform, so the hypocrisy argument also fails to hold water in terms of his parliamentary voting patterns (Hansard, 2003, 2008).

The ACMA report recognised that the broadcasting of information regarding a person's sexual preference is generally regarded by the Authority 'as material relating to a person's personal or private affairs' (2010: 9). The report also noted that privacy may in certain circumstances be expected in a public place (as, for example, in the UK decisions in *Campbell* and *Murray* (J. K. Rowling); see Whittle and Cooper, 2009: 13), and that although surreptitious filming may imply that the person being filmed had an expectation of privacy, it will not necessarily follow that the broadcasting of such footage will invade a person's privacy. In relation to the latter point, the ethical aspects of surreptitious filming by private investigators working for news media are being examined by the Leveson Inquiry, and witnesses have provided evidence about the practice. Ofcom's *Broadcasting Code* has specific provisions concerning surreptitious filming that require that it be used and broadcast only where it is warranted, and there is *prima facie* evidence of the story being in the public interest (Ofcom, 2011: 41). There are no equivalent rules in the *Commercial Television Industry Code of Practice*. I will not discuss further in this context the ethics of using surreptitious filming, other than to note that there is some suggestion in the David Campbell case that the Seven Network obtained the footage from a private investigator.

The ACMA report considered that a viewer of the news broadcast would have probably considered it a private matter relating to sexual preference, stating: 'The ACMA is satisfied that the broadcast used material relating to the Minister's personal or private affairs and invaded his privacy' (2010: 9). The report also acknowledged that the Seven Network did not dispute in its submissions that it had breached the privacy provision of the *Commercial Television Industry Code of Practice*.

ACMA found that there was 'an identifiable public interest', and despite no explicit or implied consent being obtained from the Minister prior to the broadcast by the Licensee, it found no breach of the commercial TV industry codes of practice. Its reasoning included the argument that:

> *Those holding public office will be open to greater and more frequent scrutiny in their personal lives as a very consequence of their public office. In these cases the public interest exemption to the prohibition of the broadcast of private material is more likely to apply ... to the extent that the Minister's activities were secret, the ACMA also accepts that engaging in covert activity while in a position of public responsibility or administration could make a person vulnerable to being compromised. (2010: 11)*

Having weighed the merits of the broadcaster's 'public-interest' assertions justifying intrusion into the Minister's private life, ACMA found only one to be persuasive: the Minister's resignation itself. The clear implication was that all the other explanations were only window-dressing that the broadcaster used to attempt to justify what the majority of the media commentariat saw as a blatant breach of an individual's privacy.

Tellingly, ACMA's investigation report into the code of practice breaches was silent on the implied scenario of there being no available public-interest defence had Campbell not resigned as a minister.

Since David Campbell himself was not the complainant in this matter, and therefore had no input into ACMA's decision processes, his view was not considered under the code complaint process.

The ACMA privacy guidelines review

The regulator was undoubtedly made aware through public opinion and criticism that it was sailing close to the wind in the Campbell matter. Several news polls indicated that majority opinion was critical of the footage being used, including those carried out for online news media sites such as NineMSN[3] and Yahoo!7, the latter being cited by ABCTV's *Mediawatch* on 24 May 2010. The fact that the Campbell investigation report became a case study in the regulator's 2009–11 review of privacy guidelines for broadcasters, which was underway during the Campbell matter, was perhaps an expression of the need to explain the decision to a wider audience (ACMA, 2011a: 13).

Similarly, survey research commissioned by ACMA itself (Figure 10.1) to inform the review, by delving more deeply into community attitudes concerning privacy and news and current affairs programming, found that:

> *A total of 93 per cent of media users believe it is either 'very important'*
> *(68 per cent) or 'somewhat important' (25 per cent) for broadcasters*
> *to safeguard a person's privacy in news and current affairs programs.*
> *(ACMA, 2011b: 5)*

In terms of demographic variations, the researchers noted that protecting personal privacy was 'very important' mostly for people over the age of 50 (74%), and those sampled in the 18–24 years group were the least likely to find safeguarding privacy 'very important' (53%) (ACMA, 2011b: 5). However, virtually all of those younger media users surveyed nevertheless thought protecting privacy 'somewhat important' (90%).

Of more direct relevance to the Campbell Affair was the fact that the survey sought responses regarding information gained through the use of a hidden camera, and revelations about a person's sexual preferences. Between two-thirds (67%) and three-quarters (74%) of media users considered three sample scenarios 'very intrusive' of the person's privacy (Figure 10.2) (ACMA, 2011b: 6).

Demographic variations for views regarding the use of hidden cameras in order to report sensitive or embarrassing personal information

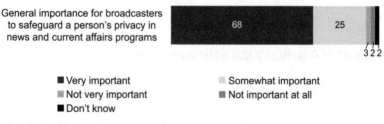

General importance for broadcasters to safeguard a person's privacy in news and current affairs programs

68   25

322

■ Very important   ▨ Somewhat important
▨ Not very important   ■ Not important at all
■ Don't know

Survey sample: n = 1,190 weighted to the Australian population.

Figure 10.1   Importance of safegaurding a person's privacy (% of media users), 2010.

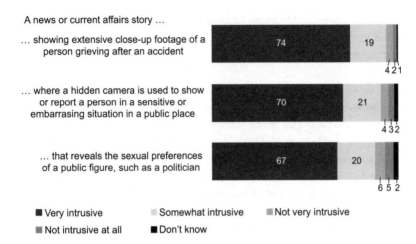

Survey sample: n = 1,190 weighted to the Australian population.

Figure 10.2   Views on the degree of privacy intrusion from the broadcast of certain personal material (% of media users), 2010.

revealed that a clear majority of people over 18 saw these practices as 'very intrusive'. Similarly, broadcasting content that reveals the sexual preferences of public figures was also regarded as 'very intrusive', a view held by more people on higher incomes in the survey sample. Thus it can be seen that even data assembled by the regulator itself, in order to inform its own review, indicate that its decision in the Campbell case was out of step with the majority of public opinion.

The back-story to the guidelines is that they were launched soon after the creation of ACMA in 2005 (the new 'convergent' regulator which replaced the previous regulatory body, the Australian Broadcasting Authority, and is modelled on Ofcom). During a speech at the launch of guidelines, the then acting Chair, Lyn Maddock (2005), explained that their purpose was to 'help raise the level of public awareness about the issues'. The guidelines were developed with the assistance of the industry. Motivated by ongoing public concern gauged through research and a relatively high level of complaints, the regulator thought it responsible to provide additional explanatory guidance on the operation of the privacy provisions within the commercial TV and radio codes of practice. The TV codes have an appended privacy advisory note, but these guidelines seek to provide additional information about perceived hotspots for all categories of broadcasters.

In her speech, Maddock cautioned that public concern about media intrusion and privacy could not easily be read off merely the number of complaints since:

> Firstly, making a complaint about an invasion of privacy may be perceived by the person involved as, in effect, repeating the invasion … it's entirely understandable that people considering making a complaint that their privacy has been invaded might decide that the benefits to be gained from proceeding with the complaint might be outweighed by the potential or perceived disadvantages. Secondly, we might expect there to be a lower level of complaints about invasions of privacy than about other matters dealt with in the media because individuals who are not directly affected are probably less likely to complain.

Rightly, Maddock noted that this was in contrast with other categories of complaints, such as bias, accuracy, and fairness, where complainants were more likely to be members of the public, as well as the individual who may have felt themselves harmed by a particular story. Three case studies were used to highlight guidelines for best practice. These examples, Maddock explained,

> illustrate the types of privacy issues we as regulators consider and illustrate the tensions between public interest and private interest. And they are examples that lead to the concern often expressed in the community about privacy and the media. (Maddock, 2005)

The harm arising from such privacy breaches, she argued, went beyond serious embarrassment to exclusion from and detriment to employment and social life. It was also a kind of harm that, unlike inaccuracy, bias, and other errors, is not able to be easily remedied by an apology or a correction.

The new privacy guidelines have been tweaked to take into account more recent investigations, and to add more detailed guidance and explanatory examples for cases involving the public interest and the privacy of public figures. In news and current affairs content concerning public figures, the broadcasting of material that invades a person's privacy may be in the public interest if it raises or answers questions about any of the following:

1. the person's appointment to or resignation from public office;
2. the person's fitness for office;
3. the person's capacity to carry out his or her duties;
4. conduct or behaviour that contradicts the person's stated position on an issue.

However, the content is unlikely to be in the public interest if a broadcast is merely distasteful, socially damaging, or embarrassing (ACMA, 2011a: 6).

Footnotes further explain the numbered points. In relation to the third, the note states: 'This approach was taken in the ACMA's investigation 2431 concerning a news report on the resignation of a NSW Minister of Parliament' (ibid. appendix 1). As discussed earlier, the main argument in the report is that ACMA exercised the public-interest exemption because they decided the Minister's resignation was in the public interest. However, this note suggests that it was actually in the public interest to invade David Campbell's privacy because it concerned questions of capacity, which is an entirely different argument.

A lack of appeal

Decisions made by ACMA under the *Commercial Television Industry Code of Practice* are not 'reviewable decisions' as defined in section 204 of the *Broadcasting Services Act 1992*. Reviewable decisions are limited to specific aspects of licensing, the control of commercial broadcasting services, variations in class licensing decisions, the imposition of new conditions, matters arising from programming and license fees, and digital conversion decisions. Applications for an appeal in these areas are made to the Administrative Appeals Tribunal at a federal level. *The Commercial Television Industry Code of Practice* has ACMA as the decision-maker already, in effect, making the decision 'on appeal', in that the decision has come to the regulator because the complainant is dissatisfied with the broadcaster's response (or a period of 60 days has lapsed without the broadcaster responding to the complaint). Arguably, this lack of appeal to a higher review body is a flawed element of the co-regulatory regime when it comes to adjudicating on such serious matters as privacy, reputation, and livelihood.

It is interesting to contemplate how such complaints would have unfolded had they arisen in the self-regulatory context of the print media. This is, of course, hypothetical, but it nonetheless highlights a number of important issues. Absent in a system of licensing of the print media (arising from English constitutional history where the removal of newspaper licensing in the late seventeenth century has generally been seen as an advance in civil liberties), there has, to date, been no news print media oversight body with statutory powers akin to ACMA. However, the question of statutory powers for regulators is now a key term of reference for both the Leveson Inquiry in the UK, and the somewhat similar Finkelstein Inquiry in Australia.

News print media and privacy

The Australian Press Council's *Statement of Principles and Privacy Standards* constitutes general advice for media practitioners, and is relied upon in the adjudication of complaints. The principles stress that, in adjudicating complaints, 'first and dominant consideration' will be given to what 'it perceives to be in the public interest' (APC, 2011a). In a recent submission to a Senate Committee inquiring into a 'Commonwealth cause of action for serious invasion of privacy', APC noted that it had 'during the last decade ... mediated a satisfactory settlement in over one hundred complaints about alleged invasion of privacy' (2011b: 1). Privacy is directly addressed in APC's *Statement of Privacy Principles*, which states:

> *News and comment should be presented honestly and fairly, and with respect for the privacy and sensibilities of individuals. However, the right to privacy is not to be interpreted as preventing publication of matters of public record or obvious or significant public interest. Rumour and unconfirmed reports should be identified as such. (APC, 2011a)*

Privacy is also addressed by the APC's *Statement of Privacy Principles* 1 and 2. They are framed in terms of fairness, honesty, and the public interest in the course of news-gathering, and more specifically focus on issues of collection (or 'gathering'), use, and disclosure of personal information. Most relevant for this chapter is Principle 1, which notes:

> *In gathering news, journalists should seek personal information only in the public interest. In doing so, journalists should not unduly intrude on the privacy of individuals and should show respect for the*

dignity and sensitivity of people encountered in the course of gathering news ... journalists and photographers may at times need to operate surreptitiously to expose crime, significantly anti-social conduct, public deception or some other matter in the public interest ... Public figures necessarily sacrifice their right to privacy, where public scrutiny is in the public interest. However, public figures do not forfeit their right to privacy altogether. Intrusion into their right to privacy must be related to their public duties or activities. (APC, 2011c)

The UK's Press Complaints Commission (PCC) has a privacy provision in the *Editors' Code of Practice*. This states:

i)   *Everyone is entitled to respect for his or her private and family life, home, health and correspondence, including digital communications.*

ii) *Editors will be expected to justify intrusions into any individual's private life without consent. Account will be taken of the complainant's own public disclosures of information.*

iii) *It is unacceptable to photograph individuals in private places without their consent.*

Note – Private places are public or private property where there is a reasonable expectation of privacy. (PCC, 2012)

Other *Editors' Code* provisions relate to privacy arising from media 'intrusion into grief or shock' (clause 5), 'children' (clause 6), and 'clandestine devices or subterfuge' (clause 10) which contains a prohibition on the use of hidden cameras, listening devices, and mobile phones. However, all these privacy provisions may be breached if there is an overriding public interest in doing so. Journalists' codes of practice in the UK (National Union of Journalists) and Australia (Media, Entertainment and Arts Alliance) take a broadly similar approach.

'In the public interest'

The phrase 'the public interest' is among the most overused and imprecise terms in media governance. This is not to doubt its enduring necessity for regulation, law, and policy, but the question is how can regulatory decision-makers in a disparate range of situations best apply it? Indeed, would a singular statutory definition be desirable? Julian Petley (in this volume) has comprehensively reviewed the UK's range of regulatory instruments that reference media scenarios and practices where a public-interest defence *may* be justified, noting that the common ground in these debates ought to be about taking action on behalf of the public, not of media defendants.

There is no shortage of assessments of the inherent risks run by the media in intruding upon people's privacy. As Whittle and Cooper put it:

> *We need a free media that can expose wrongdoing and challenge those in power, but, if the media is going to infringe privacy, it needs to take care that it is standing on the firm ground of public interest and that the means it employs to investigate are not fatally compromised either by the wrong choice of target or the manner in which the investigation is conducted. (2009: 1–2)*

Whittle and Cooper go on to make a strong argument for the need to introduce more robust definitional criteria for media activities which are claimed to be in the public interest. They argue that the public-interest justification must take into account the following considerations: citizens require information about the state and corporations in order to make informed decisions in a democracy; if citizens are to be able to trust public figures, then their actions must be open for inspection and investigation by the news media; public figures should be judged on public grounds as opposed to private ones; private beliefs and actions should not be presumed to inform how public figures behave in their work. They argue that the assumption that a private life should be protected is in itself 'a considerable and humane public good' (ibid. 98).

But despite the press's best efforts to conflate the public interest with what interests the public, a robust case can be made that the public interest is concerned mainly with the ethical implications for citizenship of the growth of unaccountable formations of media power. It therefore represents a set of vital policy and regulatory discourses that has democratic significance for citizens, and it is critically linked with media performance.

There are various definitions of the public interest, ranging from quite straightforward ones encapsulating less explicit ideas of contestation, through to those attempting to explain conflict in terms of more complex and dynamic formations of media power. For Australia's Press Council, the public interest is defined as 'involving a matter capable of affecting the people at large so they might be legitimately interested in, or concerned about, what is going on, or what may happen to them or to others' (APC, 2011a). The notion is explained in similar terms in the ACMA *Privacy Guidelines*, but seems to add a layer of vagueness which is not overly helpful in a case such as the David Campbell one:

> *The broadcast of private information or material that invades privacy, without consent, will not breach the codes if there is a clear and identifiable public interest in the material being broadcast. The public interest is assessed at the time of the broadcast. Whether something is in the public interest will depend on all the circumstances, including whether a matter is capable of affecting the community at large so that citizens might be legitimately interested in or concerned about what is going on. (ACMA, 2011a: 5-6)*

The definition is more specific in the PCC Editors' Code:

1. *The public interest includes, but is not confined to: i) Detecting or exposing crime or serious impropriety. ii) Protecting public health and safety. iii) Preventing the public from being misled by an action or statement of an individual or organization.*
2. *There is a public interest in freedom of expression itself.*
3. *Whenever the public interest is invoked, the PCC will require editors to demonstrate fully that they reasonably believed that publication, or journalistic activity undertaken with a view to publication, would be in the public interest and how, and with whom, that was established at the time.*
4. *The PCC will consider the extent to which material is already in the public domain, or will become so.*
5. *In cases involving children under 16, editors must demonstrate an exceptional public interest to over-ride the normally paramount interest of the child. (PCC, 2012)*

Nick Davies, in his written evidence to the Leveson Inquiry, expressed the view of a highly experienced practitioner on the public interest in the following terms:

> *The most important point that needs to be made about the concept of the public interest is that nobody knows what it means. I am not referring*

to the confusion between 'the public are interested in X' and 'the public have an interest in being told about X'. I am saying that nobody knows where the boundary lines are. For years, generally speaking reporters have operated in a kind of ethical mist where it wasn't particularly clear exactly what the rules were because nobody was asking us to be particularly clear. In 35 years, I think I've only twice been called to account by the PCC (and both times I have been acquitted).

For example, I believe that those journalists who claim that it is a matter of public interest that we be told about the sex lives of public figures, particularly when they are in breach of established conventions are speaking sincerely. I profoundly disagree with them. I think there is no public interest in the disclosure of people's sex lives unless there is evidence of crime.

I don't think that judicial decisions have succeeded in clarifying this in day-to-day operational terms. There are some cases where the boundaries are clear but many where they are not. One result of this enduring confusion is that I don't think I know of a single serious journalist who dares to try to take advantage of the public interest defence in Section 55 of the Data Protection Act.[4]

If journalists profess not to know what the public interest actually is, then what about those for whom they write? Morrison et al. (2007: 354–7) have undertaken extensive focus-group work and nationally representative surveys into people's ideas of what constitutes the public interest. People's responses to a set of storylines were sought (e.g. 'foods sold by a major supermarket have been contaminated by bacteria', or 'a member of a leading pop group has cosmetic surgery to change her face shape'). Morrison and his colleagues found that news items of the former kind were generally thought to be of 'majority public interest', while those of the latter kind were seen as 'minority public interest' and as playing more to personal interests. They concluded that 'for many people, public interest is understood to mean something beyond purely personal interest' and that the majority of people viewed 'gossip' media stories as not being in the public interest (ibid. 357).

Questioning modes of regulation

The Campbell affair raises broader questions about how breaches of personal privacy by the media are handled by media regulators. The inference is that the ethics of regulation itself is important, and it allows us to consider issues such as the effectiveness or otherwise of codes of practice. Questions regarding the independence and transparency of the regulator become paramount in this regard. This is an evolutionary process and will be subject to the outcome of the various reviews in Australia and the UK that I mentioned at the beginning of this chapter.

Transformations of our media and cultural industries constitute the backdrop against which any analyses of regulation need to be constructed. These changes, typically characterised as part of the process of media convergence and deregulation, have formed a part of the regulatory landscape for several years (Dwyer, 2010: 14). Regulatory agencies throughout the world have been restructuring their organisations in order better to respond to these evolving industry conditions, and this process will undoubtedly continue. The last two decades have been characterised predominantly by self- or co-regulatory forms of regulation, which have followed the political and economic vogue for deregulation. A recent comparative review of audiovisual regulation in the UK, Germany, Canada, and the US noted: 'All countries have independent or industry bodies that are involved in audiovisual media regulation via self- or co-regulation; these may relate to traditional broadcasting or new media' (ACMA, 2011c: 11). Embedded as it is in neoliberal philosophy, deregulation asserts the supremacy of 'the market' as the best mechanism for governance, and system-wide choices have been made that claim that greater public benefit flows from market-based regulatory mechanisms than from those based on the principles of public service.

Many of these debates about the fundamental structuring of institutions and processes are recurring ones. In 2000, an Australian Senate inquiry identified convergence trends and emphasised the need for regulatory frameworks that ensure that the information and communications industries 'operate in a transparent and accountable environment' (Parliament of Australia, 2000: p. x). A key recommendation of their report was:

> The decision as to what will or will not constitute 'an identifiable public interest', should not be left to purely sectarian interests. The Committee is of the view that the important balance to be struck between the 'private' and 'public' interest ought to be weighed up within the framework of a fair, independent and objective statutory regime. (Ibid. 15)

Eleven years on, a federal government review of convergence, begun in 2011, has forced a reassessment of the most appropriate modes of regulation for different intervention strategies. As one of the first steps in the review, the convergence review committee released a 'framing paper', with the chairman noting that, with profound changes in the media and communications industries set to continue, a review of the existing main policy frameworks and objectives was urgently required. From the outset the review committee noted that specific policy objectives (such as achieving a diversity of voices in news and information) could be achieved in various ways, including 'regulatory and non-regulatory approaches such as incentive/reward systems' (DBCDE, 2011: 2–3).

Constant changes in industry practices (and related practitioner values) justify reviewing approaches to intervention in the regulation of our media and communications industries. In times of commercial strains and pressures we can reasonably ask whether self-regulatory and co-regulatory modes are adequate from both citizen and consumer perspectives. Such 'light touch' regulation has rules which are formulated at least partly by industry participants, and, as critics frequently point out, this 'insider design' can lead to limitations (especially from a citizen's point of view) in this system of regulation, and in particular to a form of 'regulatory capture' in which regulator and regulated enjoy rather too close a relationship. Undoubtedly 'light touch', co-regulatory frameworks increase the risk of scandals involving the media. Take, for example, the 'Cash for Comment' affair in Australia, in light of which, in the high-profile *Commercial Radio Inquiry* of 2000, the regulator found:

> *A systemic failure to ensure the effective operation of self-regulation particularly in relation to current affairs programs including a lack of staff awareness of the Codes and their implications. (ABA, 2000: 4)*

Similarly, commercially motivated ratings wars often encourage broadcasters to maintain their market position by breaking sensational stories which may be dubious in one way or another. The David Campbell affair certainly falls into this category, and was the product of a news department that is no stranger to homophobic tales.[5] But nor did the regulator emerge well from this either, utilising the minister's resignation to provide itself with a veneer of public-interest justification for letting Seven off the hook.

The arguments in favour of this form of regulation are that it potentially avoids inappropriate use of high-end enforcement options for relatively minor infringements; it is less costly to administer; and it enables those with the knowledge of a fast-changing industry to participate directly in the rule-making. On the other hand, it allows certain matters to be moved 'off the books' of government, and thus helps the industry to protect itself from more direct legislative intervention which might be desirable from the point of view of the citizen.

In this new environment, codes of practice have become the *de rigueur* solution to warding off regulatory problems. But we can reasonably ask: how well does this approach actually deal with the full spectrum of transgressions, from relatively minor breaches to significant ones with high stakes consequences? And how well does it serve the citizens', as opposed to the media owners', interests?

A responsible media industry is able to distinguish between what will merely interest the public and issues that are of genuine public interest for citizens' welfare. Professional codes of practice, privacy standards, principles, and personal ethical frameworks are there to provide the scaffolding to guide responsible and accountable decision-making. However, in market societies, commercial media will inevitably make more difficult any straightforward application of these ethical frameworks, especially at a time of tremendous industry upheaval. The innards of this crisis are being laid bare in the multiple inquiries that we are witnessing at the time of writing.

Conclusion

In this case study of commercial television news intrusion into private life, it is evident that media regulators have invoked conceptions of privacy and the public interest to justify their actions. On one level, the consequences of these commercial media practices confirm Solove's argument that 'the harm of disclosure is not so much the elimination of secrecy as it is the spreading of information beyond expected boundaries' (2008: 145). But more importantly, beyond this, it exposes a convenient alliance of commercially competitive media interests, regulatory supervision, and moral judgement that shelters behind the rhetoric of acting in the public's interest.

Theoretically, this failure of regulation can be situated within a wider context of 'liquid modern' journalistic practices caught up in the dynamics of wider social change (Bauman, 2011; Deuze, 2008). However, ultimately, we need to draw these conclusions in relation to media practices in particular national, historical, and cultural contexts, and to recognise that 'self-' or 'co-regulatory' arrangements are the product of a specific set of political and industrial contingencies.

Notes

1   http://www.pcc.org.uk/news/index.html?article=NzcyNA (accessed July 2012).
2   http://www.abc.net.au/news/2010-05-21/campbell-sex-scandal-sparks-privacy-debate/836580 (accessed Jan. 2012).
3   http://news.ninemsn.com.au/vote-archive.aspx?year=2010 (accessed Jan. 2012).
4   http://www.levesoninquiry.org.uk/wp-content/uploads/2011/11/Witness-Statement-of-Nick-Davies.pdf (accessed Jan. 2012).
5   See, for example, e.g. 'Marsden wins defamation case against Channel 7', 27 June 2001, http://www.abc.net.au/7.30/content/2001/s320016.htm (accessed Jan. 2012).

References

Australian Broadcasting Authority (2000) *Commercial Radio Inquiry* (Sydney: Australian Broadcasting Authority).

Australian Communications and Media Authority (2010) *Channel Seven (Sydney) Pty Ltd/ATN Sydney, Investigation Report 2431* (Sydney: Australian Communications and Media Authority).

Australian Communications and Media Authority (2011a) *Privacy Guidelines for Broadcasters,* Dec. (Sydney: Australian Communications and Media Authority).

Australian Communications and Media Authority (2011b) *Australians' Views on Privacy in Broadcast News and Current Affairs: Complementary Survey Report to Community Research into Broadcasting and Media Privacy* (Sydney: Australian Communications and Media Authority).

Australian Communications and Media Authority (2011c) *International Approaches to Audiovisual Content Regulation: A Comparative Analysis of the Regulatory Frameworks,* occasional paper, May (Sydney: Australian Communications and Media Authority).

Australian Press Council (2011a) *General Statement of Principles,* Aug. (Sydney: Australian Press Council): http://www.presscouncil.org.au/general-principles (accessed Sept. 2012).

Australian Press Council (2011b) 'Submission to the Issues Paper', *A Commonwealth Cause of Action for Serious Invasion of Privacy* (Sydney: Australian Press Council).

Australian Press Council (2011c) *Statement of Privacy Principles*, Aug. (Sydney: Australian Press Council): http://www.presscouncil.org.au/privacy-principles/ August (accessed Sept. 2012).

Bauman, Zygmunt (2011) *Culture in a Liquid Modern World* (Cambridge: Polity).

DBCDE (Department of Broadband Communications and the Digital Economy) (2011) *Convergence Review: Framing Paper* (Canberra: DBCDE).

DBCDE (Department of Broadband Communications and the Digital Economy) (2012) *Convergence Review: Final Report* (Canberra: DBCDE).

Deuze, Mark (2008) 'The Changing Context of News Work: Liquid Journalism and Monitorial Citizenship', *International Journal of Communication*, 2: 848–65.

Dwyer, Tim (2010) *Media Convergence* (Maidenhead: Open University Press).

Feintuck, Mike (2004) *The Public Interest in Regulation* (Oxford: Oxford University Press).

Feintuck, Mike, with Varney, Mike (2006) *Media Regulation, Public Interest and the Law*, 2nd edn (Edinburgh: Edinburgh University Press).

Fenton, Natalie (2012) 'Telling Tales: Press, Politics, Power and the Public Interest', *Television and New Media*, 13(1): 3–6.

Finkelstein Report (2012) *Independent Inquiry into Media and Media Regulation*: http://www.dbcde.gov.au/digital_economy/independent_media_inquiry (accessed Sept. 2012).

Free TV (2010) *Commercial Television Industry Code of Practice*: http://www.freetv. com.au (accessed Sept. 2012).

Freedman, Des (2012) 'The Phone Hacking Scandal: Implications for Regulation', *Television and New Media*, 13(1): 17–20.

Hansard (2003) New South Wales Parliament Legislative Assembly. Crimes Amendment (Sexual Offences) Bill, 7 and 21 May.

Hansard (2008) Miscellaneous Acts Amendment (Same Sex Relationships) Bill, 4 June.

Kellner, Douglas (2012) 'The Murdoch Empire and the Spectacle of Scandal', *International Journal of Communication*, 6: 1169–1200.

Leveson, The Right Hon. Lord Justice (2012) *An Inquiry into the Culture, Practices and Ethics of the Press: Report*, 4 vols (London: TSO).

Maddock, Lyn (2005) Speech given by the Acting Chair of the ACMA at the launch of *Privacy Guidelines for Broadcasters*: http://www.acma.gov.au/webwr/aba/ newspubs/speeches/documents/23aug05-lmaddock-privacyguidelines.pdf.

Morrison, David, Kieran, Matthew, Svennevig, Michael, and Ventress, Sarah (2007) *Media and Values: Intimate Transgressions in a Changing Moral and Cultural Landscape* (Bristol: Intellect).

Nissenbaum, Helen (2010) *Privacy in Context: Technology, Policy, and the Integrity of Social Life* (Stanford, CA: Stanford University Press).

Ofcom (2011) *Broadcasting Code*: http://stakeholders.ofcom.org.uk/broadcasting/ broadcast-codes/broadcast-code (accessed Jan. 2012).

Parliament of Australia (2000) *In the Public Interest: Monitoring Australia's Media,* a report by the Senate Select Committee on Information Technologies, Apr.: http://www.aph.gov.au/senate/committee/it_ctte/completed_inquiries/ 1999-02/selfreg/report/index.htm (accessed Jan. 2012).

Press Complaints Commission (2012) *Editors' Code of Practice*: http://www.pcc. org.uk/cop/practice.html (accessed Jan. 2012).

Solove, Daniel (2008) *Understanding Privacy* (Cambridge, MA: Harvard University Press).

Spence, Edward, Alexandra, Andrew, Quinn, Aaron, and Dunn, Anne (2011) *Media, Markets and Morals* (Oxford: Wiley-Blackwell).

Whittle, Stephen, and Cooper, Glenda (2009) *Privacy, Probity and Public Interest* (Oxford: Reuters Institute for the Study of Journalism).

11

John Leslie: The Naming and Shaming of an Innocent Man

Adrian Quinn

On the last day of July 2003, John Leslie, a well-known television presenter, left Southwark Crown Court 'without a stain on his character'. Those were the words of Judge George Bathurst-Norman, who found Leslie not guilty on the two counts of indecent assault with which he had been charged on 18 June. Despite this, Leslie would never reclaim the television career that had effectively ended on 23 October of the previous year when he did not appear as co-presenter of *This Morning* on ITV. This was a job from which Leslie would be speedily sacked, effectively for failing to defend himself against a separate allegation of sexual assault for which he never faced charge or trial, at least not in a court. 'There have been many cases of trial by media in recent years', wrote Stephen Maguire in the *People*, 27 October 2002, 'but this particular one must be the worst'.

This chapter looks at the conscious choices of key players in the media to name and shame – seemingly with impunity – a man against whom no evidence of serious sexual assault has ever been successfully presented to a court of law. The observations offered here are informed by a review of press and broadcast commentary on John Leslie in 2002–3 and by interviews with two London media lawyers: Paul Fox, who came to act as solicitor for Leslie the summer after his name was publicly tied to an alleged sexual assault upon Ulrika Jonsson; and Duncan Lamont, who wrote a monthly column on media law for the *Guardian* from 2001 to 2007 and also works for ITV, ITN, and Channel 4 News. I focus on the role, and sometimes the culpability, of four camps in the resultant naming and shaming of John Leslie: (i) Ulrika Jonsson and her publishers; (ii) the press and broadcasters; (iii) lawyers acting for John Leslie; (iv) John Leslie himself.

The alternative tribunal

In October 2002, Pan Books published the autobiography of Ulrika Jonsson, who, like John Leslie, worked in the world of light television, with its one-word title: *Honest*. The book was serialised in the *Mail on Sunday* and the *Daily Mail* and was accompanied by a Channel 4 programme, *The Truth About Men* (17 October 2002), which was seen by an audience of 2.8 million. On 4 November 2002 the *Sun* reported that Jonsson, then aged 35, was paid nearly £1m for *Honest* and earned a further £750,000 for the *Mail* serialisation. While both the print and the television texts narrate a date rape, the book goes further than the Channel 4 broadcast in identifying the alleged assailant as a 'presenter':

> *The presenter turned up at my hotel room with flowers, and I was touched. The television was on, and as I was getting my handbag together for the date he started petting. We kissed a bit, but I was quite keen to get going so as not to miss the film, and tried lightly to dissuade him. He ignored me, by now kissing me quite hard and starting to touch my breasts and around my bum. I had been fully dressed when he arrived, but now he was slowly, yet brusquely, pulling at my clothing, despite my increasingly persistent objections. I pulled away, only for him to pull me back towards him until he eventually pushed me onto the bed.*
>
> *I landed on my back and remember saying out loud, 'No, no, don't.' This was the first point at which I began to feel fear. I felt that I had somehow lost control of him and that I didn't have the power to stop him. I panicked and raised my voice, attempting to wriggle out of his reach and repeating, 'No! No! No!' In what seemed to be no time at all he had my trousers off and he was tugging at my knickers. This was crazy, I thought. Surely he is going to stop. Can't he hear me? But just as that was going round in my head he inserted himself inside me with all the force of his big body. The words I was shouting made no noise as they left my lips; I was breathing, I knew that, but no words were coming out anymore. All that I could do was beat with my fists on his back and kick a little with my legs. He ignored me, continuing to kiss me hard. I did not reciprocate, and instead turned my head from side to side as it lay trapped between his head and the bed.*
>
> *Once he had deposited his load inside me, he climbed off me and started talking as if nothing had happened, pulling up his trousers. I remember lying very still, not even able to pull up my underwear. He urged me to*

get myself together so we could get going. I remember the sound of his voice so vividly at that point – although he was talking to himself: I was in no state to reply. Eventually I managed the words, 'I think I will just stay here', as I curled myself in a ball on the covers of the bed. He didn't seem bothered and said we should talk later. I had been raped. (Jonsson, 2002: 84–6)

The day after the broadcast of *The Truth About Men*, on 18 October 2002, Ulrika Jonsson appeared on *The Jonathan Ross Show* to plug her book which, in addition to narrating a serious assault, also goes into detail about her abortion, adultery, divorce, and mental illness. 'You've had sex with a lot of people, haven't you Ulrika?' asked Ross, drawing laughs from the studio audience. He then asks Jonsson about the 'presenter' passage in her book, saying: 'I think I know who this is. I genuinely do. I think I know who this person is.'

Then, as now, Jonsson would not be drawn on the identity of her attacker. In his column for the *Guardian* on 28 October 2002, Duncan Lamont stated that, in *Honest*, 'Ulrika was careful not to leave clues that could lead to the identification of the mystery man'. But this is not altogether correct. For many, her use of the words 'the presenter', combined with 'his big body', provided clues that led right to John Leslie's front door. As the press often reported, Leslie is six feet five inches tall and, as he arrived at court in July 2003 to be tried for rape, he was described by Martin Brunt, a crime reporter for *Sky News*, as 'probably the biggest man in Southwark'. More boldly, a *Mail on Sunday* reporter doorstepped Leslie at his home and put it to him that he was the rapist described in *Honest*. Paul Fox, John Leslie's solicitor, characterised these incremental developments in the Leslie story as 'a slow burn'. He also adds that 'the story excited the media because it appeared to be one of their own. Various names were in the bracket and then Matthew Wright made the connection.'

This connection was made explicit five days later, on 23 October, during a live discussion between Wright and fellow broadcaster Vivienne Parry on Channel Five's *The Wright Stuff*. As Wright and Parry discussed the Jonsson book, in what now seems a recklessly informal setting in which to discuss a serious sexual assault, Wright accidentally spoke of three women 'pointing the finger at John Leslie, one of them's got a book out, £16.99 in book shops'. This horrified Vivienne Parry who looked silently and incredulously at Wright, her mouth slightly agape. The journalist and broadcaster Jane Moore, who would later present *John Leslie: My Year of*

Hell for Sky, on 28 September 2003, said in that programme that Matthew Wright's slip threw 'a hand grenade into newsrooms everywhere'.

In its bulletin the next day, *Channel 4 News* reported that only two newspapers, the *Independent* and the *Telegraph*, had followed the letter of the law by not naming Leslie and thereby connecting him with the rape scene in *Honest*. In its words, the bulk of the media, beginning with the *London Evening Standard*, 'threw libel law caution to the wind' with coverage that 'ranged from broad hints, to outright name and shame'. Later, on 17 June 2003, the *Standard* was to describe Leslie as a '6ft 5in Scot [who] lost his £250,000-a-year job after refusing to respond to allegations of assault and that he took cocaine'. *Channel 4 News* itself was upfront about its editorial position, telling viewers that the programme had decided that 'the serious issues raised by the media coverage *are* in the public interest, but decided not to detail the exact nature of the allegations'. Still, it dedicated eight and a half minutes of its evening bulletin to the Leslie story. Duncan Lamont attributes the differences in print and broadcast coverage of the Leslie story to the fact that the broadcasters he was advising had no choice but to comply with the relevant broadcasting code, whereas newspapers were, of course, working to a voluntary one.

In interview, Leslie's solicitor explained that date rape, the exact nature of the allegation that *Channel 4 News* chose not to detail, dealt a killer blow to Leslie's career: 'John was a breakfast presenter and on the whole his target market was women, so this particular sort of allegation was damaging to him.' The same month, 30 other women came forward with allegations of their own, and the tabloid media provided them with what Mary Riddell at the *Observer*, 3 August 2003, called 'the alternative tribunal'. Duncan Lamont's proximity to the media as a media lawyer enables him to say with confidence that there was 'a campaign of harassment against Leslie, particularly by the newspaper group that then owned the *Evening Standard* as well as the *Daily Mail* who, quite bluntly, had it in for him'. In interview, he also confirmed that 'rightly or wrongly, John Leslie had a reputation in the media industry for being sexually athletic and aggressive'. But quoted in the *Mail*, 21 March 2009, Leslie said that the media's decision to tie him to an alleged assault on Ulrika Jonsson, covering three disturbing pages of her autobiography, amounted to the denial of due process, arguing that 'if she had said "John Leslie did not rape me" that would have put an end to it. If she had said "John Leslie did rape me" I could have defended myself.'

In a comment piece for the *Spectator* magazine on 2 November 2002, headed 'Why I am Ashamed of the British Press', the *Independent's* editor, Simon Kelner, also highlighted the serious denial of due legal process that the Leslie case represented. But he also looked reality in the face when he added: 'Perhaps this doesn't matter. In the pitiless eyes of the most powerful court in the land, justice has already been seen to be done.' Similarly, in its segment on the Leslie disclosures on 24 October 2002, ITV's *News at Ten* interviewed the disgraced former Tory MP Neil Hamilton, who had also been falsely accused of sexual assault, resulting in the jailing of the complainant for three years. 'In England we used to have a system which was called innocent unless proven guilty,' Hamilton said. 'Today, of course, you're innocent unless demonised by tabloids.'

Duncan Lamont says that Leslie was 'in effect, stitched up'. He added that certain high-profile cases, like those of John Leslie and John Terry and, more recently, Ryan Giggs provide expert London media lawyers with 'object lessons in what not to do'. At the time of Matthew Wright's slip, Leslie was represented not by Paul Fox but, from October 2002 to June 2003, by Mark Stephens, who would later represent Julian Assange. Fox explains that the decision of Leslie's then lawyers was:

> Better to say nothing than to feed the story, whereby your denial becomes the story. That's how libel lawyers get around difficult areas: They don't report the allegation, they report the denial of the allegation, thereby blaming the person who made the release in the first place. The decision was made not to make a denial. In hindsight, that decision clearly was wrong, because then it was then open season on John. Once the floodgates open, the libel laws are a very blunt weapon in essence.

Just how open was the season on Leslie was made clear when the *Sun* published an appeal headlined in capital letters 'HAVE YOU BEEN A VICTIM OF JOHN LESLIE? CALL THE SUN NEWS DESK.' Leslie's fate was sealed when, the Sunday following Matthew Wright's slip, 27 October 2002, the *Sun's* sister paper, the now defunct *News of World*, ran on its front page, under the headline 'End of the Line', a picture of Leslie snorting cocaine, taken surreptitiously six weeks earlier at a party at his home in Surrey.

While Fox speaks with hindsight, there were those at the time who explicitly questioned the wisdom of saying nothing. Writing in the *Daily Mirror*, 31 October 2002, Ros Wynne-Jones said that 'Leslie's silence damns him ... For one woman to complain about your sexual conduct is unfortunate. For 30 to looks worse than careless.' The role of spokesman for the tabloid press was assumed by Wynne-Jones's editor, Piers Morgan, who was rated the seventh most powerful man in Britain by *GQ* magazine in 2002. In the above-mentioned Sky programme, *John Leslie: My Year of Hell*, which is something of a right-to-reply for Leslie, Morgan is featured as saying that 'a lot of people that knew John Leslie thought that he was an accident waiting to happen. In the end it wasn't just an accident but a multiple motorway car crash.' And in an appearance on *Channel 4 News*, 24 October 2002, Morgan outlined his thinking on the *Mirror*'s decision to name John Leslie. Morgan, whose editorship would end nine months after Leslie's acquittal, when the *Mirror* admitted publishing hoax photographs of tortured Iraqi prisoners on its front page, deflected responsibility for naming Leslie. Asked by Krishnan Guru-Murthy why the *Mirror* chose to name Leslie, Morgan replied:

> *The decision was taken for us by television. This person's name was being bandied about on the internet, by emails to every company, and then yesterday morning a major TV programme inadvertently blurted his name out. So, millions of people very quickly knew from watching their television screens. And you can bet your life that, within an hour, the entire western world knew who it was. Everyone knew it was John Leslie. In that situation, for newspapers to simply pretend that the public don't know is to treat the public rather stupidly. John Leslie himself accepts that it was all gonna come out. I don't think we're gonna get a libel action here. I think he's much more concerned about other actions involving the allegations.*

Guru-Murthy then asks: 'Are you not worried that you could be completely ruining the life and career of an innocent man? You haven't seen any evidence against him.' Morgan replies:

> *No. I'm much more worried, and I've communicated this to John Leslie's representatives, that if he doesn't come out and defend himself pretty quickly, then the drip, drip, drip effect of anonymous allegations being printed in newspapers and talked about in the broadcast media is gonna damage him irreparably. This is one of those freak occasions where, much as we would like to pursue the normal path involving these cases, the essence of the modern media age, and the internet in particular,*

meant that everybody knew who we were talking about. And to pretend otherwise is to be, I think, vaguely ridiculous.

And let's remember that all they're doing is reporting what happened on Channel 5 yesterday morning. It is a rather freakish set of circumstances where, if his name is gonna be broadcast on national television, is it really improper of a newspaper like the Mirror or the Evening Standard, to repeat that name once it's in the public domain? It's a legal minefield. The law can't really legislate for this kind of situation.

Morgan speaks in a characteristic mixture of cliché, innuendo, and hyperbole. While it is fair to say that the entire Western world will have known of the untimely deaths of Michael Jackson and Whitney Houston, John Leslie was unknown outside the United Kingdom and possibly outside the audience for daytime television. Still, it is the view of Will Storr in the *Independent*, 23 February 2006, that in the ten months from the publication of *Honest* to John Leslie's acquittal on two charges unrelated to the attack narrated in that book, Leslie was, 'at least as far as the red-top media was concerned, the most hated man in Britain'. In affirming the view that the law cannot legislate for a scenario such as the one that both allowed and revelled in the Leslie disclosures (as well as correctly predicting that Leslie would bring no libel action), Morgan sought to legitimate exactly the 'alternative tribunal' that Mary Riddell spoke of in the *Observer*. According to this view, given the ever-present disconnection between justice and the law, the alternative tribunal provides a legitimate site in which to try 'villains' like John Leslie. Duncan Lamont disagrees, taking a very different view of the role of the news media. 'I don't think many people would say it was just, or proportionate, or balanced. The sort of things that the law and indeed the media should strive towards.'

Contempt of court

The 'strict liability' of section 2 of the Contempt of Court Act 1981 exists to ensure that media reporting does not interfere with the formal justice process and so make it impossible for a defendant to receive a fair trial. The crucial point here is that the provisions of the Act do not apply until proceedings have become active. As of October 2002, John Leslie had not been arrested for, or charged with, an assault on Ulrika Jonsson. Not until

June of the next year would Leslie be charged with two assaults on an unnamed actress. In June 2008, Leslie was again arrested on suspicion of rape, in connection with an alleged incident dating from 1995, but the case was dropped. In each case, the complainant was granted anonymity for life by the court under section 1 of the Sexual Offences (Amendment) Act 1992. On the face of it, the media did not fall foul of the strict liability rule in the Ulrika Jonsson incident, as no proceedings were active. However, Leslie's solicitor disagrees:

> *That, of itself, wouldn't necessarily have prevented a prosecution [for contempt] because there is a common law concept that if you're seen to be campaigning for someone to be prosecuted, that in itself can be contempt. It's still interfering with the justice process. So if the prosecuting authorities were minded they could have done something. You say contempt wouldn't have worked, but that's not a private right of the state. It would have been John's case that a fair trial wasn't possible in light of the pre-trial publicity. Would that have succeeded? I expect not. Certainly the state has been resistant to the idea that publicity, as such, can render a fair trial impossible, almost on policy grounds. Once you concede that it's there how, frankly, does any defendant achieve a fair trial?*

When Piers Morgan appeared on *Channel 4 News* he asked whether it was really improper of a newspaper to repeat Leslie's name once it was in the public domain. Defamation law is clear in this respect: repeating a libel constitutes a fresh instance of libel. Also speaking on the same programme, Duncan Lamont usefully clarified the legal position on defamation, stating: 'John Leslie doesn't have to *disprove* anything. The newspapers have to prove to a high standard, to a *criminal* standard, what they've chosen to publish, because these are pretty serious allegations.'

Lawyers in civil cases, including defamation, speak in terms of 'remedies'. Ten years after providing expert commentary on the Leslie case for ITN, Duncan Lamont clarified the standard legal position on this topic, explaining that 'the court's view is that there is nothing wrong with British law. You have your remedy and your remedy is that you sue for libel.' Indeed, that was Lamont's free advice to Leslie at the time, as published in the *Guardian*, 4 November 2002. Following Leslie's sacking by ITV, Lamont said:

If I was advising him I'd say sue the Sun and the Mail – he has nothing to lose. All the evidence they have only amounts to low-level sexual harassment, and that doesn't amount to a hill of beans compared with the more serious allegations that have been levelled against him.

Why, then, did John Leslie choose not to sue? Part of the reason was immediately evident to the media and also to Leslie's later lawyers. 'John Leslie's reputation has been dragged through the mire', reported Victoria MacDonald on *Channel 4 News*, 24 October 2002, and although 'the legal consensus is that he has strong grounds to sue, he would risk his private life being exposed still further'. In interview, Paul Fox repeatedly returned to the question of suing for libel, asking:

What was libel law to do? You'd sue, you'd say there's been damage to the reputation. How do you separate damage caused by one article with damage caused by another? It was all too late frankly. You either had to go in there and warn the press at the beginning, or effectively you have to abandon any thought of a civil remedy and fight the main claim, which was a criminal case.

For John, the civil remedy was to pursue them after the event. But what would the point be? And there would have perhaps been a succession of women entered into the witness box making various allegations and through the sheer weight of numbers his reputation would have been damaged. There was nothing to gain. Once his name was out there wasn't much the law could do to protect him.

It was such a fast moving show at the time. The media were united in the pursuit of John, not because they had it in for him particularly, but simply that it was a story. After the event we did look at going after them. Say, for example, we went after the Daily Mail, and they decided to dig their heels in which, by definition, they had to, you would be looking at a trial that went on for weeks and weeks and weeks. And at the end of the day, whatever happened, I expect John would be damaged. No one's private life can bear that kind of inquisition. [A court could say] 'you're not a rapist, we don't believe that, but you played fast and loose'. He'd be risking every penny he had and he could win and get ten thousand pounds. And who goes into the betting shop like that? What would it achieve? He wasn't going to get a clearer statement of his innocence than the trial judge's. He had so little to achieve.

Leslie's role in his own downfall

In the years since Leslie was named and shamed, both he and his solicitor have spoken candidly of the hand he played in his own downfall. In an appearance on the BBC3 programme *My Childhood* on 8 January 2006, Leslie confessed to the psychiatrist Linda Treliving that he had 'never learnt how to treat women with respect'. The following month, in an interview in the *Independent*, 23 February, Will Storr asked Leslie about the 30 women who had come forward with allegations about his sexual behaviour. He responded:

> *The way I judge the 30 women is that there were none before, there's been none since and they'd all been paid for what they said. I didn't even recognise half of them. However, saying all that, my behaviour with women at times was inappropriate. I was not respectful enough, was not sincere enough, was cold. I know all this sounds pig-headed but I think the majority of the women who I had met who went to the papers were those I hadn't called back and were pissed off ... but I never harmed one of those girls. I've never harmed anyone. My behaviour was not right on occasions. I shouldn't have had those girls in situations where they would feel uncomfortable, which obviously some of them did ... We're talking about women years ago who went to newspapers to make some money. I had a 10-month investigation by Scotland Yard and they found jack shit. So I can sit here and I can feel quite happy in feeling vindicated.*

However, Leslie's solicitor sees it slightly differently:

> *Without a shadow of doubt, and not to put too fine a point on it, he was a big shagger and he'd offended a lot of people. There was a feeling that he'd chanced his arm once too often. There were a lot of people in the media who weren't prepared to give him another chance. He did, somewhat naively, think that once he was clear, life would carry on as before. But that wasn't to be. That was made very clear to him. The main channels, ITV, BBC and Sky, wouldn't touch him with a barge pole. But he was riding for a fall.*

A rape trial involves, crucially, an examination of the notion of consent. In particular, the question has to be asked: did both parties consent to having sex? As Morrison Torrey has noted: 'The concept of consent is a thorny one ... perhaps more than any other single legal issue. The idea of consent concerns fundamental problems of a society in which one group dominates all others and defines legal doctrine according to its own experiences' (1995: 43). In this particular case, further confusion arose when, in a 2006 interview, Leslie confirmed that he had had consensual sex with Ulrika Jonsson shortly after arriving in London, and he made more precise his earlier denial that he was not the presenter described in *Honest*. He stated in the *Independent*, 23 February 2006:

> *There are three or four people who it could have been – basically all the people who were going around with her at that time. The problem with Ulrika is that at any point she could have come out and said, 'John is not the guy.' That would have stopped a whole lot of damage. But she didn't. She just sat on the fence and took the money. Whether you like me or hate me, that's not right.*

It is fair to say that, in the eyes of the dominant commentators in the popular press, neither Leslie nor Jonsson emerge well from the *Honest* episode. 'A pox on both their houses' cursed Richard Littlejohn in the *Sun*, 25 October 2002:

> *Ulrika's sex life is, quite literally, an open book. Mind you, Leslie's isn't exactly a closely-guarded secret. If ever two people deserved each other, it is this pair of pro-celebrity legover merchants. Would you fancy sitting on a jury and trying to choose between them?*

Conclusion

News editors described as bizarre and freakish the circumstances that led to John Leslie being tried in the media for date rape, itself a category of crime which divides opinion. Sarah Moore argues for a feminist perspective that 'allows us to recognise that "date rape" has been transformed from an issue of female disempowerment into a nebulous threat of limited ideological significance' (2011: 451). However, typically less measured in her assessment was Carole Malone, writing in the *Sunday Mirror* on 27 October 2002, a few days after Leslie was first named and shamed. She poured scorn on Jonsson and the other quasi-complainants for undermining women's liberation, remarking:

I am fascinated by the scores of women who have come forward claiming to have been abused or sexually assaulted by the TV presenter ... One woman stated that at a party Leslie tried to kiss her and threw her against a wall so forcefully that she was terrified. Not terrified enough, however, to refuse an invitation to his house that night, where they had sex and where she says he hit her so hard 'the bruises didn't fade for a week'. Yet despite this, the same girl went back to Leslie's house a week later and had sex with him again. What was the point of the women's liberation movement? Who are these women who think it's acceptable to sleep with men who scare them, who hurt them, and who physically abuse them? ... Ulrika, and sadly, some of Leslie's women, are emotional jellyfish, who complain about being abused and victimised and yet don't have the courage or self-respect to do anything about it.

But Malone also found Leslie to be complicit in his own downfall, arguing that:

If Leslie's got one ounce of sense he should forget all this talk of revenge and of suing the people he says ruined his life. He might well have been to Hell and back but it's not all down to Ulrika and the police. A lot of it is down to him. I never for one moment believed John Leslie was a rapist and he was always totally charming around me. But the past few months have revealed that at best he wasn't a very nice man around women he fancied. He was cocksure, arrogant, ... and almost always disrespectful. Worst of all he believed his celebrity entitled him to have any woman he wanted.

But Malone's argument is not rooted in the primacy of the law, nor even of the public interest, so much as in the notion of *karma*. Leslie was named and shamed, and deserved to be because, she says, 'he wasn't a very nice man'. But however bizarre and freakish the Leslie disclosures may have seemed at the time, both of the media lawyers interviewed for this chapter fully agree that a recurrence of a John Leslie-type scenario is altogether possible. Duncan Lamont remembers the *Honest* episode as:

A sordid tale and one, unfortunately, that one can see happening again. That kind of thing sells vast numbers of newspapers. And that's not a criticism because it's very important to have a powerful and free and energised media. But I hope that journalists are in the business of reporting fairly and accurately, with vigour and bravery but also a sense of proportion and not gratuitous intrusion.

Data from the *Guardian* support Lamont's judgement. On 1 November 2002, it reported that, in the week of the Leslie disclosures, the *Mail* and the *Express* increased their sales by 7% (or 300,000 copies), with the *Daily Mirror* and the *Sun* swelling theirs by an additional 4% and 5% respectively. The *News of the World* shifted an additional 200,000 copies.

At the end of an emotional statement outside Southwark Crown Court – a statement that began with the words 'I am an innocent man' – a reporter asked Leslie: 'Are you gonna get your job back?' With tears in his eyes, and holding hands with his mother and his then girlfriend, Abi Titmuss, Leslie responded: 'Who knows? You tell me.' In the estimation of the *Express*, 8 September 2003, to which Leslie had agreed to sell his story the previous May for £550,000, the *Honest* episode had left him 'unemployed and unemployable'. Any lingering doubts about the end of Leslie's media career were ended early in 2004 when a sex tape featuring Leslie, Abi Titmuss, and another woman was made public. To this, Titmuss responded by selling her story, or 'confession', to the *News of the World* for £50,000. John Leslie would not get his job back and he eventually returned to his native Edinburgh to pursue a career in property development under his birth name John Leslie Stott. The decision to sack Leslie was attributed to ITV boss David Liddiment, now one of 12 members of the BBC Trust. In an article in the *Guardian*, 4 November 2002, Liddiment explained:

The crux of our decision to end his contract was that by not defending himself against widespread and disturbing allegations he compromised his ability to do the job and effectively disqualified himself. In the end we had to face the fact that the trust between him and the audience had been broken.

Liddiment thus passes the blame onto that nebulous entity the audience, whose tastes are invoked and assumed a great deal more than they are actually researched. In the article he denies 'bowing to trial by media', but asserts that 'in the end all broadcasters have a duty to protect that bond of trust with viewers at all costs. What it comes down to is not what will the papers say but what will the viewers think.' Though slightly further away from television's coal face, Duncan Lamont nonetheless paints a similar picture of the price paid by sinners working in front of the camera, confirming that:

> *The media, and especially television, are the most po-faced and unforgiving organisations. If you do wrong in any other area, there's the rehabilitation of offenders. In politics you can be forgiven, you can rebuild. But in media if you're damaged – if the preception is that you're not appropriate for the channel or the programme – then you're toast.*

Not long after John Leslie lost his job, the same fate befell Piers Morgan. In an interview on 29 March 2009 for his ITV series, *Life Stories,* Morgan revisited the publication of *Honest* with Ulrika Jonsson, but she refused to be drawn on the subject of John Leslie, saying only that 'trial by media is incredibly awful', adding that it was 'a bad mistake' for the term 'the presenter' to appear in *Honest.* And just as Piers Morgan had shifted the blame onto Channel 5 and the *Evening Standard,* and David Liddiment had passed it on to the audience, so Jonsson suggested that it was the publishers and not she who insisted that the word 'presenter' appear in the book. But, just as in 2002, Jonsson would still not deny that John Leslie was her attacker.

For critical observers of the media, 2011 will be remembered as the year of the so-called 'Super-Injunction spring', the residual fallout from the WikiLeaks exposures, the closure of the *News of the World,* and the start of the Leveson Inquiry. 2012 saw Rebekah Brooks, Andy Coulson, and others face charges of phone hacking. Among the charges are that between October 2002 and July 2006, Greg Miskiw from the *NotW* newsdesk conspired with the private investigator Glenn Mulcaire to hack into the voicemail messages of Abi Titmuss and John Leslie. Since losing his television career, Leslie has surfaced occasionally, including an appearance on 5 May 2010 on David Aaronovitch's *Devil's Advocate* series on BBC Radio 4 where, surprisingly, he argued in favour of the motion that 'celebrities have no automatic right to private life', opposing Toby Young.

What I have attempted to show here is that the naming and shaming of John Leslie came about due to the actions, and in some cases the inactions, of his initial lawyers, national newspaper editors, Leslie himself, and, ultimately, the author and publisher of *Honest.* In an English court, two verdicts are possible, guilty or not guilty – with a third, not proven, possible under the law of Leslie's native Scotland – the so-called 'bastard verdict'. What I have tried to show here is that trial by media, requiring as it does the extensive excavation of private behaviour, is not an anomaly in a system of justice that is otherwise functioning nicely. When reporting on John Leslie, sections of the press decided they knew better than the legal system, under which Leslie was arrested, charged, and acquitted of serious sexual assault; it also granted anonymity for life to his accuser. The whole object of trial by media is a kind of 'natural justice', or rather street justice, which an orthodox trial can neither accommodate nor provide when the matter is largely one of sinning, which Leslie did often, rather than criminality, and of this there has been no evidence offered in the ten years since Leslie's acquittal.

References

Unless indicated otherwise, the quotations from Paul Fox and Duncan Lamont are taken from interviews conducted by the author on 8 December 2011 and 20 June 2012 respectively.

Jonsson, Ulrika (2002) *Honest* (London: Pan Books).
Moore, Sarah E. H. (2011) 'Tracing the Life of a Crime Category', *Feminist Media Studies*, 11(4): 451–65.
Torrey, Morrison (1995) 'Feminist Legal Scholarship on Rape: A Maturing Look at one Form of Violence Against Women', *William and Mary Journal of Women and the Law*, 44(14): 35–49.

12

The Two Cultures

John Lloyd

Evidence has emerged over the past five years of reporters, working with private investigators, hacking into the mobile phones of those they were following for a story. A case in 2006 at the *News of the World*, involving the hacking of the phones of the royal princes William and Harry, resulted in prison sentences for the paper's royal correspondent, Clive Goodman, and the private investigator Glenn Mulcaire. News International, the British publishing arm of the US-based News Corporation led by Rupert Murdoch, said that the correspondent was a rotten apple.

However, largely due to the work of the *Guardian*, much, much more evidence of phone hacking at the paper was progressively uncovered. When it was reported that one of the victims of hacking had been Milly Dowler, a 13-year-old abducted and murdered in 2002, public outrage rose, and on 13 July 2011, the Prime Minister announced that an inquiry would be set up, with a relatively wide brief, chaired by Lord Justice Leveson. That sat in session from October 2011 to July 2012, and took evidence from a wide spectrum – journalists, victims of journalism, lawyers, and others. At the time of writing, the government is attempting, with considerable difficulty, to formulate a response to Lord Justice Leveson's report which is acceptable to parliament, the press and the public.

It is a large exercise, and has taken a large amount of media space. Yet, as Paul Dacre, the editor-in-chief of the *Daily Mail* and the *Mail on Sunday*, remarked to the Inquiry, much else that is more important is happening all about us: the Euro crisis, the crisis in Syria, the rise in unemployment. The Inquiry was established because phones were hacked – relatively minor crimes; and it is suspected that policemen were bribed – more serious, but so far only allegations and also, in the scheme of things, not huge matters. Even if they were, why – it could be asked – could not the issue be handled by the police inspectorate, and the courts? Why the extended paraphernalia of a public hearing, a massive inquiry?

I want to say why that is.

First, because there is a widespread view that the tabloid culture is pestilential. In his submission to the Inquiry, the former judge, Sir Stephen Sedley, argued that while Britain can boast of some of the best journalism in the world, it also has – as he put it – 'the most intrusive and foulmouthed papers in the world. Where else would a major daily run a headline "Up yours, Delors", or protest loudly about its freedom to publish humiliating stories which have no news value and are of interest only for their salacity?'[1]

When the tabloid journalists protest, as they loudly have, that the Inquiry is in part an expression of the views of that part of British society which doesn't read tabloids but think they are dreadful, there is a point to that. A large number of people do think the tabloids are dreadful. They think they have become largely outposts of the celebrity culture, that they have a strong line in running sex scandals – mostly, too, among celebrities but not always – and that the news they carry, when it is not sex and celebrity, is often distorted and sometimes flat wrong.

They also believe that the popular press, especially that owned by Rupert Murdoch – the *Sun*, the *Times*, the *Sunday Times,* and formerly the *News of the World*, closed last year to limit the damage done to News Corporation, now succeeded by the *Sun on Sunday* – has had an improper armlock on the political class – both Labour and Conservative.

Indeed, tabloid editors thought so too. In the most outspoken piece of evidence given to the Inquiry – or rather, to a seminar before the Inquiry proper started – the former *Sun* editor Kelvin McKenzie said that:

> *After all, the only reason we are here is due to one man's action; Cameron's obsessive arse kissing over the years of Rupert Murdoch. Blair was pretty good, as was [Gordon] Brown. But Cameron was the daddy ... there was never a party, a breakfast, a lunch, a cuppa or a drink that Cameron and Co would not turn up to in force if the Great Man or his handmaiden Rebekah Brooks was there. There was always a queue to kiss their rings. It was gut wrenching.*

His evidence was published in the London *Evening Standard* on 12 October 2011, at virtually the same moment that he delivered his speech;

it was headed 'I only checked the source of one story when I was *Sun* editor ... and that landed me with £1m bill for Elton libel'.

If the political class is or was to a significant extent in thrall to the Murdoch press, that is clearly a reason for real concern. Indeed, the relationship between the press and politicians was one of the explicit terms of the Inquiry's appointment, and was the subject of its fourth module. Much that was revealed there was distinctly uncomfortable for the political class, and especially for the government.

But there is also a deeper debate; it is a cultural and social debate which is not often made apparent, but it is one which underlies many of the concerns of the Inquiry, and indeed beyond. That is, that there is a large division in society, and among journalists and others, over whether or not it is right to expose the private activities – some would say sins – of individuals, especially individuals with prominence in public life. Those who argue that they should be revealed are usually, and have long been, dismissed as wishing to profit from gossip: and so they do, because gossip, sex, and celebrity sell papers. This is a point to which I'll return.

But first I want to deal with the moral argument, which I believe, in the face of much scepticism, is a real one. The scepticism was well expressed, in her evidence to the Inquiry, by the journalist and social activist Joan Smith. She argued that there were, essentially, two cultures – not those referred to by C. P. Snow in his Rede lecture over 50 years ago, when he said that there was a scientific culture and a humanities culture, and that they rarely met nor did they understand each other – but two cultures in journalism. One, which she practises – it was a fairly self-serving statement – which was responsible, evidence-based, non-intrusive and was concerned, in the main, with the serious issues facing society; the other is a tabloid culture which is 'so remorseless, its appetite is so unable to be filled, that the people involved have lost any sense that they're dealing with human beings'. In her view the tabloid press seems to 'live in a kind of 1950s world where everyone's supposed to get married, stay married and if anything happens outside that, then it's a story'.[2]

Smith is in a long line of commentators who see in the tabloid press little or nothing of any worth. In a famous essay written in 1890 in the *Harvard Law Review* by Samuel Warren and Louis Brandeis on 'The Right to Privacy', the two legal scholars and practitioners argued for a new law because of 'the evil of invasion by the newspapers, long keenly felt', and because 'the press is overstepping in every direction the obvious bounds of propriety and decency' with an obsessive triviality which 'destroys at once robustness of thought and delicacy of feeling. No enthusiasm can flourish, no generous impulse can survive under its blighting influence.' They end ringingly: 'The common law has always recognised a man's house as his castle, impregnable, often, even to its own officers. Shall the courts thus close the front entrance to constituted authority and open wide the back door to prurient or idle curiosity?'[3]

Yet this growing new respect for privacy in the face of a ruthless press – remember that in the US, this was the time of Gordon Bennett, William Randolph Hearst, and Joseph Pulitzer, yellow press barons all – developed on the back of certain assumptions which Warren and Brandeis shared. In an essay – 'The Rights of the Citizen to His Own Reputation' – published in the same year, E. L. Godkin, the writer and founder of the *Nation* magazine, wrote that 'the most effective deterrent for matrimonial infidelity, next after consideration for the children, is fear of social reprobation. This is the one terror of the dissolute, or depraved, or light minded, and thus does most for the maintenance of the family bond.'[4]

We should recognise that there are two moral assumptions clashing here. One sees the abuse of privacy as the crime, and the sanctity of the family, or the individual, as needing to be preserved, by regulation and law, from the inquiry of the press. The other sees the intrusion of the press as benign, since its object is to expose moral turpitude. The first is held, broadly speaking, by the 'establishment' – politicians, the judiciary, the upmarket press; the second by the tabloids. That clash remains very much alive. Though privacy, including the privacy of those who have what would have been considered (and still are by some) deviant personal relationships, has not been generally recognised as a right in law, the much greater revelatory powers of the internet mean that in practice it is now often rendered null and void – especially when the interest from sections of the public is very high, as in the topless photographs of the Duchess of Cambridge.

This has left Justice Leveson with a very unenviable task: that of Canute, to tell the tide to stop.

Notes

1   http://www.levesoninquiry.org.uk/wp-content/uploads/2012/02/Submission-by-Sir-Stephen-Sedley.pdf.

2   http://www.levesoninquiry.org.uk/wp-content/uploads/2011/12/Transcript-of-
    Morning-Hearing-21-November-2011.pdf.

3   http://groups.csail.mit.edu/mac/classes/6.805/articles/privacy/Privacy_brand_
    warr2.html (accessed Aug. 2012).

4   http://www.archive.org/stream/scribnersmag08editmiss/scribnersmag08edit
    miss_djvu.txt (accessed Aug. 2012).

Index

RISJ/I.B.TAURIS PUBLICATIONS

CHALLENGES

Transformations in Egyptian Journalism
Naomi Sakr
ISBN: 978 1 78076 589 1

Climate Change in the Media: Reporting Risk and Uncertainty
James Painter
ISBN: 978 1 78076 588 4

Women and Journalism
Suzanne Franks
ISBN: 978 1 78076 585 3

EDITED VOLUMES

Media and Public Shaming: The Boundaries of Disclosure
Julian Petley (ed.)
ISBN: 978 1 78076 586 0 (HB); 978 1 78076 587 7 (PB)

*Political Journalism in Transition: Western Europe in a
Comparative Perspective*
Raymond Kuhn and Rasmus Kleis Nielsen (eds)
ISBN: 978 1 78076 677 5 (HB); 978 1 78076 678 2 (PB)

Transparency in Politics and the Media: Accountability and Open Government
Nigel Bowles, James T. Hamilton and David A. L. Levy (eds)
ISBN: 978 1 78076 675 1 (HB); 978 1 78076 676 8 (PB)

The Ethics of Journalism: Individual, Institutional and Cultural Influences
Wendy N. Wyatt (ed.)
ISBN: 978 1 78076 673 7 (HB); 978 1 78076 674 4 (PB)